Words That Make New Jersey History

A project of the New Jersey Historical Commission

Words That Make New Jersey History

A PRIMARY SOURCE READER

Expanded Edition

Edited by Howard L. Green

RIVERGATE BOOKS

AN IMPRINT OF RUTGERS UNIVERSITY PRESS
NEW BRUNSWICK, NEW JERSEY

Second paperback printing, 2009

Library of Congress Cataloging-in-Publication Data

Words that make New Jersey history : a primary source reader / edited
by Howard L. Green — Expanded ed.
    p.   cm.
  Includes bibliographical references and index.
  ISBN 978-0-8135-3849-5 (cloth)   ISBN 978-0-8135-3850-1 (pbk.)
    1. New Jersey—History—Sources.   I. Green, Howard L., 1948–
F134.W59   1994
974.9—dc20   94-8927
                                                                   CIP

British Cataloging-in-Publication information available

For Julie who keeps me thinking
and for Sarah and Aaron who force me to explain well

Contents

SECTION THREE
The Early Republic   71

SECTION FOUR
Liberty and Justice for All   93

Contents ix

Acknowledgments

Anyone who undertakes a large project such as this incurs many debts, nearly too many to mention. At the risk of offending a friend by omission of her or his name, I want to thank the following people for their advice, support, or help. Without exception, everyone I talked to while I was working on this collection responded to me graciously, thoughtfully, and with enthusiasm. Their generosity improved this work. Its weaknesses are my fault.

Thanks to: Ron Becker, Henry Bischoff, Bernie Bush, Marilyn Campbell, Marcia Carlisle, Sue Cobble, David Cohen, Sue Crilley, Charles Cummings, Bill Fernekes, Sue Finkle, Joel Gardner, Bill Gillette, Steve Golin, Brian Greenberg, Doug Greenberg, Rita Heller, Gail Hunton, Barbara Irvine, Dan Jones, Cassandra John, Mark Lender, Roz Libby, Bob Lupp, Dick McCormick, Bob Morris, John Murrin, Mary Murrin, Karl Niederer, Lee Parks, Barbara Petrick, Mary Alice Quigley, Jack Reynolds, Roger Shatzkin, Don Sinclair, Paul Stellhorn, Sol Stetin, Joe Stringer, Evelyn Tayor, Pat Thomas, Carol Tomson, George Tselos, Peter Wacker, Dick Waldron, Burt Weltman, Julie Williams, Lorraine Williams, Giles Wright.

Introduction

When I started work on this project, my purpose was twofold. First of all, in the spirit of both the state law defining the high school history requirement and the Core Course Proficiencies in Social Studies adopted by the New Jersey Department of Education, I wanted to equip teachers of United States history to incorporate the history of New Jersey into their survey courses.[1] But just as American history can be taught in a nearly infinite variety of ways, so, too, there are many ways to tie New Jersey history to U.S. history. I hoped to provide a flexible tool that would lend itself to many diffeent ways of making the story of New Jersey's past part of the sweep of American history. I also hoped the collection would be flexible in another way, so it would be useful to teachers who use a range of pedagogical styles and who work with many different kinds of students.

My second aim was to help students read and interpret the primary documents of the past. I believe this is one of the most important aspects of teaching history. The study of history ought to develop in students the capacity for analysis and judgment. It ought to train students to detect bias, to weigh evidence, and to evaluate arguments. All of this can be well done through the use of primary source materials. Moreover, whatever shape the global workplace of the future takes, in order to succeed in it participants will need high-level verbal and conceptual skills. The importance of communication through the written word will not diminish, nor will the importance of critical thinking abilities. I know of no better means to improve verbal skills and sharpen thinking abilities than to help students work on comprehending, interpreting, and analyzing historical documents.

Beyond these two interrelated primary goals, I had an ulterior motive. I believe that a book of this sort can contribute to a general improvement in the quality of the United States history survey by supplementing the basic texts generally in use. I envisaged a collection that would use New Jersey history to help survey courses do a better job exploring values and important social issues.

With these goals in mind, it was harder to decide what not to put in than the other way around. There are literally thousands of challeng-

1. NJSA 18:35-1 requires a "two-year course of study in the history of the United States, including the history of New Jersey, to be given to each student during the last four years of high school."

ing, intriguing documents that might have gone into this volume. Why did I choose what I did? I used four standards.

1. The documents had to fit the main themes of a representative course in United States history. I am aware that the idea of a representative course may be somewhat naive. No two school districts structure their programs in precisely the same way. But I also know that teachers are besieged by demands for new things to include in the curriculum. I hope that this volume will not be seen as a new demand, but as a way to help teachers do, in a somewhat new and better way, what they are already doing.

2. The documents had to be readable at a high school reading level, realistically defined. This definition, of course, is no simple matter. Reading levels in high schools vary enormously. One finds in New Jersey schools a range of students. There are those who can read advanced, technical material in fields that interest them. There are others who read elementary school–level materials only with difficulty.

I have tried to select materials that represent a range of reading levels, cutting off only the extremes. Students who read at an elementary school level will probably find much of the material in this reader challenging, although some selections may be appropriate for such students, if chosen with care by a patient teacher. Conversely, there may not be too much here for the genuinely advanced student. However, since historical complexity often lies more in the questions one asks of the past than in the inherent difficulty of a document, many of these selections will lend themselves to assignments for advanced students.

3. The documents overall had to reflect the cultural pluralism that New Jersey has exhibited since the days of its founding. The documents here included, to the extent this was possible given my two previous priorities, give voice to the men and women of New Jersey's past: rich and poor, black and white, immigrant and native-born. They give voice to a broad spectrum of people from New Jersey's past and reflect my sense of the social realities of that past.

4. Last, but by no means least, and related to the previous objective, I wanted the documents to illustrate my basic sense of United States history. In my view our past has been a long struggle over who is and who is not to be a beneficiary of the egalitarian promise offered in the central texts of the republic. It is an unfinished struggle, arguably one that can never be finished. I have tried to select documents that reflect this view on two levels. Our national history has first of all witnessed a struggle over what our democracy is to stand for. But even as agreement over this is reached, from period to period, there

has generally followed a no-holds-barred, shirt-sleeves-rolled-up-to-the-elbows fight over who is to benefit from the new arrangements. I hope the documents I have chosen reflect some of this.

The title of the book may be misleading to some readers. What does it mean to "make history"? In English our term is ambiguous. We have two different kinds of makers of history. The men and women of the past made history, certainly, but equally certainly the writers of today make history by what they choose to (not) write about. I hoped to conjure some of this ambiguity by the title. I am trying to broaden the definition of who makes history in two ways. I want readers to understand that history is what historians say it is. I also want them to see that many different people have made United States and New Jersey history.

Anyone with a passing familiarity with the primary sources of the past will recognize that these documents are heavily edited. I have modernized spellings throughout and omitted much extraneous and tangential material through generous use of the ellipsis. Although purists may object, I believe that given my objectives for this project, this was appropriate. My editorial aim was to deflect attention from matters such as changing styles of writing, punctuation, and spelling and aim it instead at the ideas and issues brought up in the documents. I do not mean to suggest that changing rhetorical styles and modes of expression are unimportant or even ultimately entirely separable from content. They are not. But for the purposes of this collection I felt it was more important to get students dealing more directly with the essence of the material. Students who pursue further study in history will have ample opportunity to hone their abilities to read and interpret unedited historical documents.

Some basic questions can be asked of any historical document; these questions form a template that may be used as a starting point with these materials.

- What type of document is it?
- When was it created?
- Who wrote it?
- What can you say about this person?
- At what audience was the document aimed? How do you know this?
- What are the document's main points?
- Why do you think it was written? What evidence do you find in the document for your conclusion?
- Based on it, what can you say about life in New Jersey at the time the document was written?
- What questions would you like to ask the author if you could speak with him or her?

This list of questions is far from exhaustive, but it is a starting point. Any student who learns to ask (and to begin to answer) these, or similar, questions of the material in this book will be learning the rudiments of what it means to study history and the lessons one may draw from it.

European Exploration and Settlement

NOTABLE EVENTS

1524	Giovanni da Verrazano explores the mid-Atlantic region
1607	Jamestown colony settled
1609	Henry Hudson reaches the Delaware River and New York Harbor
1619	First Africans arrive in Virginia
1620	Pilgrims reach Cape Cod
1621	Dutch West India Company chartered
1624	First Dutch settlements at New Amsterdam
1626	Peter Minuit buys Manhattan Island
1629	Dutch settlement at Pavonia (Jersey City)
1630	Puritan emigration from England begins
1638	New Sweden colony founded
1648	George Fox starts the Society of Friends
1656	Dutch capture New Sweden
1664	England conquers New Netherland; the Duke of York grants New Jersey to Berkeley and Carteret
1676	New Jersey divided into East Jersey and West Jersey
1677	Concessions and Agreements of West Jersey drafted
1681	Pennsylvania chartered
1683	First tavern in the Jerseys opens at Woodbridge
1687	Sir Isaac Newton publishes *Principia Mathematica*, establishing the laws of modern physics
1692	Witchcraft hysteria in Salem, Massachusetts

"Between Hope and Fear": A Legend of the First Lenape Encounter with Europeans

We don't know precisely how many native people were living in the land that became New Jersey when Europeans first arrived in the early seventeenth century to explore its coasts and trade for its natural resources. Estimates range from six or eight thousand to fifteen or twenty thousand. A century or a century and a quarter later the number of Native Americans had fallen to a few hundred. Thus the Lenape, as they knew themselves, or Delaware Indians, as the English called them, experienced the same nightmarish population decline that befell all Native Americans in the first century after European arrival. Historians and anthropologists think that wherever in the "New World" Europeans set foot, the native population was reduced approximately 90 percent within one century. The rapid decline of native populations all over the Western Hemisphere may have been the greatest demographic catastrophe in history.

We have only a few sources that describe the Native Americans who inhabited what is now New Jersey when Europeans first began to arrive. Sources that suggest what the natives thought and felt are even scarcer. It can be debated how much the following excerpt reflects Lenape thinking at the time of their first contact with European traders, but the document is a good introduction to the care with which historical sources must be read.

This account was first published in 1819—roughly two centuries after the events it purports to describe—by John G. E. Heckewelder, a Moravian missionary who lived among the Delaware for many years. Heckewelder argued it was "a correct account of the tradition existing among them." Since he is generally considered a reliable source, we may accept this statement. The question is how much had the story altered over the years. Archaeological evidence, for example, suggests that the Lenape had contact with other Indian groups along the coast, so it is probable that they had heard of big floating houses containing white men before they saw one.

A great many years ago when men with a white skin had never yet been seen in this land, some Indians who were out fishing . . . espied at a great distance something remarkably large floating on the water, and such as they had never seen before. . . . They . . . could not agree

John Heckewelder, *History, Manners and Customs of the Indian Nations Who Once Inhabited Pennsylvania and the Neighboring States* (1819; reprint ed., New York: Arno Press and the New York Times, 1971), 71–75.

upon what it was; some believed it to be an uncommonly large fish or animal while others were of opinion it must be a very big house floating on the sea. At length the spectators concluded that this wonderful object was moving towards the land and that it must be an animal or something else that had life in it. . . . They sent off a number of runners and water men to carry the news to their scattered chiefs, that they might send off in every direction for the warriors. . . .

[They] concluded it to be a remarkably large house in which the Mannitto (the great or supreme being) himself was present, and that he probably was coming to visit them. . . . Every measure was taken to be well provided with plenty of meat for a sacrifice. The women were desired to prepare the best victuals. All the idols or images were examined and put in order, and a grand dance was supposed not only to be an agreeable entertainment for the great being, but it was believed that it might, with the addition of a sacrifice, contribute to appease him if he was angry with them. The conjurers were also set to work to determine what this phenomenon portended and what the possible result of it might be. . . .

Distracted between hope and fear, they were at a loss what to do; a dance, however, commenced in great confusion. While in this situation, fresh runners arrived declaring . . . that it is positively a house full of human beings, of quite a different color from that of the Indians and dressed differently from them; that in particular one of them was dressed entirely in red, who must be the Mannitto himself. They were hailed from the vessel in a language they did not understand, yet they shout or yell in return by way of answer. . . . Many are for running off to the woods but are pressed by others to stay in order not to give offense to their visitor, who might find them out and destroy them. The house . . . at last stops and a canoe of a smaller size comes on shore with the red man, and others, in it. . . .

The chiefs and wise men, assembled in council, form themselves into a large circle towards which the man in red clothes approaches with two others. He salutes them with a friendly countenance and they return the salute after their manner. They are lost in admiration; the dress, the manners, the whole appearance of the unknown strangers is to them a subject of wonder. But they are particularly struck with him who wore the red coat all glittering with gold lace, which they could in no manner account for. He, surely, must be the great Mannitto, but why should he have a white skin?

Meanwhile, a large hackhack[1] is brought by one of his servants, from which an unknown substance is poured out into a small cup or

---

1. Some kind of container, possibly a gourd.

glass, and handed to the supposed Mannitto. He drinks, has the glass filled again, and hands it to the chief standing next to him. The chief receives it, but only smells the contents and passes it on to the next chief who does the same. The glass or cup thus passes through the circle without the liquor being tasted by anyone, and is upon the point of being returned to the red-clothed Mannitto when one of the Indians, a brave man and a great warrior, suddenly jumps up and harangues the assembly on the impropriety of returning the cup with its contents. It was handed to them, says he, by the Mannitto that they should drink out of it as he himself had done. To follow his example would be pleasing to him; but to return what he had given them might provoke his wrath and bring destruction on them. And since the orator believed it for the good of the nation that the contents offered them should be drunk, and as no one else would do it, he would drink it himself, let the consequence be what it might. It was better for one man to die, than that a whole nation should be destroyed. He then took the glass, and bidding the assembly a solemn farewell, at once drank up its whole contents.

Every eye was fixed on the resolute chief, to see what effect the unknown liquor would produce. He soon began to stagger and at last fell prostrate on the ground. His companions now bemoan his fate, he falls into a sound sleep, and they think he has expired. He wakes again, jumps up, and declares that he has enjoyed the most delicious sensations and that he never before felt himself so happy as after he had drunk the cup. He asks for more, his wish is granted; the whole assembly then imitate him, and all become intoxicated.

After this general intoxication had ceased . . . the man with the red clothes . . . distributed presents among them, consisting of beads, axes, hoes, and stockings such as the white people wear. They soon became familiar with each other, and began to converse by signs. The Dutch made them understand that they would not stay here . . . but would pay them another visit the next year, when they would bring them more presents, and stay with them awhile. But as they could not live without eating, they should want a little land . . . in order to raise herbs and vegetables. . . .

They went away as they had said, and returned in the following season when both parties were much rejoiced to see each other. . . .

As the whites became daily more familiar with the Indians, they at last proposed to stay with them and asked only for so much ground for a garden spot. . . . The white and red men lived contentedly together for a long time, though the former from time to time asked for more land, which was readily obtained. . . . The Indians began to believe that they would soon want all their country, which in the end proved true.

"Draw the Indians to Our Service": Instructions for the Director of New Netherland (1625)

The region that encompasses what became New Jersey was the only part of British North America whose first European inhabitants were not English. Early in the seventeenth century the Swedes had the first settlement, a trading outpost on the lower Delaware, but it was uprooted by the Dutch, who were the dominant commercial power in the world in those years.

In 1621 the Dutch West India Company began to do business in the Atlantic world. Although trade was its primary objective, colonization was permitted by the government of Holland, known as their High Mightinesses, the States General. New Netherland, the Company's outpost in North America, was a relatively unpromising piece of a vast empire that stretched from Indonesia and Africa to Brazil and the Caribbean islands.

The investors' basic concerns may be read in the following excerpt from the instructions that the Company gave to the director of the New Netherland undertaking, Willem ver Hulst.

First, he shall take care that divine service be held at the proper times, both on board ship and on land, . . . and see that the community there is properly served by him in the ministration of holy baptism, in reading sermons, [offering] prayers . . . and that the Indians be instructed in the Christian religion. . . . He shall also prevent all idolatry, in order that the name of God and of our Lord and Savior, Jesus Christ, be not blasphemed therein by any one, and the Lord's Sabbath be not violated, but that by the example of godliness and outward discipline on the part of the Christians, the heathen may the sooner be brought to a knowledge of the same. . . .

He shall also see that no one do the Indians any harm or violence . . . or condemn them in any way. . . . They [should] be shown honesty, faithfulness, and sincerity in all contracts, dealings, and intercourse, without being deceived by shortage of measure, weight, or number, and that throughout friendly relations with them be maintained. . . .

A.J.F. Van Laer, *Documents Relating to New Netherland, 1624–1626, in the Henry E. Huntington Library* (San Marino, Calif.: Henry E. Huntington Library and Art Gallery, 1924), 36–67.

Whereas we have received and examined a report about the condition of a certain island to be called the High Island,[1] situated about twenty-five miles up the South River,[2] below the first falls, we deem it expedient, unless a still more suitable place be found, to settle there all the families together with the hired farmers and the cattle that will be sent hither. . . .

In case any Indians should be living on the aforesaid island or make any claim upon it, or upon any other places that are of use to us, they must not be driven away by force or threats, but by good words be persuaded to leave, or be given something therefore to their satisfaction, or else be allowed to live among us, a contract being made thereof and signed by them in their manner, since such contracts upon other occasions may be very useful to the Company.

And for the better security of the trade and the exclusion of foreign nations, he is to consider whether it would not be practicable so to contract with the natives of the country in various districts as would make them promise us to trade with no one but those of the Company, provided that we on our part should bind ourselves to take all the skins which they could bring us upon such terms as would be considered reasonable, or at such price as we have hitherto bought them. . . .

He shall by small presents seek to draw the Indians to our service, in order to learn from them the secrets of that region and the condition of the interior, but not feed them in idleness or give in too much to their wanton demands.

He shall also as far as feasible avoid getting into any dispute with the French or English, and especially avoid all acts of violence, unless he be obliged to defend himself and those who are committed to his charge against open aggression.

But if any persons belonging to a foreign nation . . . attempt to trade with the Indians, he shall spoil the market for them by [outbidding them]. . . .

He shall endeavor to increase the trade in skins and other articles that are obtained in the country, and at the place of trading with the Indians have a cabin erected so that the goods may be stored therein, and at a suitable time he shall send one or more sloops thither to carry on trade. . . . He shall not neglect to send as a sample some deerskins and other skins that are prepared by the Indians, also such things as the Indians make of them according to their ingenuity.

1. Probably Burlington Island, in the Delaware River opposite Burlington City.
2. The Delaware River. The Hudson River was called the North River.

He shall give the colonists and other free persons full permission to trade in the interior and to catch the animals with the skins, but they must deliver up the said skins and goods to the Company at the price for which we obtain them at the trading-place from the Indians, and he shall not permit them, by selling the skins [to others], to make the Company pay a higher price for them.

DOCUMENT 3

"Many Eyes Will Be Upon You": A Letter to West Jersey Quakers (1676)

In 1664 the English drove the Dutch from New Amsterdam. In 1676 New Jersey was split into two provinces: East Jersey and West Jersey. In West Jersey, William Penn led a group trying to establish a Quaker colony. Within a few years Penn's attention shifted to the western shore of the Delaware River, to what became the state that bears his name. But at the time the letter excerpted here was written, West Jersey was the focus of efforts to establish a Quaker commonwealth in the New World.

Quakers, or the Society of Friends as they are more formally known, believe that all humans are capable of receiving direct guidance from God. Contrary to the Puritans, at whose hands Quakers experienced persecution in England and in the New World, in Quaker belief all individuals are equally capable of finding God (which they call achieving one's "inner light") and thereby obtaining salvation. Men and women are equal in Quaker eyes and they do not believe in showing deference to those of higher social standing.

George Fox, the author of this letter, was the founder of the Society of Friends. He visited West Jersey in the late 1670s.

My dear friends in New Jersey, and you that go to New Jersey,

My desire is that you may all be kept in the fear of God and that you may have the Lord in your eye in all your undertakings. For many eyes of other governments or colonies will be upon you. . . . Let your lives and words and conversations be as becomes the gospel, that you may adorn the truth and honor the Lord in all your undertakings. Let that only be in your eye and then you will have the Lord's blessing and increase, both in basket and field and storehouse. And at your lyings down you will feel him and at your goings forth and comings in. . . . [1]

After you are settled you may join together and build a meeting-house. And do not strive about outward things; but dwell in the love of God, for that will unite you together and make you kind and gentle one towards another; and to seek one another's good and welfare, and to be helpful one to another; and see that nothing be lacking among you, then all will be well. And let temperance and patience and kindness and brotherly love be exercised among you, so that you may abound in virtue and the true humility.

1. Here Fox echoes Deuteronomy 6:7.

George Fox, *A Collection of Many Selected and Christian Epistles, Letters and Testimonies* (Philadelphia, 1831). 121–122.

Religious Freedom in Early New Jersey (1676/77, 1683)

Settlements in North America generally began for either economic or religious reasons. The economic factor tended to dominate in the Chesapeake region, the religious in New England. New Jersey was a middle colony in more ways than geography. The history of its settlement reveals a mixture of motives.

The proprietors (the term refers to individuals who had been given land in the New World by the English Crown) hoped to promote immigration to increase the value of the real estate they had been given. They wanted to profit by selling their land to settlers whose religious beliefs they shared. They lured potential settlers with many enticements: economic opportunity, representative self-government, and religious liberty.

The economies of East and West Jersey were quite similar, but their social compositions differed. In West Jersey the Quakers were seeking refuge from English persecution. In East Jersey Puritans from Long Island and New England hoped to reassert Puritan orthodoxy. They were joined by Scots Presbyterians.

The excerpts that follow, although they focus primarily on religious freedom, reflect the broader cultural differences between the Quakers of West Jersey and the Puritans and Presbyterians of East Jersey. Each passage is drawn from a source that was intended to be the organic law of its province. These documents had two main purposes. Not only were they to attract settlers to the area, they established the basic plan by which the colony was to be governed.

The Concessions and Agreements of West Jersey, from which this first passage comes, was the most libertarian document of its age. It granted complete religious freedom in simple language. Although religious liberty was widely available outside New England, no other colony spelled out the matter this plainly.

In the East Jersey document religious freedom was somewhat restricted. It was granted to those who believed in God, thus excluding atheists. Furthermore, office holding was reserved for Christians. Although no official church was established in East Jersey, before 1700 several towns supported ministers at public expense. When the two provinces merged to become the Royal Colony of New Jersey in 1702, East Jersey precedents were adopted for the most part.

Julian P. Boyd, ed., *Fundamental Laws and Constitutions of New Jersey, 1664–1964* (Princeton: D. Van Nostrand, 1964), 72–85, 120–121.

The Concessions and Agreements of the Proprietors, Freeholders, and Inhabitants of the Province of West New-Jersey in America (1676/77)[1]

No men . . . upon earth have power or authority to rule over men's consciences in religious matters. Therefore it is consented, agreed, and ordained that no person or persons whatsoever within the said Province . . . shall be any way, upon any pretence whatsoever, called in question or in the least punished or hurt . . . for the sake of his opinion, judgment, faith or worship towards God, in matters of religion. But that all and every such person and persons may . . . at all times freely and fully have and enjoy . . . the exercise of their consciences in matters of religious worship throughout all the said Province.

The Fundamental Constitutions for the Province of East New-Jersey in America (1683)

All persons living in the province who confess and acknowledge the one almighty and eternal God and hold themselves obliged in conscience to live peaceably and quietly in a civil society shall in no way be molested or prejudged for their religious persuasions and exercise in matters of faith and worship. Nor shall they be compelled to frequent and maintain any religious worship, place or ministry whatsoever. Yet it is also hereby provided that no man shall be admitted a member of the great or common council,[2] or any other place of public trust, who shall not profess faith in Christ-Jesus, and solemnly declare that he doth no ways hold himself obliged in conscience to endeavor alteration in the government, or seeks the turning out of any in it or their ruin or prejudice . . . because they are in his opinion heretics, or differ in their judgment from him. Nor by this article is it intended that any under the notion of this liberty shall allow themselves to avow atheism, irreligiousness, or to practice cursing, swearing, drunkenness, profaneness, whoring, adultery, murdering or any kind of violence, or indulging themselves in stage plays, masques, revels, or such like abuses.[3] For restraining such and preserving of the people in diligence and in good order, the great council is to make more particular laws, which are punctually to be put in execution.

1. Under the Julian calendar, which was in use by the English until 1752, a new year began in late March. Thus, for example, February came late in 1676 by one reckoning, and early in 1677 by our count.
2. Colonies were ruled by a governor, a royal or great council appointed to advise the governor, and a common council or assembly elected by the inhabitants.
3. The Puritans considered theater pagan and offensive in the sight of God. Some argued it had been concocted by the Devil, others that it was a Catholic invention. All the theaters in England were closed during the Civil War, which began in 1642.

DOCUMENT 5

"Wealth Circulates Like the Blood": William Penn's Account of the Delaware Indians (1683)

William Penn is one of the towering figures of colonial America. He is best known as a Quaker leader and the founder of Pennsylvania, his "Holy Experiment." The passage excerpted here reflects two other significant points about Penn's life. His first connection with America was with New Jersey, and his dealings with Indians were marked by truthfulness and humanity.

In 1676, when West Jersey came into the hands of Quakers, Penn was one of the trustees designated to manage the property. Later he was also among the large group of investors who got title to East Jersey. Penn's association with New Jersey ended when he was granted a large tract of land north of Maryland by King Charles II in repayment of a debt the King owed to Penn's father.

The enlightened Indian policy that was to highlight Penn's years in Pennsylvania was already evident in this comparatively early essay, written shortly after he left West Jersey.

In this excerpt one can read a nearly anthropological imagination combined with a genuine respect for Indian ways of life on the land. The idea that the natives of the New World were descendants of the Ten Lost Tribes of Israel was not unique to Penn.

Of their customs and manners there is much to be said; I will begin with children. . . . If boys, they go fishing till ripe for the woods, which is about fifteen; then they hunt, and after having given some proofs of their manhood, by a good return of skins, they may marry. . . . The girls stay with their mothers and help to hoe the ground, plant corn, and carry burdens. . . .

The age they marry at, if women, is about thirteen and fourteen; if men, seventeen and eighteen. They are rarely elder.

Their houses are mats or bark of trees set on poles, in the fashion of an English barn, but out of the power of the winds, for they are hardly higher than a man; they lie on reeds or grass. In travel they lodge in the woods about a great fire with the mantle of duffel[1] they wear by day wrapped about them, and a few boughs stuck round them.

1. Heavy cloth.

Albert Cook Myers, ed., *William Penn: His Own Account of the Lenni Lenape or Delaware Indians* (Moylan, Pa., 1937).

Their diet is maize, or Indian corn, divers ways prepared: sometimes roasted in the ashes, sometimes beaten and boiled with water, which they call hominy; they also make cakes, not unpleasant to eat. They have likewise several sorts of beans and peas that are good nourishment; and the woods and rivers are their larder.

If a European comes to see them, or calls for lodging at their . . . wigwam they give him the best place and first cut. If they come to visit us, they salute us with an *Itah* which is as much as to say, "good be to you," and set them down. . . . Maybe they speak not a word more, but observe all passages. If you give them anything to eat or drink, well, for they will not ask; and be it little or much, if it be with kindness, they are well pleased. Else they go away sullen, but say nothing. . . .

Some of the young women are said to take undue liberty before marriage, . . . but when married, chaste. When with child they know their husbands no more till delivered; and during their month they touch no meat. They eat [it], but with a stick, lest they should defile it. . . .

In liberality they excel, nothing is too good for their friend; give them a fine gun, coat, or other thing, it may pass twenty hands before it sticks. . . . Wealth circulates like the blood, all parts partake and though none shall want what another has, yet exact observers of property. . . .

They care for little, because they want but little. . . . A little contents them. In this they are sufficiently revenged on us. If they are ignorant of our pleasures, they are also free from our pains. They are not disquieted with bills of lading and exchange, nor perplexed with chancery-suits and exchequer-reckonings. We sweat and toil to live; their pleasure feeds them; I mean, their hunting, fishing, and fowling and this table is spread everywhere. They eat twice a day, morning and evening. . . .

In sickness impatient to be cured . . . especially for their children, to whom they are extremely natural. . . . If they die, they bury them with their apparel, be they men or women, and the nearest of kin fling in something with them, as a token of their love. Their mourning is blacking of their faces, which they continue for a year.

Their government is by kings, which they call Sachems, and those by succession . . . of the mother's side. . . . Every king has his council, and that consists of all the old and wise men of his nation, which perhaps is two hundred people. Nothing of moment is undertaken, be it war, peace, selling of land, or traffick, without advising with them and . . . with the young men too. It is admirable to consider how powerful the kings are, and yet how they move by the breath of their people. . . .

bones. The meat that we eat does not do us good, we always are in fear. We have not the benefit of the sun to shine on us, we hide us in holes and corners. . . .

We are willing to have a broad path for you and us to walk in, and if an Indian is asleep in this path the Englishman shall pass by and do him no harm; and if an Englishman is asleep in this path, the Indian shall pass him by, and say, 'He is an Englishman, he is asleep; let him alone he loves to sleep.' It shall be a plain path; there must not be in this path a stump to hurt our feet. . . .

Some are apt to ask how we can propose safely to live amongst such a heathen people as the Indians, whose principles and practices lead them to war and bloodshed and our principles and practices lead us to love enemies . . . and if smitten on one cheek to turn the other. We being a peaceable people whose principles and practices are against wars and fighting.

I answer that we settled by the Indians' consent . . . and bought the land of them that we settle on, which they conveyed to us by deeds under their hands and seals, and also submitted to several articles of agreement with us: not to do us any injury. But if . . . they break these covenants and agreements . . . they may be . . . proceeded against as other offenders: to be kept in subjection to the magistrate's power, in whose hand the sword of justice is committed, to be used by him for the punishment of evil doers. . . . The power of the magistrate's sword, which is not to be used in vain . . . may be used against such as raise rebellions and insurrections against the government of the country, be they Indians or others. Otherwise it is in vain for us to pretend to magistracy or government.

"Ample and Happy Livelihoods": West Jersey in 1698

Whether a colony was an investment or a religious experiment, its success depended on the steady arrival of new settlers. Pamphlets promoting the attractions of various settlements in the New World were therefore very common. They tended to paint very flattering portraits of the areas they were promoting.

The pamphlet excerpted here was published in London in 1698 by Gabriel Thomas, who had resided in the area for approximately fifteen years. Thomas's work bore the title "An Historical and Geographical Account of the Province and Country of Pennsylvania and West Jersey in America." It depicts the area at the dawn of the eighteenth century and includes a detailed description of the region's natural resources.

My chief design in writing this short account of West New Jersey, is to inform all (but especially the poor) what ample and happy livelihoods people may gain in those parts, whereby they may subsist very well without either begging or stealing. . . . They have a fair prospect of . . . living very plentifully and happily, which medium of life is far better than lingering out their days so miserably poor and half starved; or whipping, burning, and hanging for villainies, they will have little temptation . . . to perpetrate here. . . .

The first inhabitants of this country were the Indians. . . . Their chief employment is in hunting, fishing, . . . making canoes . . . and bowls, in all which arts they are very dexterous and ingenious. Their women's business chiefly consists in planting . . . corn and pounding it to meal . . . [to] . . . make bread. . . . They also make Indian mats, ropes, hats, and baskets (some of curious workmanship) of their hemp, which there grows wild and natural in the woods in great plenty. . . .

The Dutch and Swedes inform us that they are greatly decreased in number to what they were when they came first into this country. And the Indians themselves say that two of them die to every one Christian that comes in here. . . .

Burlington is now the chief town . . . having a great many stately

Gabriel Thomas, "An Historical and Geographical Account of the Province and County of Pennsylvania and of West Jersey in America" (1698; reprint ed., *Proceedings of the New Jersey Historical Society*, n.s. 8, no. 1 [January 1923]:2–12).

brick houses in it. . . . Likewise in the said town there are very many fine wharves and large timber yards, malt houses, brew houses, bake houses, and most sorts of tradesmen. . . .

A ship of four hundred tons may sail up to this town in the River Delaware . . . and several fine ships and vessels . . . have been built there. . . .

There are water men who constantly ply their ferry boats . . . to the city of Philadelphia in Pennsylvania and to other places. . . .

There are several meetings of worship in this country, viz., the Presbyterians, Quakers, and Anabaptists. . . .

They have wheat, rye, peas, oats, barley, rice, etc., in vast quantities. Also Indian corn, peas, and beans, likewise English hemp and flax. . . . Pumpkins, cashews, watermelons, muskmelons, cucumbers, squashes, carrots, artichokes, potatoes, turnips, garlic, onions, and leeks grow there in greater plenty than in England. . . .

Of fish they have whales, sturgeon, cod . . . flat fish, rock, shad, cat[fish], eels, perch, and many other sorts in prodigious shoals. And wild waterfowl, as geese, ducks, swans, are very numerous, even beyond all expectation. . . .

There are otters, beavers, foxes . . . wild cats, raccoons . . . and also that cunning creature the possum. . . . Likewise there were some wolves and bears, but now they are very rare to be seen, by reason the Indians destroy them. . . . There are great numbers of wild deer . . . free and common for any to kill and take. And for wild fruits there are chestnuts, filberts, hickory-nuts, grapes, mulberries, strawberries, raspberries, huckleberries, and cranberries, with several sorts of plums, and all those fruits in great plenty being free for anybody to gather.

Now I am coming to the planted fruit trees, as apples, pears, apricots, quinces, plums, cherries, gooseberries, currants, and peaches, from which last they distill a liquor . . . much like rum or brandy. . . . They have likewise great stocks of horses and hogs raised in the woods. . . . Their plow shears require but small reparation, wearing out but little. They harrow[1] their ground with a wooden-tined harrow, and twice over does the business. . . .

In this country also is great plenty of working timber, as oaks, ash, chestnuts, pine, cedar, walnut, poplar, fir. . . . 'Tis far cheaper living . . . here than in England, and either men or women that have a trade or are laborers, can, if industrious, get near three times the wages they commonly earn in England.

---

1. A harrow is an implement that levels the earth and breaks up large clods of earth. Harrowing is done after plowing.

To the Speediest Improvement of the Province: Queen Anne's Instruction to Lord Cornbury (1702)

The earliest governors of New Jersey were chosen by the proprietors to run the colony in their behalf. But affairs were so chaotic that these men were often unable to maintain order. Hoping that royal rule might stabilize the colony and thus enable the proprietors to capitalize on their investments, in 1702 the proprietors handed over to the Crown their authority to govern. Queen Anne appointed her cousin Edward Hyde, Lord Cornbury, governor of New York and New Jersey, making Lord Cornbury New Jersey's first royal governor.

This excerpt from the instructions provided to the new governor gives a sense of what the Crown hoped for from its colonies. (See also document 2.)

The inhabitants of our said province have of late years been unhappily divided, and by their enmity to each other our service and their own welfare has been very much obstructed. You are . . . to avoid the engaging yourself in the parties which have been formed amongst them, and to use such impartiality and moderation to all, as may best conduce to our service and the good of the colony. . . .

And in order to the better consolidating and incorporating the two divisions of East and West New Jersey into and under one government, our will and pleasure is that . . . you call together one general assembly for the enacting of laws for the joint and mutual good of the whole; and that the said general assembly do sit in the first place at Perth Amboy, in East New-Jersey and afterwards . . . at Burlington, in West New-Jersey; and that all future general assemblies do sit at one or the other of those places alternatively. . . .

And our further will and pleasure is that the general assembly . . . consist of four and twenty representatives . . . and that no person shall be capable of . . . sitting in general assemblies who shall not have one thousand acres of land of an estate of freehold in his own right . . . and that no freeholder shall be capable of voting in the election of such representative who shall not have one hundred acres of land of an estate of freehold in his own right. . . .

You shall propose to the general assembly of our said province the

William A. Whitehead et al., eds., *Archives of the State of New Jersey* [hereafter, *ASNJ*], 1st ser., vol. 2 (Newark, 1881), 506–536.

passing of such act or acts whereby the right . . . of the . . . general proprietors to the soil of our said province may be confirmed . . . together with all such quit-rents[1] as have been reserved . . . or shall become due. . . . And you are further to take care that . . . the particular titles and estates of all the inhabitants of that province . . . be confirmed and settled . . . as shall tend to the best and speediest improvement or cultivation of the same. . . .

You shall not permit any other person or persons besides the said general proprietors or their agents to purchase any land whatsoever from the Indians. . . .

You are to permit a liberty of conscience to all persons (except Papists)[2] so they may be contented with a quiet and peaceable enjoyment of the same, not giving offence or scandal to the government. . . .

You shall send an account unto us . . . of the present number of planters and inhabitants, men, women and children, as well masters as servants, free and unfree, and of the slaves in our said province, as also a yearly account of the increase or decrease of them and how many of them are fit to bear arms in the militia of our said province. . . .

You shall take care that all planters and Christian servants be well and fitly provided with arms . . . and when, and as often as shall be thought fit, mustered and trained whereby they may be in a better readiness for the defense of our said province under your government. . . .

You are from time to time to give an account . . . what strength your bordering neighbors have, be they Indians or others . . . and of the condition of their plantations. . . .

You shall take especial care that God Almighty be devoutly and duly served throughout your government. The *Book of Common Prayer*, as by law established, read each Sunday, and Holy-day, and the blessed sacrament administered according to the rites of the Church of England.[3]

You shall be careful that the churches already built here be well and orderly kept, and that more be built, as the colony shall by God's

1. In England quitrents, a feudal remnant, were fees paid instead of obligations of service that a tenant might have owed the landowner. In America quitrents were payments made by inhabitants of a tract of land to the owners of the land, usually the proprietors but sometimes the Crown.
2. Followers of the Pope, Roman Catholics. Anti-Catholicism ran deep among adherents of the Church of England. Although their rituals were similar, Anglicans saw in Catholic obedience to the authority of the Pope the agency of a foreign power.
3. The official church in England.

blessing be improved. And that, besides a competent maintenance to be assigned to the minister of each orthodox church, a convenient house be built at the common charge for each minister, and a competent proportion of land assigned to him, for a glebe[4] and exercise of his industry. . . .

You are to take care that drunkenness and debauchery, swearing and blasphemy be discountenanced and punished. And for the further discountenance of vice and encouragement of virtue and good living (that by such example the infidels may be invited and desire to partake of the Christian religion) you are not to admit any person to public trusts and employments in our said province under your government, whose ill fame . . . may occasion scandal. . . .

You are to give all due encouragement and invitation to merchants and others who shall bring trade unto our said province or any way contribute to the advantage thereof and, in particular, the Royal African Company of England.

And whereas we are willing to recommend unto the said company that the said province may have a constant and sufficient supply of merchantable Negroes at moderate rates in money or commodities, so you are to take especial care that payment be duly made and within a competent time. . . .

And you are yearly to give unto us . . . an account of what number of Negroes our said province is yearly supplied with and at what rates. . . .

You shall endeavor to get a law passed for the restraining of any inhuman severity . . . and that provision be made therein that the wilful killing of Indians and Negroes may be punished with death and that a fit penalty be imposed for the maiming of them.

You are also, with the assistance of the council and assembly, to find out the best means to facilitate and encourage the conversion of Negroes and Indians to the Christian religion. . . .

You are to encourage the Indians upon all occasions so as they may apply themselves to the English trade and nation, rather than to any other of Europe. . . .

Forasmuch as great inconveniences may arise by the liberty of printing in our said province you are to provide by all necessary orders that no person keep any press for printing nor that any book, pamphlet, or other matters whatsoever be printed without your especial leave and license first obtained.

---

4. Cultivable land assigned to a parish church.

Royal Colony to Statehood

NOTABLE EVENTS

1732   Stagecoach line operates between Burlington and Perth Amboy

1738   New Jersey receives a royal governor

1739   George Whitefield tours, igniting Great Awakening

1741   Slave revolt scare in New York

1743   American Philosophical Society established to promote scientific advancement

1745   Decade of land riots begins

1746   The College of New Jersey (Princeton University) chartered

1758   Indian reservation established at Brotherton, first in North America

1760   George III becomes King of England and Ireland

1763   Treaty of Paris signed, ending Seven Years' War

1765   Stamp Act

1766   Queen's College (Rutgers University) chartered

1773   Boston Tea Party

1774   First Continental Congress meets; cargo of tea burned in Greenwich

1775   Pennsylvania Quakers form first antislavery society in the world

1776   Tom Paine's *Common Sense*; Declaration of Independence; British capture New York; Battle of Trenton; first New Jersey constitution written

1777   Articles of Confederation adopted by Continental Congress; Battle of Princeton

1781   Revolutionary War fighting ends; Articles of Confederation ratified

1783   Continental Congress meets at Princeton

1785   John Fitch's steamboat, first in America, plies the Delaware River

1787   Constitutional Convention meets; Federalist Papers appear

1788   Constitution ratified

Selected New Jersey Population Statistics, 1726–1784

Year	1726	1738	1745	1784
Population (× 1,000)	32	47	61	149
% Female	47	46.9	44.7	n.a.
Race				
% White	92	91.6	92.5	n.a.
% Black	8	8.4	7.5	n.a.

SOURCE: Peter O. Wacker, *Land and People, A Cultural Georgraphy of Preindustrial New Jersey: Origins and Settlement Patterns* (New Brunswick, N.J.: Rutgers University Press, 1975), 413–416.

"Lusty and Well Set": Runaway Servants in the Early Eighteenth Century

In order to exploit the resources of the New World, many workers were needed; the need for labor was a recurring theme during the colonial period. The extent to which a system known as indentured servitude was used to provide this labor force is often overlooked. Approximately half of all the people who came to the North American colonies south of New England were indentured servants. Terms of servitude varied, but generally someone traded a commitment to work for a master for a number years in return for passage to America. In New Jersey the usual term was four years.

Servants frequently broke the terms of their contracts by running away before their time was up. The following notices are representative of many that appeared in the newspapers of New York, Philadelphia, and even Boston.[1] They provide many details of daily life in the early eighteenth century.

Run away from Samuel Dennis, Junior of Shrewsbury in Monmouth County, December 18, 1722, a servant man named James M'Curdy, aged about twenty-two years. He came from Ireland in the vessel that was cast away . . . this month at Manesquan. He is of a low stature, indifferent,[2] thick set. [He] speaks English and Irish, he can read and write. He has with him some books, two or three shirts, a large felt hat, an old yellowish wig, . . . a threadbare blue coat the buttonholes bound, a cinnamon-colored vest, an old pair of leather breeches, sheep-colored black stockings with several holes in them, and an old pair of round-toe shoes. Whosoever can take up the said servant or secure him so that his master may have him again shall have a pistole[3] reward besides reasonable charges.

1. New Jersey did not have a newspaper printed within its boundaries until 1777.
2. Average, not special, in size or appearance.
3. A European gold coin, in this case probably from France or Spain.

The American Weekly Mercury, January 1, 1722. Reprinted in *ASNJ*, 1st series, vol. 11, Newspaper Extracts, 1704–1739 (Paterson, 1894):68–69.

The American Weekly Mercury, August 25, 1726. Reprinted in *ASNJ*, 1st series, vol. 11, Newspaper Extracts, 1704–1739 (Paterson, 1894):109.

The Pennsylvania Gazette, July 24, 1735. Reprinted in *ASNJ*, 1st series, vol. 11, Newspaper Extracts, 1704–1739 (Paterson, 1894):422.

Run away on August 29, 1726, [from] Doctor John Browne in York Road, West Jersey, a servant woman, named Sarah Parker or Sartin, supposed to be . . . conveyed away by one Richard Sartin, who served his time at French Creek in Pennsylvania, at the Iron Works, who pretends that he is her husband but is not. She is a little thin person, having on a calico gown striped with blue, or a black and white one of wool and worsted, a new bonnet, and other tolerable good clothes. Whosoever takes up said servant woman and secures her to her said master, shall have forty shillings as a reward and all lawful charges.

Run away June 30, 1735, from David Heldreth of Middletown in Monmouth County East New Jersey, a servant woman named Martha Barnes, about thirty-six years of age, lusty and well set, long, thin, . . . tawny complexion, light hair, and blue eyes, with one tooth out before and great ringworms[4] on her breast and arms. Had on a pair of low leather-heeled shoes and two striped homespun petticoats and has since altered the rest of her clothes. Whosoever takes up the said servant so that she may be had again, shall have twenty shillings reward and reasonable charges paid.

---

4. A contagious skin disease caused by a parasitic fungus. So named because the skin blotches are ring-shaped, the disease was once quite common, but today is rare.

"Too Much Indulged": Glimpses of Slavery (1716–1763)

Although the enslavement of Africans did not become the chief source of labor in the North as it did in the South, colonial New Jersey knew slavery. There is evidence of slavery in New Jersey as early as 1680, although surely the Dutch had kept slaves before the English conquest. A census published in 1738 revealed that nearly 12 percent of the population of the counties of old East Jersey was made up of slaves.[1] In Bergen County, which then included what are now Hudson County and part of Passaic County, one inhabitant in five was a black slave.

The following excerpts from items found in the newspapers of New York and Philadelphia illustrate some aspects of the slavery system. The first item suggests that in New Jersey, as elsewhere, one of the factors that underlay the development of black slavery was the failure of Indian slavery. The next item suggests that even slaves who were ill equipped to survive on their own in a foreign environment chose to trust themselves to fate rather than to remain in bondage.

The third item is an account of the aftermath of an alleged slave rebellion in Somerville. It is not clear if there really was such a plot, but evidently one man was hanged in retaliation, several had their ears cut off, and others were whipped. The potential for slave revolt was a constant fear that frequently spilled over, as it did here, into unfounded claims that the rebellious slaves had sexual designs on the white women of the community.

The fourth item describes a cargo of recently arrived slaves. New Jersey's

1. There were four efforts to count the population of colonial New Jersey. None gives any information about free blacks. I am assuming here that all African Americans were enslaved in these years. Undoubtedly there were free blacks in the colony and their number was probably increasing over the course of the eighteenth century.

The Boston News-Letter, July 23–30, 1716. Reprinted in *ASNJ,* 1st series, vol. 11, Newspaper Extracts, 1704–1739 (Paterson, 1894):41.

The American Weekly Mercury, July 14–26, 1727. Reprinted in *ASNJ,* 1st series, vol. 11, Newspaper Extracts, 1704–1739 (Paterson, 1894):105–106.

New York Gazette, March 25, 1734. Reprinted in *ASNJ,* 1st series, vol. 11, Newspaper Extracts, 1704–1739 (Paterson, 1894):340–342.

Pennsylvania Journal, May 27, 1762. Reprinted in Elizabeth Donnan, *Documents Illustrative of the History of the Slave Trade to America* (New York: Octagon Books, 1965), 3:455.

Pennsylvania Journal, October 13, 1763. Reprinted in *ASNJ,* 1st series, vol. 24, Newspaper Extracts, 1762–1765 (Paterson, 1902):251–252.

slave markets (Perth Amboy and Camden) were busy because the import duties on Africans were lower there than in New York and Pennsylvania. The last item is a runaway notice for a talented man who seems to have served as a uniformed house servant.

This is to give notice that on July 16, 1716, run away from his master, David Lyell, an Indian man named Nim. He lately belonged to Mr. James Moore. He is about one and twenty years of age and is a short, broad-shouldered fellow. His hair has been lately cut off, he has a swelling on the back of his right hand, and can do something at the carpenter's trade. He has with him two new shirts, a new waistcoat,[2] breeches of white, coarse linen . . . [and] a homespun coat. [He] wears a hat, shoes, and stockings. It is believed he endeavors to get on board some vessel. Whoever takes up the said Indian in the Jerseys . . . shall have forty shillings and charges; and if in any other government five pounds if they give but notice where he is, so that his master may have him again. Direct to David Lyell in New York, or at Amboy in New Jersey.

Notice is hereby given that there is come to the house of John Leonards at South River Bridge, near Amboy . . . a Negro man, who was forced to the said house for want of sustenance. He is a middle-sized man, talks no English or feigns that he cannot. He calls himself Popaw. His teeth seem to be filed or whet sharp. He will not tell his master's name. Whosoever owns the said Negro may have him from the said Leonard on coming or sending for, paying according to reward (if any be), . . . and also reasonably for his diet till fetched.

I . . . think it necessary to . . . warn all masters of Negroes not to be too careless of their own safety with respect to their slaves, which now begin to be numerous, and in some of our colonies too much indulged. . . .

The Negro of one Hall at Raritan having drank too much, accosted one Reynolds on the road and told him the Englishmen were generally a pack of villains, and kept the Negroes as slaves, contrary to a positive order from King George. . . . Reynolds was surprised at the freedom and independence of this fellow and told him he was a great

---

2. A vest.

rascal to talk in that manner. The Negro answered that he was as good a man as himself and that in a little time he should be convinced of it.

This was the first . . . suspicion of a Negro plot. Upon Reynolds's information . . . he and another Negro was taken up, tried, condemned, and one hanged. . . . It appeared that the design of these Negroes was this. That so soon as the season was advanced that they could lie in the woods, one certain night . . . every Negro in each family was to rise at midnight, cut the throats of their masters and sons (but not meddle with the women, whom they intended to plunder and ravish the day following), and then set all their houses and barns on fire, kill all the draft horses, and secure the best saddle horses for their flight towards the Indians in the French interest.

How easy this design might have been put in practice if it had not been discovered, I leave every one to judge, and how very necessary it is for every colony to make proper laws and ordinances for their own security. . . . Great fatality attends the English dominion in America from the too great number of that unchristian and barbarous people being imported and then by some too much indulged in their vices.

Just imported from the River Gambia in the schooner Sally, Bernard Badger, Master, and to be sold at . . . Cooper's Ferry,[3] opposite to this city, a parcel of likely men and women slaves, with some boys and girls of different ages. . . .

It is generally allowed that the Gambia slaves are much more robust and tractable than any other slaves from the coast of Guinea, and more capable of undergoing the severity of the winter seasons in the North American colonies, which occasions their being vastly more esteemed and coveted in this province and those to the northward, than any other slaves whatsoever.

Run away from Raritan Landing, October 3, 1763, being a middle-sized mulatto[4] slave, born in this country, about twenty years of age, has a very wide mouth, bushy hair (lately cut off), walks with his knees bending forward. His clothes are a French soldier's coat, almost new, which had been white, but dyed (not pressed) together with the lining of a brown color, bordering upon the olive, a new vest, lined

3. Camden. "This city" refers to Philadelphia.
4. An offspring of one black and one white parent.

with white, which had also been made for a French soldier, both altered to fit him, with brass buttons, also an old blue coat, an old leather jockey cap, and trousers of tow cloth.[5]

He is an extremely handy fellow at any common work, especially with horses and carriages of almost any sort, having been bred to it from a little boy, and to the loading and unloading boats; a good deal used to a farm; can do all sorts of house work and very fit to wait upon a gentleman; speaks very good English and Low Dutch, also pretty good High Dutch; is noted for his sense and particularly for his activity at any thing he takes in hand.

It is supposed he will endeavor to pass for a freeman, and get away in the country, or go with some vessel to any part, so as not to be overtaken; all persons are forbid harboring of him, and all masters of vessels taking him on board.

Any person that will bring him to his master, Cornelius Low, of Raritan Landing, near New Brunswick, or secures him in any of his Majesty's jails, giving notice thereof, so that he may be had again, shall have ten dollars reward, and more if it can be reasonably demanded with proper charges.

5. Coarsely woven cloth made out of scratchy flax or hemp fibers.

"Died with the Cancer": A Puritan Gravestone in Monmouth County (1730)

Culturally and intellectually, Puritanism is a foundation stone of American life. Although primarily associated with New England, the Puritan influence in colonial New Jersey was strong. Gravestones such as that pictured here provide powerful reminders of the Puritan presence in New Jersey. This stone was found in the middle 1960s at an unidentifed location in Monmouth County by photographer William F. Augustine.

Grave markers were the only highly decorated artifacts the Puritans produced, which suggests that thinking about death played a large part in Puritan life. We may interpret the images on the stones to help us understand Puritan ideas about death.

The three images at the top of this stone—a death's head, crossed bones, and an hourglass—were quite common. Puritans were Calvinists; they believed that God decreed who was damned and who was saved. What one did in this world had no bearing on one's place in the hereafter according to the strict Calvinist. Death, although inevitable, was so fearful because the moment of truth was at hand and nothing one might have done in life determined whether one was facing a heavenly eternity or damnation.

The hourglass represented the passage of time, the inevitable coming of the fateful showdown. The crossed bones and the grim death's head with its prominent teeth, ghastly eyes, and narrow chin suggest the dread of this terror-filled moment. Because one's life had no bearing on one's fate at the end, there was no way to meet death calmly.

Not surprisingly, the language of the epitaph fit the Puritan scheme as well. It was only the body of Mr. Clark that was interred at this location; his soul had begun its fateful journey.

The eighteenth-century concept of cancer (not so different from our own) fit, too. The term meant an incurable growth that spread indefinitely—it might even return after removal—and in the course of its growth the tumor would eat away whatever part of the body it had lodged in. Death was a virtual certainty for cancer victims. Alexsander Clark had no more control over the malignancy that was corroding his body than he did over his ultimate fate.

Monmouth County oversize folder, William F. Augustine Collection, Rutgers. Reproduced by permission of the Department of Special Collections and University Archives, Rutgers University Libraries.

Fraudulent Claims: The Land Riots of 1746

In the late 1740s rioting was widespread in New Jersey. The disputes primarily concerned who had legal title to the land, but other social and religious tensions were involved as well.

The riots generally were attempts to intimidate rent collectors or to prevent the jailing of someone for trespassing or nonpayment of rent. Sometimes there would be a cycle of violence. Colonial authorities might arrest a man they had caught hunting or chopping wood on land not his to use. A small riot would result in his release. The leaders of this riot would be apprehended, and a second, larger mob might free these men. The first excerpt used here, from a New York newspaper, describes such a riot in which a mob freed the leader of a previous melee, along with others then in prison.

The basis of the confusion in land titles lay in the origins of the colony eighty years earlier. In the middle of the eighteenth century the issue had become so complicated that it was difficult to know who owned what land, who had permission to live on or work a particular tract, and who might owe rent to whom.

Sometimes disputes involved two parties, both of whom believed they had received, by purchase or gift, titles from those who had been empowered by the Crown to dispose of the property. This confusion was possible because in the early years of the colony more than one individual was given authority to make land grants. At other times the dispute involved parties with entirely different conceptions of what property ownership meant. Some settlers believed, as reflected in the second passage included here, that unworked land belonged to God and that those who worked the soil had a natural right to it.

On the other hand, those who believed their right to the land stemmed from the Crown, through the proprietors, argued that only the Crown could grant land. They felt that people who were farming or hunting or cutting wood on land not theirs were committing not only the theft of property, but treason as well, by challenging the authority of the Crown. This concern is suggested in the third passage, a brief excerpt from Governor Jonathan Belcher's message to

New York Weekly Post Boy, January 20, 1746. Reprinted in *ASNJ*, 1st series, vol. 11, Newspaper Extracts, 1704–1739 (Paterson, 1894):286–287.

The New York Weekly Post Boy, June 9, 1746. Reprinted in *ASNJ*, 1st series, vol. 12, Newspaper Extracts, 1740–1750 (Paterson, 1895):308–309.

"Message of Governor Belcher to the Council and Assembly of New Jersey." Reprinted in *ASNJ*, 1st series, vol. 7 (Newark, 1883): 68–69.

ASNJ, 1st series, vol. 7 (Newark, 1883):193–197.

the legislature, and in the fourth, wherein the proprietors appeal to the King to intercede because they doubt the local authority's ability to deliver justice.

We have just now received the following account of a very extraordinary riot at Newark. . . . One Nehemiah Baldwin, with two others, were apprehended . . . for being concerned in a former riot and committed to jail. In the morning one of them offered to give bail and the Sheriff, for that purpose, took him . . . to the Judge. But on their way thither a great number of persons appeared, armed with cudgels,[1] coming down from the back settlements, who immediately rescued the prisoner in a very violent manner. . . . The Sheriff retreated to the jail . . . to guard it. But by two o'clock in the afternoon the mob, being increased to about three hundred strong, marched with the utmost intrepidity to the prison, declaring that if they were fired on, they would kill every man. After breaking through the guard, wounding and being wounded, they got to the jail, which they broke open, setting at liberty all the prisoners they could find, as well debtors and others, and then marched off in triumph, using many threatening expressions against all those who had assisted the authority. Several of the guard as well as of the mob were much wounded and bruised, and it is thought one of the latter is past recovery. What may be the consequence of this affair, is not easy to guess.

No man is naturally entitled to a greater proportion of the earth than another; but though it was made for the use of all, it may nevertheless be appropriated by every individual. This is done by the improvement of any part of it laying vacant, which is thereby . . . made the property of that man who bestowed his labor on it, from whom it cannot afterwards be taken without breaking through the rules of natural justice; for thereby he could be actually deprived of the fruits of his industry.

Yet if mankind, who were designed by the Almighty to be tenants in common of the habitable globe, should agree to divide it among themselves into certain shares or parts, the contract will be binding by the laws of nature and ought, therefore, to be inviolably observed. Such a division has been attempted by the treaties made between the several Princes and States of Europe, with regard to the vast desert of America. But each Prince stipulated, or ought to be understood to have stipulated, for the general benefit of the people under his government and not for his particular profit. The Kings of England al-

1. Thick sticks or clubs.

ways held the lands in America . . . in trust for their subjects; which lands, having lain uncultivated from the beginning of the world, were therefore, as free and as common for all to settle upon as the waters of the rivers are to all to drink. Yet to prevent the confusion that would follow on every man's being his own carver, governors were, from time to time, appointed by the Crown, to parcel out to the subjects as much land as each could occupy. But the mischief of it was, that the best parts . . . have been granted to a few particulars, in such exorbitant quantities that the rest of the subjects have been obliged to buy it for their use, at an extravagant price: A hardship, that seems as great, as if they had been put under the necessity of buying the waters of the rivers.

I have received sundry complaints from numbers of persons who say they are unjustly disturbed in the possession of their lands. . . . I wish both houses would so far reconsider the matter as to . . . be able to report what may be proper to be done by the legislature to bring an end to the disorders and confusions that have so long subsisted in the province . . . to the dishonor of God, in high contempt for the King's authority and of the good and wholesome laws of this province. As it well becomes rulers to encourage and support them that do well so it is their indispensable duty to be a terror to evildoers. . . . Assaults and batteries, breaking open the king's jails . . . must soon bring things to this question: whether his Majesty's authority shall be supported in this province of New Jersey or whether a number of rioters shall take the government into their own hands.

New Jersey . . . was granted by King Charles the Second to His Royal Highness James, Duke of York, and by him conveyed to Lord Berkeley and Sir George Carteret in the year 1664 who began to plant and improve the same. . . . Sir George Carteret . . . made considerable improvements and brought into the province great numbers of inhabitants to whom he gave lands as an encouragement, upon small rents.

The . . . eastern part . . . of New Jersey, together with the powers of government, were . . . afterwards conveyed to twenty-four persons who were called the general proprietors and who went on in planting and improving the said Province at their own very great cost and charge. . . .

The said proprietors exercised the powers of government in the said province from the time of their grant in 1664 till the year 1702, when they made a surrender thereof to the Crown, reserving to themselves the rents and soil and all things granted them as aforesaid, the government only excepted.

But . . . great numbers of men . . . entered into a combination to subvert the laws and constitution of the province and to obstruct the course of legal proceedings. . . . They . . . endeavoured to infuse into the minds of the people that neither Your Majesty nor your noble progenitors, Kings and Queens of England, had any right whatsoever to the soil or government of America and that Your Majesty's and their grants thereof were void and fraudulent. Having by those means associated to themselves great numbers of the poor and ignorant part of the people of this province, they . . . broke open the jail of the County of Essex and took from thence a prisoner . . . and have since that time gone on . . . dispossessing some people of their estates . . . plundering the estates of others who do not join with them . . . breaking open Your Majesty's prisons as often as any of them are committed and rescuing their accomplices from thence and . . . travelling often in armed multitudes to different parts of this province for those purposes. . . .

Your Majesty's petitioners having in vain applied to the legislature here for that protection which they think themselves entitled . . . and having not the least hopes or expectations that their persons or properties will be protected by their own legislature do find themselves under a necessity of laying this their petition at the feet of Your Most Sacred Majesty the gracious guardian and protector of all Your faithful subjects.

DOCUMENT 13

Sacred Friendship: Excerpts from the Journal of Esther Edwards Burr (1754–1757)

We know very little about the day-to-day lives of colonial women. Few read and fewer wrote; often those who could write were discouraged from doing so by their husbands.

Esther Edwards was the daughter of Massachusetts minister Jonathan Edwards, a leader of the Great Awakening and perhaps the most important theologian in eighteenth-century America. When she was twenty she married—after a five-day courtship—Aaron Burr, the president of the College of New Jersey, a man sixteen years her senior. She bore two children; the second, Aaron Burr, Jr., served as Vice President of the United States during Thomas Jefferson's first term, though he is probably most famous for the 1804 duel in Weehawken, during which he shot and killed Alexander Hamilton.

Esther Edwards Burr was not representative of the women of provincial New Jersey, but her letters to her friend Sarah Prince reflect important issues in the lives of many women of the day. In the letters excerpted here, Burr touches on work, marriage, the bonds of sisterhood, and relations between men and women.

Esther Edwards Burr died at twenty-six, shortly after having been inoculated against smallpox. The last item included here is an excerpt from the moving passage Sarah Prince recorded in her diary when she learned of the death of her dear friend and correspondent.

October 5, 1754

I write just when I can get time. . . . I can't get much for I have my Sally to tend and domestic affairs to see to and company to wait of, besides my sewing. . . . I am really hurried.

I don't much wonder that . . . some folks would want to break the friendship between us. It was what I expected, so forewarned, fore-armed. . . .

I look on the ties of friendship as sacred and I am of your mind that it ought to be a matter of solemn prayer to God; where there is a friendship contracted that it may be preserved.

Carol J. Karlsen and Laurie Crumpacker, eds., *The Journal of Esther Edwards Burr: 1754–1757* (New Haven: Yale University Press, 1984), 50, 78–79, 178, 194–195, 257, 307–308. Copyright © 1984 by Yale University Press. Reprinted by permission.

January 6, 1755

I think we go along much as we used to last winter. I hope you have not forgotten. . . . Mr. Burr [has] gone to Elizabethtown as he used to all the cold days last winter (for you must know the weather is very cold.) . . .

Pray, what do you think everybody marries in, or about winter for? . . . I really believe 'tis for fear of laying cold and for want of a bed-fellow. . . .

December 20, 1755

I am perplexed about our public affairs. The men say (though not Mr. Burr, he is not one of that sort) that women have no business to concern themselves about 'em, but trust to those that know better and be content to be destroyed because . . . they did all for the best. Indeed, if I was convinced that our great men did act as they really thought was for the glory of God and the good of the country, it would go a great ways to make me easy.

April 16, 1756

I never was so near being angry at you in my life. . . . You must pardon my severity for I am too warm about it. . . .

You would not have the man act like a fool, would you? Well, why will you oblige him to either become a fool or give up the affair. . . . I wonder in the name of honesty what business you had to run away time after time when you knew he was a coming. You may repent it when it is too late. . . .

You should consider my dear that he does not . . . know the reasons of your conduct. 'Tis most likely that he thinks that you dislike him or else that you are a mortal, proud creature which must sink you in his opinion. . . . No man likes a woman the better for being shy when she means the very thing she pretends to be shy of.

April 12, 1757

I have had a smart combat with Mr. Ewing[1] about our sex. He is a man of good parts and learning but has mean thoughts of women. He began the dispute in this manner. Speaking of Miss Boudinot,[2] I said she was a sociable, friendly creature. . . . Mr. Ewing says: she and the Stocktons[3] are full of talk about friendship and society and such stuff—and made a mouth as if much disgusted. I asked what he

1. John Ewing, a College of New Jersey tutor.
2. Annis Boudinot, a poet and friend of Burr's.
3. Abigail and John Stockton and their son Richard, probably. Annis Boudinot married Richard Stockton in late 1757.

would have 'em talk about; whether he chose they should talk about fashions and dress. He said: things that they understood. He did not think women knew what friendship was. They were hardly capable of anything so cool and rational as friendship.

My tongue you know hangs pretty loose, thoughts crowded in so I sputtered away for dear life. You may guess what a large field this speech opened for me. I retorted several severe things upon him before he had time to speak again. He blushed and seemed confused. . . . We carried on the dispute for an hour. I talked him quite silent. . . . One of the last things that he said was that he never in all his life knew or heard of a woman that had a little . . . learning, . . . but it made her proud to such a degree that she was disgustful to all her acquaintance.

April 21, 1758

God in holy but awful severity has again struck at one of my principal springs of earthly comfort in taking from me the beloved of my heart, my dearest friend, Mrs. Burr. . . . My whole prospects in this world are now changed. My whole dependence for comfort in this world gone. . . . She knew and felt all my griefs. She laid out herself for my good. . . . Her natural powers were superior to most women, her knowledge was extensive of men and things, her accomplishments fine, her prudence, forethought and sagacity wonderful; her modesty rare. In friendly quality none exceeded her. . . . How faithful? How sincere? How open hearted? How tender? . . . And she was mine. Oh the tenderness which tied our hearts. Oh the comfort I have enjoyed in her, almost seven years. Oh the pleasant days and nights we have spent in opening our whole souls and pouring them into each other's breasts. . . . Oh the pleasure of seeing, hearing, loving, writing, conversing, thinking we took in each other. Oh the lovely pattern she set for me. . . . But she is gone. Fled this world forever. . . . And with her went almost the all in which I had summed up my earthly good. Oh painful separation. Oh desolate world. How barren art thou now to me. . . . My earthly joy is gone. Not only so, but my God hides His face. . . . What shall I do?

DOCUMENT 14

A Harmony of Practice and Principle: John Woolman Objects to Military Service (1757)

John Woolman was born in Rancocas (Burlington County) in 1720. One of thirteen children and largely self-educated, Woolman became a Quaker minister when he was twenty-three. He was an influential opponent of slavery whose pamphlet Some Considerations on the Keeping of Negroes *(1754) is the first important abolitionist work. After his death in 1772, the Philadelphia Yearly Meeting renounced slavery and disowned those of its members who refused to free their slaves. This was a measure of Woolman's influence.*

The passage here is excerpted from John Woolman's journal, one of the masterpieces of colonial American writing. In this excerpt, which demonstrates both his characteristically simple style and his spiritual idealism, Woolman discusses two separate but related incidents having to do with the Seven Years' War.[1] In the first section Woolman discusses the calling up for possible military service of a number of Quaker young men. He displays sensitivity to the officers involved and impatience with young men whose pacifism seemed insincere. In the second instance Woolman is forced to decide what to do when he is asked to provide lodging for a soldier. In each case Woolman seems to relish the opportunity to put his convictions to the test.

Orders came to . . . draft the militia and prepare a number of men to go . . . to the relief of the English at Fort William Henry[2]. . . . Shortly after, there came orders to draft three times as many to hold themselves in readiness to march when fresh orders came. . . . There was a meeting of the military officers at Mount Holly who agreed on a draft,

1. Known in the colonies as the French and Indian War, the Seven Years' War ran from 1756 to 1763. It was part of a much longer struggle between the British and French empires. Native Americans tended to side with the French because they saw the British as principally responsible for their loss of autonomy. The inhabitants of the British colonies were unenthusiastic about the war, hoping that London would wage it without asking for too much from them.
2. A British fort at the head of Lake George in upstate New York. It fell to the French in 1757 after a brief siege.

Phillips P. Moulton, ed., *The Journal and Major Essays of John Woolman* (New York: Oxford University Press, 1971), 87–89. Reprinted by permission of Phillips P. Moulton.

and orders were sent to the men so chosen to meet their respective captains at set times and places, those in our township to meet at Mount Holly, amongst whom were a considerable number of our Society.

My mind being affected herewith, I had fresh opportunity to see and consider the advantage of living in the real substance of religion, where practice does harmonize with principle. Amongst the officers are men of understanding who have some regard to sincerity where they see it; and in the execution of their office, when they have men to deal with whom they believe to be upright-hearted men, to put them to trouble on account of scruples of conscience is a painful task and likely to be avoided as much as may be easily. But where men profess to be so meek and heavenly minded . . . that they cannot join in wars, and yet by their spirit and conduct in common life manifest a contrary disposition, their difficulties are great at such a time. . . .

Men who are insincere, pretend[ing] scruple of conscience in hopes of being excused from a dangerous employment, they are likely to be roughly handled. In this time of commotion some of our young men left the parts and tarried abroad till it was over. Some came and proposed to go as soldiers. Others appeared to have a real tender scruple in their minds against joining in wars and were much humbled under the apprehension of a trial so near. . . .

At the set time when the captain came to town some of those last mentioned went and told in substance as follows: That they could not bear arms for conscience sake, nor could they hire any to go in their places. . . . At length the captain acquainted them all that they might return home for the present and required them to provide themselves as soldiers and to be in readiness to march when called upon. This was such a time as I had not seen before, and yet I may say with thankfulness to the Lord that I believed this trial was intended for our good, and I was favored with resignation to Him. The French army, taking the fort they were besieging, destroyed it and went away. The company of men first drafted after some days' march had orders to return home, and these on the second draft were no more called upon on that occasion. . . .

Orders came to some officers in Mount Holly to prepare quarters a short time for about one hundred soldiers. An officer and two other men, all inhabitants of our town, came . . . to speak with me to provide lodging and entertainment for two soldiers, there being six shillings a week per man allowed as pay for it. The case being new and unexpected, I made no answer suddenly but sat a time silent, my mind being inward. I was fully convinced that the proceedings in wars are inconsistent with the purity of the Christian religion, and to be hired to entertain men who were then under pay as soldiers was a difficulty with me. I expected they had legal authority for what they did, and after a short time I said to the officer, "If the men are sent here for entertainment, I believe I shall not refuse to admit them into my house, but the nature of the case is such that I expect I cannot keep them on hire." . . .

Though they spoke of two, there came only one, who tarried at my house about two weeks and behaved himself civilly. And when the officer came to pay me I told him that I could not take pay for it, having admitted him into my house in a passive obedience to authority. . . . As I turned from him he said he was obliged to me, to which I said nothing, but thinking on the expression I grew uneasy, and afterwards being near where he lived I went and told him on what grounds I refused pay for keeping the soldier.

"Orderly and Useful Subjects": The Brotherton Indian Reservation (1759)

By the middle of the eighteenth century only a small group of Lenapes remained in New Jersey. Although most sought to adapt to the Anglo-American way of life, some sided with the French during the Seven Years' War.[1] A 1756 raid on settlements in Sussex County forced the leaders of New Jersey to deal with the Indians.

The document excerpted here is a report of Governor Francis Bernard on his efforts to establish an Indian reservation (arguably this nation's first) in the Pinelands. The mixture of motives—controlling on one hand, humanitarian on the other—that underlay much Indian policy is reflected in this document.

I went to Burlington County to lay out the Indian Town there. . . . By agreement with the Indians south of Raritan, they released all their claims in the province, in consideration of a tract of 3,000 acres to be purchased for their use. This purchase was made and the Indians are removed to the place. It is a tract of land very suitable for this purpose, having soil good enough, a large hunting country and a passage by water to the sea for fishing. It is out of the way of communication with the wild Indians and has a sawmill upon it which serves to provide them with timber for their own use and to raise a little money for other purposes.

To this place I went with . . . the commissioners for Indian affairs, where we laid out the plan of a town, to which I gave the name of Brotherton and saw a house erected being one of ten that were ready prepared. Afterwards [I] ordered lots of land to be laid for the Indians to clear and till, the land already cleared . . . to remain in common until they have acquired . . . separate property by their own industry. We also made an appointment of a house and lands for a Minister, I having engaged Mr. Brainerd,[2] a Scotch Presbyterian, for that purpose. . . .

The next day I had a conference with the chiefs at which they

1. See John Woolman, "A Harmony of Practice and Principle," document 14, note 1.

2. John Brainerd, a missionary for the Scottish Society for the Propagation of Christian Knowledge, was appointed minister and superintendent. He remained at Brotherton until 1768.

ASNJ, 1st ser., vol. 9 (Newark, 1885), 174–176.

expressed great satisfaction at what had been done for them. I assured them that the same care of them should be continued and exhorted them to order, sobriety and industry. The whole number of them at present does not amount to 200; and when we have gathered together all in the province they will not be 300. If I can but keep them from being supplied with rum, for which there are laws strict enough, I shall hope to make them orderly and useful subjects.

No Taxes Without Consent: New Jersey and the Stamp Act (1765)

The Stamp Act was the first direct tax on the colonies passed by Parliament. It was designed to defray the rising costs of colonial military defense. The Act hit lawyers, merchants, and tradesmen the hardest, but it touched virtually every colonist because it required the purchase of a tax stamp for nearly every transaction in the economic life of the colonies. In addition, the law required that the stamps be purchased with scarce hard currency and called for violators to be prosecuted in vice-admiralty courts, which afforded no trials by jury.

In New Jersey opposition to the law developed gradually between its passage in March 1765 and its scheduled implementation in November of that year. The colony's lawyers carried on their practices without using the stamps, a passive means of resistance that was emulated in other colonies. But the tactic was controversial because many felt that rather than continuing to work, the lawyers should cease their practices and endeavor to bring the commerce of the colony to a halt, a more active form of resistance.

The colonial assembly issued in late November a series of protest resolutions, which are excerpted below; citizens organized themselves as Sons of Liberty to coordinate local protests around the province. An excerpt of the organizing document of the Sons of Liberty in New Brunswick is provided here as well.

The Stamp Act crisis raises a number of issues. The assembly in its "Resolves" took pains to stake out an argument on constitutional grounds. The fundamental question the legislators raised was what power Parliament could exercise over a lawfully elected legislature.

The Sons of Liberty, or Liberty Boys as they were popularly known, consisted in New Jersey largely of farmers, lawyers, and merchants. Concerned with keeping the protest within appropriate limits, the New Jersey Liberty Boys were not a vehicle for radical protest as they were in colonies such as New York and Massachusetts.

The late act of Parliament called the Stamp Act is found to be utterly subversive of privileges inherent in, and originally secured by, grants

Edmund Morgan, ed., *Prologue to Revolution: Sources and Documents on the Stamp Act Crisis, 1764–1766*. Published for the Institute of Early American History and Culture, Williamsburg, Virginia. (Chapel Hill: University of North Carolina Press, 1959), 59–60, 115–116. Copyright © 1959 by the University of North Carolina Press.

. . . from the Crown of Great Britain to the settlers of this colony. In duty therefore to ourselves, our constituents, and posterity, this House think it absolutely necessary to leave the following resolves on our minutes.

Resolved . . . that his majesty's subjects inhabiting this province are, from the strongest motives of duty, fidelity, and gratitude, inviolably attached to his royal person and government, and have ever shown, and we doubt not ever will, their utmost readiness and alacrity in acceding to the constitutional requisitions of the Crown, as they have been from time to time made to this colony.

Resolved . . . that his majesty's liege[1] subjects in this colony are entitled to all the inherent rights and liberties of his natural-born subjects within the Kingdom of Great-Britain.

Resolved . . . that it is . . . essential to the freedom of a people, and the undoubted right of Englishmen, that no taxes be imposed on them but with their own consent. . . .

Resolved . . . that the people of this colony are not . . . represented in the Parliament of Great Britain. And if the principle of taxing the colonies without their own consent should be adopted, the people here would be subjected to the taxation of two legislatures, a grievance unprecedented, and not to be thought of without the greatest anxiety.

Resolved . . . that the only representatives of the people of this colony are persons chosen by themselves, and that no taxes . . . can be imposed on them . . . but by their own legislature. . . .

Resolved . . . that as the tranquility of this colony has been interrupted, through fear of the dreadful consequences of the Stamp Act, that therefore the officers of the government, who go on in their offices for the good and peace of the province, in the accustomed manner while things are in their present unsettled situation, will, in the opinion of this House, be entitled to the countenance of the Legislature. And it is recommended to our constituents to use what endeavors lie in their power to preserve the peace, quiet, harmony and good order of the government; that no heats, disorders, or animosities may in the least obstruct the united endeavors that are now strongly engaged, for the repealing of the act above mentioned, and other acts affecting the trade of the colonies.

At a meeting of the Sons of Liberty of the city of New Brunswick . . . it was resolved:

That we will cheerfully embark our lives and fortunes in the defense of our liberties and privileges.

---

1. Owing allegiance to royal authority.

That we will resist . . . all illegal attempts to deprive us of our indubitable rights and for that reason will, to the last extremity, oppose the exercise of the Stamp Act in the colony.

That we will contribute all in our power to preserve the public tranquility, so far as it may be preserved, consistent with the principles already professed.

That we will do our utmost to support and defend the officers of government in this colony who shall act agreeable to the above resolves.

That we shall always be ready, with hearts and hands, to assist the neighboring provinces in opposing every attempt that may be made to deprive them and us of those privileges and immunities which God and nature seem to have intended us.

And lastly, that we do bear his Majesty, King George the Third, true allegiance and will at all times faithfully adhere to his royal person, and just government, and heartily defend him from every attempt to injure his person, crown, or dignity.

DOCUMENT 17

Affectionate Father, Dutiful Son: Benjamin and William Franklin and the Coming of the American Revolution

It is easy to lose sight of the personal dimension of large historical events. The correspondence between Benjamin Franklin and his son, William, illustrates the human impact of the gulf that gradually grew between the interests of the American colonists and the British Crown.

William Franklin was Benjamin Franklin's son by a now unknown woman. Father and son developed a close relationship over the years. They shared far more than the famous experiment with the kite. When William was appointed Royal Governor of New Jersey, Benjamin was in London representing the interests of the colonies. Father and son both loved the Crown and believed that it was possible to keep the interests of King George III in harmony with those of the American colonies. The following excerpts from correspondence between and about William and Benjamin show what happened as this became impossible.

In the fall of 1773 when these letters began, harmony was becoming harder to sustain. Although their personal relationship remained close as their politics began to diverge, strains were becoming apparent. In February 1774 Benjamin Franklin urged his son to resign his governorship, although the salary was William's only means of support; in May Benjamin predicted trouble for William if he continued to try to serve the conflicting interests of colony and Crown.

After their sharp disagreement over the tea protest in Boston, the correspondence between father and son grew less frequent and seldom returned to politics. By the end of 1775 all correspondence between them seems to have ended. The next letter included here is from William's wife to her father-in-law requesting his aid in removing Franklin from the house arrest under which he was held in Connecticut. The elder Franklin's attitude is suggested by the last two pieces of correspondence, one with William Temple Franklin, Benjamin's grandson, and one to a friend describing William's circumstances. After the war father and son met just once, despite William's desire to reconcile. Shortly before he died, Benjamin disinherited his only son.

William B. Willcox, ed., *The Papers of Benjamin Franklin* (New Haven: Yale University Press, 1976–1983), 20:436–437, 21:75, 211–212, 237–238, 285–287, 22:551–552, 612–613, 23:314. Copyright © 1976–1983 by Yale University Press. Reprinted by permission.

London, October 6, 1773
Dear Son,

I am indeed of opinion that the Parliament has no right to make any law whatever binding on the colonies. That the King, and not the King, Lords and Commons collectively, is their sovereign; and that the King . . . is their only legislator. I know your sentiments differ from mine on these subjects. You are a thorough government man, which I do not wonder at, nor do I aim at converting you. I only wish you to act uprightly and steadily. . . . If you can promote the prosperity of your people and leave them happier than you found them, whatever your political principles are, your memory will be honored. . . .

I am ever your affectionate father.

London, February 2, 1774
Dear Son,

As there is no prospect of your being ever promoted to a better government, and that you hold has never defrayed its expenses, I wish you were well settled in your farm. It is an honester and a more honorable, because a more independent, employment. You will hear from others the treatment I have received.[1] I leave you to your own reflections and determinations upon it and remain ever,

Your affectionate father.

May 7, 1774
To William Franklin:

I don't understand it as any favor to me or to you, the being continued in an office by which with all your prudence you cannot avoid running behind hand, if you live suitably to your station. While you are in it I know you will execute it with fidelity to your master, but I think independence more honorable than any service. . . . In the state of American affairs which from the present arbitrary measures is likely soon to take place, you will find yourself in no comfortable situation, and perhaps wish you had soon disengaged yourself.

July 3, 1774
To Benjamin Franklin:

I cannot but think it very extraordinary that neither the Assembly of Massachusetts Bay nor the town of Boston have so much as inti-

1. Benjamin Franklin was stripped of his job as deputy postmaster general of the colonies and publicly humiliated because he was responsible for the release of some letters written by Massachusetts's governor, Thomas Hutchinson, and lieutenant governor, Andrew Oliver. Hutchinson and Oliver had urged the restriction of the liberties of Massachusetts.

mated any intention or desire of making satisfaction to the East India Company and the officers of the customs when by doing those two things, which are consistent with strict justice, and by declaring that they will not hereafter attempt to hinder the landing at Boston any goods legally imported, they might get their port opened in a few months. But if they are to wait . . . until the grand question is settled between the two countries, they may as well never have their port opened, for by that time their trade will have got into another channel and most of their merchants . . . either ruined or removed. Besides they ought first to do justice before they ask it of others. . . . Their making reparation to those whom they have injured would besides . . . do credit to their cause. . . .

The family were all well when I left Burlington. . . . I am ever your dutiful son.

London, September 7, 1774
Dear Son. . . .

I do not, so much as you do, wonder that the Massachusetts have not offered payment for the tea. 1. Because of the uncertainty of the Act which gives them no surety that the port shall be opened on their making that payment. 2. No specific sum is demanded. 3. No one knows what will satisfy the Custom House officers, nor who the "others" are that must be satisfied, nor what will satisfy them. . . . As to "doing Justice before they ask it," that should have been thought of by the legislature here, before they demanded it of the Bostonians. They have extorted many thousand pounds from America unconstitutionally, under cover of Acts of Parliament, and with an armed force. Of this money they ought to make restitution. . . . But you who are a thorough courtier, see everything with government eyes. . . .

With love to Betsey, I am, ever your affectionate father.

Amboy, August 6, 1776

I will not distress you by enumerating all my afflictions, but allow me dear Sir to mention that it is greatly in your power to relieve them. Suppose that Mr. Franklin would sign a parole not dishonorable to himself and satisfactory to Governor Trumbull,[2] why may he not be permitted to return into this province and to his family? Many of the officers that have been taken during the war ha[ve] had that indulgence shown them and why should it be denied to him? His private affairs are unsettled, his family distressed and he is living very un-

2. Jonathan Trumbull (1710–1785), governor of Connecticut from 1769 until 1784. Trumbull was the only colonial governor to be continued in office after independence was declared.

comfortably and at a great expense, which he can very ill afford at present. Consider my dear and honored Sir that I am now pleading the cause of your son, and my beloved husband. If I have said, or done anything wrong I beg to be forgiven. I am . . . your dutiful and affectionate daughter, Elizabeth Franklin

Philadelphia, September 19, 1776
Dear Billy,

I received yours of the 16th, in which you propose going to your father, if I have no objection. I have considered the matter and cannot approve of your taking such a journey at this time, especially alone, for many reasons which I have not time to write. I am persuaded that if your mother should write a sealed letter to her husband, and enclose it under cover to Governor Trumbull of Connecticut, acquainting him that it contains nothing but what relates to her private family concerns, and requesting him to forward or deliver it (opening it first if he should think fit), he would cause it to be delivered safe without opening. I hope you do not feel any reluctance in returning to your studies. This is the time of life in which you are to lay the foundations of your future improvement and of your importance among men. If this season is neglected, it will be like cutting off the spring from the year. . . .

My love to your good Mama, and respects to her friends in the family. . . .

Your affectionate grandfather.

[1777]
To Dr. Ingen Hausz,

You inquire what is become of my son, the Governor of New Jersey. As he adhered to the party of the King, his people took him prisoner and sent him under a guard to Connecticut, where he continues but is allowed a district of some miles to ride about, upon his . . . honor not to quit this country. I have with me here his son, a promising youth of about seventeen, whom I brought with me, partly to finish his education, having a great affection for him, and partly to have his assistance as a clerk, in which capacity he is very serviceable to me.

"No Fences Left": War-Torn New Jersey (1777)

New Jersey is called the "cockpit of the revolution" because it was the scene of so much warfare. The state was badly torn up during the war, as this passage indicates.

In August 1777, Ebenezer Hazard was surveyor of the post office, based in Philadelphia. The journey he describes here was undertaken in pursuit of his duties, possibly searching for locations at which to construct new post offices.

The devastation of war had its greatest impact on the individuals directly affected. But it also weakened overall public morale, which in New Jersey was sorely tested. As the war dragged on the citizens of the state became increasingly demoralized. At war's end large areas of the state were in ruins.

After the war New Jersey's slow recovery contributed to the state's ready acceptance of the stronger frame of government proposed in the Constitution.

Trenton has suffered by the enemy, but not near so much as might have been expected: all the fences about it have been destroyed. The ferry house was burned down. . . . When General Washington attacked the enemy at Trenton,[1] numbers of the Hessians hid themselves in cellars and others wanted to do so but were driven out by the inhabitants.

Princeton looks like the picture of desolation. Several houses have been burned there: not a pew is left in the Meeting House, and a large brick chimney has been built where the pulpit stood; the windows of this house have all been broken. The College[2] is in a very ruinous situation, but this suffered more from the licentiousness of our own troops than from the ravages of the enemy; the latter knocked down a study in each room, but the former destroyed the library, damaged the orrery,[3] broke down the pews and rostrum in the hall, cut the

1. The Battle of Trenton, December 26, 1776.
2. The College of New Jersey, now Nassau Hall, Princeton University.
3. An apparatus that used movable balls to represent the position of the planets and their moons; planetarium.

Fred Shelley, ed., "Ebenezer Hazard's Diary: New Jersey During the Revolution," *New Jersey History* 90 (Autumn 1972):171–179. Reprinted in Larry R. Gerlach, *New Jersey in the American Revolution, 1763–1783: A Documentary History* (Trenton: New Jersey Historical Commission, 1975), 299–302. Reprinted by permission of the New Jersey Historical Commission.

pillars which supported the gallery, stole all the pipes of the organ, destroyed an elegant whole length picture of George II,[4] and defaced that of Governor Belcher.[5] . . . There are no fences left in Princeton.

Passed through Kingston, Rocky Hill, Grigg's Town, and Somerset Court House[6] to Morris Town. These are small villages. Kingston is so shabby a place that even an enemy could hardly deface it; the fences, however, have been destroyed. . . .

Great devastation was made by the enemy at Somerset Court House: the Dutch and Presbyterian churches (framed buildings) were stripped of their pulpits and pews, their doors and windows were broken, and the boards torn off the outside so as to leave the frames bare. Several dwelling houses were destroyed. The thatch was torn off of barns and barracks, and two orchards were cut down that booths might be made for the soldiers, of the branches of the trees. The enemy's advanced guard was kept in an orchard just back of the court house; their main body laid about half a mile farther on a beautiful rising ground: their booths still remain there. . . .

Rode through . . . Springfield . . . a small village . . . situated between two brooks which, on account of the mud at bottom, are impassable except at the bridges. To this place the enemy came but had not time to do any mischief, being disturbed and driven away before night by the militia. In their way from Elizabeth Town to this place the enemy took out of their houses a Mr. Nathaniel Morris and William Richardson, as rebels (as they termed it); they pinioned them and brought them to Springfield. When they found an engagement was likely to come on, they tied them both together and placed them in front; they remained there during the battle and neither of them received any damage. The enemy being driven off, they were released. The officer who ordered them to be placed there is supposed to have been killed or mortally wounded (and carried off), as he has not been heard of since.

The chief damage Newark sustained appears to have been the destruction of fences. The enemy violated the chastity of some of the female inhabitants here and in the vicinity. A woman of seventy was among the victims of their brutal lust.

4. King of England, 1727–1760.
5. Jonathan Belcher, governor of New Jersey, 1747–1757.
6. Now Millstone.

"How Terrible This Civil War Raged": The Journal of Nicholas Collin (1778)

British General Sir William Howe occupied Philadelphia in late September 1777. Howe's troops then defeated Washington's at Germantown, north of Philadelphia, in early October. After that the American forces retreated to Valley Forge, where they spent the winter near starvation, as is well known. The British troops, although in somewhat better shape than the Americans, were in want of provisions too. Southern and central New Jersey was no-man's-land, the site of repeated skirmishes and raids as rival foraging parties traversed the region. Neither side was very successful in rounding up food or supplies, but the passions of local citizens on both sides were inflamed.

Nicholas Collin, whose journal is excerpted here, was pastor of the Swedish Lutheran Church at Penn's Neck (now Swedesboro in Gloucester County). He described the difficult state of affairs in the southwestern part of the state.

On the last of February the American general Wayne[1] passed through here with a detachment of three hundred men, of whom the greater part were miserably clothed, some without boots, others without socks. . . . A regiment of English infantry came to attack him, but he had then already escaped. These troops had come in running march the last half mile and the militia in Swedesboro had hardly time to escape. . . . The English soldiers are undisciplined and cannot always be controlled. This was one of the main reasons for their slight success, because often both friend and foe were robbed in the most despicable manner, and sometimes with the permission of the officers.

From this time on until the end of June, when the English army left Philadelphia,[2] conditions here were in a rather wretched state. It

1. General Anthony Wayne was in charge of American troops who were foraging for supplies to support the army camped at Valley Forge. The British supply brigade was under the command of Lieutenant Colonel Robert Abercromby.
2. The British Army occupied Philadelphia on September 26, 1777. They left under General Sir Henry Clinton in June 1778 after the British revised their military strategy, planning to confine their major battles to the South: Virginia, North and South Carolina, and Georgia.

Amandus Johnson, ed., *The Journal and Biography of Nicholas Collin, 1746–1831* (Philadelphia: The New Jersey Society of Pennsylvania, 1936), 243–249. Reprinted in Larry R. Gerlach, *New Jersey in the American Revolution, 1763–1783: A Documentary History* (Trenton: New Jersey Historical Commission, 1975), 302–305. Reprinted by permission of the New Jersey Historical Commission.

looked as though America would soon be conquered. The people around here began, as early as last autumn, to trade with [the] English in order to obtain specie coin, as well as sugar, tea, syrup, and strong liquors, which are much used here. . . . The severest laws were passed against such trading and caused many people to suffer. These, in order to take revenge, and others to avoid punishment, went over to the English side. A fort on the Jersey shore, which commands the river, had already been seized by the Englishmen.[3] . . . This fort proved a convenient refuge for all those and others, who had changed their opinion, either from conviction or through fear and hope, so that as early as the middle of November a great number of so-called refugees had taken up arms for the King.[4] Everywhere distrust, fear, hatred, and abominable selfishness were met with. Parents and children, brothers and sisters, wife and husband were enemies to one another. The militia and some regular troops on one side and refugees with the Englishmen on the other were constantly roving about in smaller or greater numbers, plundering and destroying everything in a barbarous manner—cattle, furniture, clothing, and food; they smashed mirrors, tables, and china, etc., and plundered women and children of their most necessary clothing, cut up the bolsters and scattered the feathers to the winds, burned houses, whipped and imprisoned each other. . . .

At the end of March, fifteen persons were arrested, who had traded with the English.[5] . . . They were kept imprisoned for one night . . . and the next morning they were marched off under guard to the country. Orders had been given to the guards that if they encountered any English troops [they] should shoot the prisoners and then retreat.

At daybreak on April 4, three hundred refugees and English troops arrived in three divisions to surround the militia, which escaped with great difficulty. They burnt down the schoolhouse for the simple reason that their friends had been kept prisoners there. I remonstrated with them how unchristian and wicked this behavior was and that it was the worst disservice they could do to their King. The officers

3. Fort Mercer, an earthwork fortification at Red Bank, Gloucester County. With its sister, Fort Mifflin on Port Island, the two forts controlled the Delaware. They fell to the British in November 1777.
4. During this period a large number of locals joined a Loyalist unit called the West Jersey Volunteers.
5. In this region General Washington was instructed by the Continental Congress to bring to trial by court-martial anyone apprehended within thirty miles of a British garrison on suspicion of trading with or supplying information to the enemy.

agreed to this, but said that they were unable to keep proper military discipline. . . .

In the morning on Easter Day a terrific cry was heard near the church. When I came out I saw a terrible sight. A man . . . was tied to a pine tree and was being whipped. He fainted at times, but when he recovered, the flogging continued. . . . Some days later he died. His crime was that he had profited by the forbidden trade.

In the month of May a division of American troops was stationed in Swedesboro for some weeks. Although the weather was fine they nevertheless took up their quarters in the church and filled it with filth and vermin. . . . Many members of the congregation . . . suffered injury in various ways by this frenzy.

James Stillman, a strong old Swedish Republican, very rich, lost most of his cattle. Peter Loch, the widow Henricson, also Swedes, Thomas Batton, an Englishman, and many others also suffered much. . . . One Biddle, of a Swedish mother, lost his house through fire laid, as was thought, by a night party of refugees and Englishmen, who mistook him for his uncle, a zealous Republican, who robbed, whipped and imprisoned people in a tyrannical manner.

On the opposite side the militia pillaged . . . Jan Dericson, an old, kind, and quiet man; Jacob and Anders Jones who had traded with the English; . . . Isaac Jostason, a Swede, who had gone over to the Royal Army, after he had begun to trade, but had for a long time previously been a strong Republican and officer in the militia; . . . [and] John Halton, a native Englishman, belonging to the Episcopal Church, an inspector of the customs in the lower part of Jersey. . . . This man had for a long time been unpopular, simply because of his occupation and was truly devoted to his King and nation. . . .

From all this it is apparent how terrible this civil war raged, although during the whole time only one man was shot because both parties fought not like real men with sword and gun, but like robbers and incendiaries. The fact that no important detachments were stationed here contributed greatly toward such barbaric license, as the province was too wild and of less importance, so that straggling parties under lesser and poor officers were allowed to proceed according to pleasure.

A State of Substantial Farmers: John Witherspoon's Notes on New Jersey (c. 1785)

In late 1780 François Marbois, a French official in Philadelphia, circulated a list of questions among members of the Continental Congress. Marbois's questionnaire made its way to Thomas Jefferson, whose response, Notes on Virginia, *is one of the most important books written on America in the late eighteenth century.*

The questions also reached John Witherspoon, one of New Jersey's most distinguished citizens. Witherspoon was president of the College of New Jersey, a signer of the Declaration of Independence, a member of the Continental Congress, and a national leader of the Presbyterian church. Although his response to Marbois, excerpted below, is not in Jefferson's league, it provides a succinct picture of New Jersey society as the Revolutionary War drew to a close.

The number of inhabitants in New Jersey at present is certainly not less than two hundred thousand. . . . There are Negroes, but they are certainly not above one seventh or one tenth part of the whole.[1] The Negroes are exceedingly well used, being fed and clothed as well as any free persons who live by daily labor.

There is no profession of religion which has an exclusive legal establishment. . . . All professions are tolerated and all Protestants are capable of electing and being elected, and indeed have every privilege belonging to citizens. There are in New Jersey, English Presbyterians, Low Dutch Presbyterians, Episcopalians, Baptists, Quakers. The two first, except the difference of the national connection of the one with the church of Scotland and the other with the church of Holland, and the language, are of the same principles as to doctrine. They have the same worship and government and they are by far the most numerous. There is a great majority of the present legislature of these two denominations. Formerly the Quakers, though not the majority, had considerable influence; but since the late contest with Great Bri-

1. According to the United States Census of 1790 the population of New Jersey was 184,000, of whom approximately one in thirteen was an African American.

John Witherspoon, "A Description of the State of New Jersey," *Works*, vol. 4 (Philadelphia, 1802), 403–412. Reprinted in *Report of the New Jersey Commissioners on the Centennial Exhibition* (Trenton: Naar, Day & Naar, 1877), 399–409.

tain they are fewer in number and altogether without power. The Episcopalians are few. The Baptists are Presbyterians in all other respects, only differing in the point of infant baptism; their political weight goes the same way as the Presbyterians; their number is small.

There is at Princeton a college, which had originally a royal charter, begun in 1748. . . . It was in a flourishing state before the war, having about one hundred and fifty undergraduates and other scholars; but was entirely desolated, and the house made a wreck by the confusion of the times—first by the English army, which entirely scattered the scholars and took possession of the house; and afterwards by the American army making it a barrack and hospital. It now begins to recover, having of undergraduates and scholars about sixty. . . .

There is also in New Jersey a college, whose charter name is Queen's College, set up by the Low Dutch, with a particular view to preserve their language and all the peculiar customs of the Church of Holland. They have no building as yet, but have carried on their instruction sometimes at Brunswick, sometimes elsewhere. . . .

There are few men of letters in the State of New Jersey, except those who belong to law, physic,[2] or theology; and many of these professions are often taken up without a liberal education. The state consists almost wholly of substantial farmers. There has been formerly known, especially when the Quakers had some power, a prejudice against learning. That prejudice begins to wear off. . . .

I cannot at present recollect any customs peculiar to the State or that from their singularity deserve notice. New Jersey was first peopled by the Low Dutch, at least the eastern part of it. Their language is continued there as yet, though wearing out. They are a remarkably clean people and frugal. They use their slaves and other servants with great humanity, often not scrupling white and black to eat together. People from all the other States are continually moving into and out of this state, so that there is little peculiarity of manners. . . .

New Jersey being in general settled by farmers with a great equality of rank and even possessions, no considerable manufactures are established in it. There are, however, tradesmen dispersed through it of almost every kind. The farmers, being frugal and plain in their manners, always made both linen and woollen cloth for their own families and their servants. They have given greater attention to this matter within these five or six years that the differences with Great Britain have subsisted. I believe . . . that there is not one in ten of the members of the legislature of New Jersey who is not clothed in the manu-

2. The medical profession; hence our term *physician*.

facture of his own family for the greater part, and many of them have no other clothing of any kind. At this time a great quantity of very good cloth is made in the families. Some tradesmen in different places make for sale, but not much. There are some very considerable dealers in leather and still a greater number in hats. All iron tools are well made here, but not for exportation out of the State.

From the situation of New Jersey, there is hardly any foreign trade carried on directly from it. The merchants in Trenton, Brunswick, Bordentown, and several other places have boats . . . with which they trade to Philadelphia or New York. . . . Such of our merchants as are concerned in foreign trade, being almost always joined in company with some of the large cities above mentioned. . . .

The best seaport in the State of New Jersey is Amboy, which can receive vessels of as great burden as New York. There has never been as yet any great foreign trade at Amboy. The vicinity of New York has probably been a hindrance to it. . . .

The productions of New Jersey and the sources of its wealth are grain of every kind . . . horses, cattle, salted beef and pork and poultry. In times of peace great quantities of all these are sent to the West Indies and flax seed to Europe, shipped, however, more commonly in Philadelphia or New York than any port in New Jersey. The city of Philadelphia receives a great proportion of its provisions, including vegetables of every kind, from New Jersey. The soil of that part of New Jersey which is opposite to Philadelphia is exceedingly proper for gardening and derives much of its value from its proximity to that city.

The State of New Jersey is obliged to draw from Europe and other parts tea, sugar, wine, spirits. Before the war they purchased considerable quantities of English cloth, both linen and woollen, because cheaper than they could manufacture it . . . and because many tradesmen and others had not the materials of manufacture. All articles of finery they must purchase if they use them—linens, gauzes, silks, and velvet.

"The Slave of the State": The Petition of Negro Prime for His Freedom (1786)

A complicated story is told in this document. Absalom Bainbridge of Princeton sided with the British during the Revolutionary War. He fled New Jersey for the security of English protection in what is now Brooklyn, taking his slave, Prime, with him. In 1778 Prime ran away from Bainbridge and returned to the Princeton area, where he became the charge of Jacob Bergen, who was responsible for Loyalist property that had been confiscated. Bergen asked the legislature what to do with Prime and was advised to put him in the army. During the Revolutionary War Prime drove wagons for the army, assuming he was free.

In 1784 John Vanhorne appeared, claiming to have purchased Prime in 1777 or 1778. After two years' delay the court ruled that Vanhorne did not own Prime, the state of New Jersey did.

The petition excerpted below was filed on Prime's behalf, probably by William Churchill Houston, an intermittent member of the Continental Congress from New Jersey and an opponent of slavery. The legislature granted Prime "the blessings of liberty" by manumitting him in November 1786. We don't know what became of him thereafter.

The humble and earnest petition of Negro Prime shows:

That your petitioner heretofore belonged to Absalom Bainbridge. . . .

That the said Absalom Bainbridge adhered to the enemies of this state and of the United States in the month of December 1776, in consequence of which defection his estate became forfeited.

That your petitioner remained for some time at Princeton and was sometime in the family of Mr. John Taylor of Monmouth, father to the wife of the said Absalom Bainbridge, whence he was taken over to Long Island where the family of the said Absalom Bainbridge resided within the enemy's lines, but from which place your petitioner escaped and returned to the neighborhood of his former residence in the year 1778.

That your petitioner, having with other parts of the estate of the said Absalom Bainbridge, come into the possession of Jacob Bergen,

The Petition of Negro Prime, 1786, box 15, Manuscript Collection, New Jersey State Archives, Trenton. Reprinted in *Princeton History*, no. 10 (1991):65–66. Reprinted by permission of the Department of State, New Jersey State Archives.

Esquire, one of the Commissioners of Forfeitures for the County of Somerset, he humanely declined setting up your poor petitioner for sale like a beast of the stable, and applied to . . . the legislature then sitting at Princeton who seemed to be of opinion that though no law provided for cases of this kind, there was something very inconsistent in contending for liberty under an appeal to heaven and at the same time selling, for account of the public, the bodies and service of human beings into perpetual bondage. In the result Mr. Bergen told your petitioner he might go into the public service, which he did and served as a wagoner in the American army for a long time during the late troubles.

That in the month of June 1784, your petitioner being then in the neighborhood of Trenton earning his bread as a day laborer under the pleasing persuasion that he was a free subject of the state, he was seized and forcibly carried off by Mr. John Vanhorne . . . under pretext of a purchase from the aforesaid John Taylor, who alleged that he purchased your petitioner from the wife of the said Absalom Bainbridge in the year 1777. . . .

Your petitioner having obtained a Habeas Corpus,[1] his case was argued before the Supreme Court, when the Justices were of the opinion that the law would not authorize the manumission of your petitioner. But Moore Furman, Esquire, agent of forfeiture for the County of Hunterdon, having in the meantime applied to the court . . . claiming your petitioner as the property of the state, the court ordered that your petitioner should remain in custody of the law, until an issue could be tried between the state and the said John Vanhorne.

That in the term of May 1786 . . . a verdict and judgment passed in favor of the state, and your petitioner, by order of court, was delivered into the hands of Mr. Furman.

Thus is your poor petitioner the slave of the state of New Jersey and liable to be sold as their property. But he earnestly implores that he may be delivered from a situation so distressing, and by the compassion and munificence of the . . . legislature, entitled to that liberty to defend, secure, and perpetuate which the fields of America have been dyed in the blood of her citizens.

Were your poor petitioner to be sold, his price would scarcely amount to the fifth part of a copper penny to each taxable in the state and your poor petitioner can not believe that one person can be found who would not willingly contribute the fifth part of a penny to release

1. A legal judgment that a person is being illegally held and must be released.

a human being from a bondage which must otherwise continue until his eyes are closed in death. . . .

Your petitioner, therefore, most humbly prays that the . . . legislature, being ascertained of the truth of the facts set forth in his petition, will grant him leave to present a bill for his emancipation.

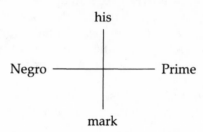

DOCUMENT 22

"Is This Liberty?": The Petition of Rachel Wells (1786)

The Revolutionary War left much devastation in its wake. Widows left destitute by the war were often in particularly difficult circumstances. The following petition concerns a very interesting case. Rachel Wells, a sculptor in wax, loaned the Continental Congress a considerable sum of money in support of the war effort. Repayments of such loans were administered by the states. New Jersey passed a law that required its citizens to have had continuous residence to qualify for repayment. Wells, because she had left the state briefly during the war, was unable to receive her repayment and was thus destitute.

In this petition she asks Congress to pay the interest she was due on the loan. I do not know the outcome of Wells's request, but it is unlikely that it was granted.

To the honorable Congress,

I, Rachel, do make this complaint, who am a widow far advanced in years and dearly have occasion of the interest for that cash I lent the states.

I was a citizen in the Jersey when I lent the States a considerable sum of money, and had I justice done me it might be sufficient to support me in the country where I am now, near Bordentown. I lived here then . . . but . . . I went to Philadelphia to try to get a living, as I can't do nothing in Bordentown in my way. . . . I . . . was there in the year 1783 when our Assembly was pleased to pass a law that no one should have any interest that lived out of Jersey state. I have sent in a petition to the Assembly. They say it lies in your breast as the cash was lent to you. They gave me a form of an oath which runs thus: that I was a resident [of New Jersey] when I put the cash into the office and was in the year 1783 and am still. I can swear that I was then and am now, but in 1783 I was not.

Now gentlemen, is this liberty? Had it been advertised that he or she that moved out of the state should lose his or her interest, you might have some plea against me. But I am innocent: [I] suspected no trick. I have done as much to carry on the war as many that sit now at

The Petition of Rachel Wells, May 18, 1786, M-247, roll 56, item 42:VIII, 354–355, Papers of the Continental Congress. A facsimile of this petition is provided in Linda Kerber, *Women of the Republic: Intellect and Ideology in Revolutionary America* (Chapel Hill: University of North Carolina Press. 1980), 88–89.

the helm of government and no notice taken of me before this. One of your Assembly borrowed £300 in gold of me just as the war commenced, and now I can neither get interest nor principal nor even security. Why? Because they have passed a law. . . .

I had suffered by the English which . . . I can bear, but to be robbed by my countrymen is very trying to nature. My dear sister Wright[1] wrote to me to be thankful that I had it in my power to help on the war, which is well enough. But then this is to be considered, that others get their interest. Why then a poor old widow to be put off who am thus stripped? . . .

I think, gentlemen, that I can ask for my interest. . . . Can't there be an order given to our Assembly that the widow Rachel Wells in and of the Jersey state may have the interest of her cash that she lent the state in 1778, and [the Assembly] not make good that law made in 1783. I heartily pity others that are in my case that can't speak for themselves. May God direct you: there is gold enough and to spare. God has spread a plentiful table for us and you gentlemen are the carvers for us. Pray forget not the poor weaklings at the foot of the table. The poor soldiers has got some crumbs that fall from their master's table— some 2/6, some 2/3 on the pound. Why not Rachel Wells have a little interest? If she did not fight, she threw in all her might which brought the soldiers food and clothing and let them have blankets, and since that she has been obliged to lay upon straw and glad of that. . . .

I do expect to hear something to my satisfaction very soon. That I may say before I leave this world that the states did me justice, though I never expect to see the principal, is the prayer of your humble servant Rachel Wells.

1. Rachel Wells's sister was Patience Wright, a well-known sculptor who worked in wax. Wright was in London during the Revolutionary War years, part of an elevated social circle that included the King and Queen. She is reputed to have aided the American cause by transmitting to America, concealed in her wax statues, intelligence she picked up among her friends.

Liberty, a Delusive Dream: Abraham Clark on Republicanism (1786)

No sooner was the War for Independence brought to a victorious conclusion than fears developed that the liberty and independence so recently won could be easily lost. The republic was fragile because it depended on virtuous citizens who were willing to sacrifice their private, selfish interests for the good of the whole community. We call these, and the related ideas of the leaders of the Revolution, republicanism.

Two of republicanism's staple ingredients were the stubborn quest for independence—personal and political—and the related belief that farming and handicraft production were the most moral of all livelihoods, because they offered autonomy and economic self-sufficiency.

Abraham Clark was one of New Jersey's truest republicans. He wrote this anonymous pamphlet to urge the state to remain true to republican principles by promoting an economy of farmers and artisans.

No doubt every true friend to the United States has beheld us emancipate from under a yoke of British oppression with a glow of pleasure; and with much delight have I seen when we rose to independence; but let us not stop here or our boasted liberty may prove but a delusive dream and we may awake in fetters more grievous than the yoke we have shaken off. . . .

I will . . . inquire who are the people and what the means by which we may rise to wealth and renown.

Is it the Ministers of the Gospel? Their counsels are very good . . . and we ought conscientiously to attend on their instruction. . . . But nevertheless we are not to look to them for a subsistence, much less for affluence.

Is it by physicians that we can obtain what we seek? They are very necessary in some cases, and may help to that health we need; at best they are the least of two evils.

Must we go to taverns to support us? Some times we may have reason to thank God for the sight of them; but very commonly people may curse the day they entered into them.

The True Policy of New Jersey, Defined (Elizabethtown, 1786). Rutgers. Reprinted by permission of the Department of Special Collections and University Archives, Rutgers University Libraries.

Our lawyers are the wise men and no doubt would wish to be the leading men. . . . May we not look to them as the chief support and defense of the state? They may be useful in some cases, but let us beware of them, for . . . the remedy is commonly worse than the disease. True to their client is their profession, and what is their God but money. . . .

If a man has defrauded, stole, murdered, or committed any other offense contrary to law and humanity, or owes a just debt, they, according to their profession, will be true to him for his money, and if by any art, evasion, or deception the jury can be led astray or kept from the knowledge of the truth and thereby justice does not take place, they think themselves worthy of honor. . . . May we not call them the worst of two evils?[1]

But may we not depend on our merchants to furnish us with riches, honor, and every necessary and convenience to live?

It is generally supposed that . . . increase of trade promises advance in riches and the decline of trade forebodes a diminution of gain. . . . But we should remember . . . that circumstances alter cases. If we look at England . . . or any other place which buys foreign goods and sells to foreigners, that nation or city will undoubtedly gain by trade. For they sell for an advanced price which stops in their hands or if they sell their own produce or manufacture to foreigners, then what they get for it is their own. . . .

The case is the same . . . with a private man who, if he buys and sells to others, it is expected he is increasing in wealth or if he produces from his farm or manufacturing and sells to a greater amount than he buys, his estate is increasing; otherwise if he trades largely for the consumption of his own family and his produce or manufactures do not sell to the amount of what he purchases, his trade is a damage to him for he is spending his estate and is in the road to poverty. . . .

The state of New Jersey is so situated that we cannot be a merchant to buy goods and sell the same to other nations or states, so that whatever goods we import we consume amongst ourselves, therefore every article that we purchase from . . . any other part of the world out of the bounds of this state takes the full price which it cost . . . out of it; from which we may judge what . . . damage our merchants are to us by importing and selling so many foreign goods. . . . If we can . . . stop . . . our importation of foreign goods, but especially superflu-

---

1. In the chaos following the war, many New Jerseyans were in serious financial difficulty. People were holding worthless paper currency; there were land foreclosures and debt imprisonments. Much of the hostility against lawyers may be attributed to their work on behalf of those who were ending up with the property in question.

ities and . . . promote our own manufactures so much as that we shall sell to a greater amount than we buy, our silver and gold will be increasing in the same proportion.

By this we may discover where our great strength lies—who the men and what the mean[s] by which we . . . may stand firm and independent. It undoubtedly is the husbandman and mechanic. By them . . . and only them can we obtain food and raiment;[2] by them alone has New Jersey changed from a howling wilderness to pleasant fields, gardens, towns, and cities; and by no others but them can we obtain riches and honor. And as much as the husbandmen and mechanics are increased in number, encouraged and led to industry and frugality, so much is the true interest of the state advanced.

2. Clothing.

The Early Republic

NOTABLE EVENTS

1791	Society for Establishing Useful Manufactures incorporated
1792	Bill of Rights adopted
1794	Whiskey Rebellion
1798	Alien and Sedition Acts
1803	United States Supreme Court (*Marbury* v. *Madison*) upholds judicial review; Louisiana Purchase
1804	Vice-President Aaron Burr kills Alexander Hamilton in a duel at Weehawken; gradual abolition of slavery enacted in New Jersey
1804–1806	Lewis and Clark expedition
1807	Fulton's steamboat, *Clermont*; suffrage in New Jersey extended to all white male taxpayers, denied to women and African Americans
1808	Congress prohibits African slave trade
1812–1815	War of 1812
1819	Commercial panic, many bank failures
1820	Missouri Compromise
1823	Monroe Doctrine
1824	*Gibbons* v. *Ogden* decision on regulation of interstate commerce
1825	Erie Canal completed; Morris Canal excavation begins
1826	American Society for the Promotion of Temperance founded
1828	Workingmen's parties appear; legislature approves funds for education

Selected New Jersey Population Statistics, 1790–1820

Year	1790	1800	1810	1820
Population (× 1,000)	184	211	246	278
% Female	45.1	45.5	45.5	49.3
Race				
% White	92.4	91.9	92.3	92.8
% Black	7.6	8.1	7.7	7.2
% Urban	0	0	2.4	2.5
People per square mile	24.8	28.5	33.1	37.4
N.J. % of U.S. population	4.7	4.0	3.4	2.9

SOURCE: This and subsequent tables derived from U.S. Department of Commerce, Bureau of the Census, *Historical Statistics of the United States: Colonial Times to 1970* (Washington, 1975).

"A Moral Certainty of Success": The Society for Establishing Useful Manufactures (1791)

In December 1791 Alexander Hamilton, secretary of the treasury in the Washington administration, submitted to Congress his famous Report on the Subject of Manufactures. *This report, the work of Hamilton and his assistant secretary, Tench Coxe, rejected the commonly held view that the new nation could prosper as a purely agricultural society. Hamilton and Coxe proposed instead that the nation devote itself to manufacturing.*

In a section on cotton the report announced an undertaking "with a capital . . . expected to be . . . at least half a million dollars . . . for prosecuting, on a large scale, the making and printing of cotton goods." This was the Society for Establishing Useful Manufactures (SEUM), whose prospectus is excerpted here. The principals in the corporation had already chosen a location at the Great Falls of the Passaic River. This site had a number of advantages: it was close to New York, which offered a domestic market for the company's products and a port for export; the falls provided marvelous water power to run the machinery; and the political climate in New Jersey seemed favorable for the venture.

But such a radical challenge to the idea that the good society was composed primarily of independent farmers and self-employed artisans, an idea that had animated so many of the revolutionaries, did not go unchallenged. The second document in this section contains excerpts from letters of "A Farmer" attacking the plan. The letters were written by George Logan, a prominent Philadelphia doctor and later a U.S. senator from Pennsylvania.

The third document contains excerpts from a critique of the Logan letters written by Tench Coxe. In later years, however, Logan and Coxe became allies.

The SEUM was not a success. The superintendent the corporation recruited fell into serious financial trouble, and little was built beyond the water

Harold C. Syrett, ed., *Papers of Alexander Hamilton* (New York: Columbia University Press, 1966), 9:144–156. Reprinted by permission.

"Five Letters Addressed to the Yeomanry of the United States: Containing some observations on the dangerous scheme of Governor Duer and Mr. Secretary Hamilton, to establish national manufactories," *American Museum* 12 (September 1792): 161, 162–164; *American Museum* 12 (October 1792):216–217.

"Observations on the Preceding Letters by a Freeman," *American Museum* 12 (October 1792):217–221.

channels engineered by Pierre L'Enfant, the designer of Washington, D.C.
But it has a claim on our attention as the focus of a debate over the political
economy of the new nation. (See document 23.)

The establishment of manufactures in the United States . . . [is] of the
highest importance to their prosperity. . . . That community which
can most completely supply its own wants is in a state of the highest
political perfection. . . . A nation . . . cannot possess much active
wealth but as the result of extensive manufactures. . . .

The dearness of labor and the want of capital are the two great
objections to the success of manufactures in the United States.

The first objection ceases to be formidable when it is recollected
how . . . the proportion of manual labor in a variety of manufactures
has been decreased by the . . . application of machines—and when it
is also considered to what an extent women and even children in the
populous parts of the country may be rendered auxiliary to undertakings of this nature. It is also to be taken into calculation that emigrants
may be engaged on reasonable terms in countries where labor is cheap
and brought over to the United States.

The last objection disappears . . . by a proper application of the
public debt. Here is the resource which has been hitherto wanted. . . .
A direction of it to this object may be made a means of public prosperity and an instrument of profit to adventurers in the enterprise. . . .

An association of the capitals of a number of individuals is an obvious expedient—and the species of capital which consists of the
public stock is susceptible of dispositions which will render it adequate to the end. . . .

To effect the desired association, an incorporation of the adventurers must be contemplated as a means necessary to their security. . . . There is scarcely a state which could be insensible to the
advantage of being the scene of such an undertaking. But there are
reasons which strongly recommend the state of New Jersey for the
purpose. It is thickly populated—provisions are there abundant and
cheap. The state having scarcely any external commerce and no waste
lands to be peopled can feel the impulse of no supposed interest hostile to the advancement of manufacturers. Its situation seems to in-
sure a constant friendly disposition. . . .

As soon as it is evident that a proper capital can be formed, means
ought to be taken to procure from Europe skillful workmen and such
machines and implements as cannot be had here in sufficient perfection. . . .

It is conceived that there would be a moral certainty of success in
manufactories of the following articles: paper and pasteboard; paper
hangings; sailcloth and other coarse linen cloths, such as sheetings,

shirtings, diaper . . . the printing of cottons and linen . . . women's shoes of all kinds; thread, cotton and worsted stockings; pottery and earthen ware . . . hats; ribbons . . . carpets; blankets; brass and iron wire. . . . The employment of the labor-saving mills and machines is particularly contemplated. In addition to the foregoing a brewery . . . may be thought of. . . .

The corporation shall be at liberty to make and vend all such articles as shall not be prohibited by law: provided that it shall only trade in such articles as itself shall manufacture in whole or part or in such as shall be received in payment or exchange therefor. . . . The stock and other property of the corporation to be exempt from taxes. . . .

The subscribers . . . will . . . contribute . . . for the purpose of establishing a company for carrying on the business of manufactures in . . . New Jersey, if an incorporation can be obtained from the said state on advantageous terms, according to the general principles of the plan aforesaid. . . .

We do hereby . . . appoint . . . our attorneys . . . to make application on our behalf . . . for an act or acts of incorporation. . . . And further to take such measures at our joint expense as shall appear to them necessary and proper for engaging workmen in the several branches of manufacture mentioned in the said plan.

Five letters addressed to the yeomanry of the United States: containing some observations on the dangerous scheme . . . to establish national manufactories.

Letter 1

Every act of the government should be equally favorable to all the citizens. . . . A legal government . . . is founded on the rights of man. It is equitable because common to all; it is useful because it can have no other object than the general good; and it is solid and durable because secured by the voice of the people.

Such a government will protect and defend, with its whole force, the person and property of every one of its members.

Letter 2

Measures of the general government of the United States . . . are tending . . . to undermine the liberties of our country—to strip the farmer, the mechanic . . . and useful laborer of all influence and of all importance. . . .

A government may waste the public money in erecting palaces, statues, etc. and the evil is but temporary; but when it assumes principles injurious to the rights of the people, and by arbitrary laws inter-feres in the occupations of its citizens, liberty is but a name. . . . The practice is oppression. . . .

It may be thought improper at this early period to offer any obser-vations on the . . . report of the Secretary of the Treasury on manufac-tures. . . . [But] experience justifies a belief that the principles of this report will . . . be adopted. . . . The Secretary of the Treasury and his friends . . . have already paved the way by procuring one of the most unjust and arbitrary laws . . . (enacted by the commonwealth of New Jersey) that ever disgraced the government of a free people—a law granting to a few wealthy men the exclusive jurisdiction of six miles square and a variety of unconstitutional privileges highly injurious to the citizens of that state. . . . Is it just that a numerous class of citizens . . . should be sacrificed to a wealthy few who have no other object in view than to add to their ill-gotten and enormous wealth?

Such being the nature of this corporation, can it be doubted whether it . . . subverts the principles of . . . equality of which free-men ought to be so jealous? Whether it establishes a class of citizens with distinct interests from their fellow citizens? Will it not, by foster-ing an inequality of fortune, prove the destruction of the equality of rights and tend strongly to an aristocracy?

There are two kinds of inequality, the one personal, that of talent and virtue . . . the other that of fortune which must exist because property alone can stimulate to labor. . . . But though it be necessary, yet in its excess it is the great malady of civil society. The accumula-tion of that power which is conferred by wealth in the hands of the few is the perpetual source of oppression . . . of the mass of man-kind. . . . The preference of partial to general interests is the greatest of all public evils; it should therefore have been the object of all laws to repress this malady; but it has been their perpetual tendency to aggravate it. . . . Laws . . . cannot equalize men—no; but ought they . . . aggravate that inequality they cannot cure? Laws cannot inspire unmixed patriotism: but ought they, for that reason, to foment the corporation spirit which is its most fatal enemy? . . .

It is not the distinctions of titles which constitutes an aristocracy; it is the principle of partial association. The American aristocrats have failed in their attempts to establish titles of distinction by law, yet the destructive principles of aristocracy are too prevalent among us and ought to be watched with the most jealous eye.

Letter 5

When Britain had power, she exerted it to restrain the growth of American manufactures. That country may now accomplish by finesse what she is no longer able to effect by force. The national manufactory . . . will give the company an opportunity of monopolizing many raw materials already procured with difficulty, particularly in the hatting and tanning business. Their workmen—being exempt from taxes, militia duty, and enjoying other privileges—will draw off the journeymen from private manufactures, beneficially scattered through the different parts of the country. . . .

The citizens of the United States engaged in the cultivation of the ground comprehend nine-tenths of its inhabitants. This numerous, laborious, and useful class of citizens have never come forward to government to solicit partial privileges; have never sought to be incorporated as a distinct body; much less do they require a violation of the rights of a numerous and respectable class of citizens, personally engaged in manufactories.

The yeomanry of America only desire what they have a right to demand—a free unrestricted sale for the produce of their own industry; and not to have the sacred right of mankind violated in their persons, by arbitrary laws, prohibiting them from deriving all the advantages they can from every part of the produce of their farms.

Tench Coxe responds to "the Farmer."

An idea has been circulated that Congress have granted exemptions, privileges and bounties to the New Jersey Society for Promoting Useful Manufactures. . . .

The whole of the advantages possessed by the New Jersey manufacturing company are under a law of that state. . . .

The assembly of New Jersey have exhibited a cautious delicacy, worthy of the legislators of a free and intelligent people, in expressly providing that the place or district shall not become incorporated if a majority of the taxable inhabitants shall signify to the governor their dissent from . . . the incorporation. So that, if on mature deliberation, they do not like the powers of the corporation, or if they are in general principles against any sort of incorporation, they have ample power to prevent it. This, fellow citizens, is the law which the Farmer tells you, "grants to a few wealthy men the exclusive jurisdiction of six square miles and a variety of unconstitutional privileges. . . ."

The origin and design of the New Jersey manufacturing society has been frequently . . . misrepresented. In the year 1791 . . . the Secretary of the Treasury formed the plan. It was represented that one of the great objections to manufactures in the United States was the want of money. . . . A union of many individuals was the only mode that could be adopted. . . . It was certainly a prudent method as each would take care not to subscribe so largely as to hurt himself, if a failure should take place. The subscribers, to avoid risking more than their subscriptions, were, of course, to apply for an incorporation; and it was not at all probable the sum would have been subscribed without one. . . . As New Jersey has very little foreign commerce, it was presumed that both her legislature and her citizens would promote so valuable a branch of internal trade. The latter have . . . subscribed handsomely; and the state, knowing that these enterprises are attended with great expense . . . with risk and sometimes with loss, authorized the company to raise by lottery $100,000. . . . Their real estate was exempted from state taxes for ten years, and their stock, or personal property, altogether. These taxes . . . will be very small under the state laws; and they will be so remote, that the manufacturers in other parts of the union cannot be sensible of their effects.

The Farmer's suggestion that the company will . . . undersell is not . . . plausible. . . . Merchants and manufacturers do not use their occasional advantages for the absurd purpose of underselling their neighbors for a short time but to increase their own substance and stock; and if they were to sell cheaper for it, the . . . consumers, that is "the great body of the yeomanry" about whose interest the Farmer wishes to appear very anxious, would be benefited by it.

A Great Export of Cider:
A Traveler's Observations (1794)

Frenchman Theophile Cazenove was an agent of the Holland Land Company when he traveled across New Jersey in October 1794, looking for real estate in which his employers could invest. Cazenove was a close student of American economics. His advice was sought by Napoleon's minister, Charles Talleyrand, during the negotiation with the Jefferson administration over the Louisiana Purchase.

This excerpt from the journal that Cazenove kept during his trip provides a detailed picture of the New Jersey economy during the early years of the nation. Among the issues on which he sheds some light are blacks in slavery and freedom; indentured servants; tenant farmers; and the cider and applejack business.

At Chatham . . . the ground is easily sold for ten pounds or twenty-five dollars per acre. The meadows yield one to one and a half tons per acre of hay, which sells at Newark for five pounds a ton. Two oxen haul one ton. . . .

Generally the farms are from two hundred to two hundred fifty acres; the farmers try mostly the raising of cattle. They sell their bulls, four years old, at from fifty to sixty dollars each; their cows, four years old, from twenty to thirty dollars each—for the Philadelphia and New York markets. The wood has almost all been cut down in this district. You have to pay two dollars a cord for walnut for burning; butter, one shilling. A pair of good oxen for plowing bring twenty to thirty pounds, fifty to seventy-five dollars, a horse for farm work, twenty-five pounds. There (as everywhere in Jersey) all the servants are black slaves; a good dependable Negro, eighteen to twenty-five years old, costs one hundred pounds or two hundred fifty dollars; a good, dependable Negro woman, eighteen to twenty-five years old, seventy pounds. You have to pay five shillings for a day's work by a white workman at harvest time; three or four shillings in the spring; wages of a white farmhand, thirty to forty pounds per year, and you must also treat him politely. . . .

At Hanover . . . three residents . . . of Philadelphia have bought . . .

Rayner Wickersham Kelsey, ed., *Cazenove Journal, 1794*, Haverford College Studies, no. 13 (Haverford: Pennsylvania History Press, 1922), 3–17.

farms which they lease for one half of the produce and furnish half of the expenses: horses, cattle, implements. . . .

At Morristown . . . a cord of wood is obtainable . . . for ten shillings for oak, fourteen to fifteen for walnut; salt ten to twelve shillings a bushel; . . . butcher's meat one and a half cents a pound; for boarding i.e. lodging, food, and a single room, two dollars per week. . . . A workman [is] easy to find for four shillings a day.

Many free negroes . . . hire out by the month in the summer for three pounds, and three shillings a day. The free negro women are hired for four shillings per week. Few houses to be found for rent, almost every house inhabited by the owner. . . .

Black River.[1] . . . The hollows between the hills make fairly good pasture. . . . Many large orchards of apple trees, the product of which is important for the farmer, who generally distills his cider.

They calculate that eight bushels of apples make one barrel of cider; the barrel is of thirty-two gallons, and these thirty-two gallons of cider make four gallons of spirits, which they sell for six shillings or seventy-five cents a gallon.

Since Jersey farmers have started to distill their cider, it is impossible to get any of it unless you pay what the distillery pays them. Today they ask fifty or sixty shillings per hogshead, which a few years ago you got for twenty. A hogshead measures one hundred four gallons.

An acre of land, planted with from sixty-five to seventy apple trees, twenty feet apart, produces in good years two hundred fifty bushels of apples. This great produce encourages every farmer to enlarge his orchard. . . .

A workman at harvest time, six shillings per day—at other times four—now, in October, you find some for three shillings.

There is a great export of spirits of cider to New York, and from there to the south; and the excise,[2] instead of stopping the distilleries, has attracted attention to the advantages of this manner of making the best of this poor ground and so good for apple trees. Each farmer has been planting nurseries for two years; so they are much pleased with the bargain. . . .

The lack of neatness and of furniture in the farmhouses, the lack of gardens and improvements . . . [the] dilapidated state of the vine-

---

1. Now Chester.
2. The Whiskey Tax of 1791 placed an excise on distilled liquor such as that described here made from apples. Designed to both raise revenue and reduce alcohol consumption, the measure provoked to armed resistance farmers in western Pennsylvania who made distilled spirits from their grain. Their protest is known as the Whiskey Rebellion.

yards which are, however, large and productive, comes from the lack of taste and sensibility on the part of the farmers. The wives have the care of the house, and besides they have a number of children: five, six, seven, eight. So they have more work than they can do, with no help, except one or two old and dispirited colored women. That is why the wives are indifferent, tired. . . . It is plain how, from father to son, is passed on this astounding indifference to the comforts of life. . . . The farmer, having no opportunity to use his extra money in improvements, they buy more land around, and the pride of being considered a large land-owner is the only thing that rouses them.

Except for a few inland inhabitants, who have lived for a long time, from father to son, on their farms . . . most of them have, either themselves or their fathers, come to America from Germany, Scotland, and especially Ireland, poor, from among the poorest country-people, and spent their first years in servitude (as is the custom for that class) from two to six years, and then become mechanics or farmers, and brought up their children as they were brought up.

Every Child Shall Be Free, But . . .: The Gradual Abolition of Slavery (1804)

With passage of the law excerpted here, New Jersey became the last state in the North to abolish slavery. The terms of the abolition were so slow that there remained eighteen slaves (technically indentured servants for life) to be enumerated in the 1860 federal census.

The item that here precedes the statute comes from a petition in support of the bill presented to the legislature by the Society for Promoting the Gradual Abolition of Slavery. It summarizes the main arguments for the gradual-abolition approach. On one hand, chattel slavery could not be defended in a land of freedom. On the other hand, respect for private property was equally an American principle.

The last paragraph of the law introduces an element not mentioned in the abolitionist petition: support for abandoned children. The law provided that the state would pay the costs of support of any abandoned children, relieving local taxpayers of this burden. This provision was probably what made the difference between defeat six years earlier of a similar bill and passage in 1804. A slave owner might abandon the child of a slave on the grounds that it was not worthwhile to support the child only to manumit him at twenty-one or twenty-five. If an owner did this, the overseer of the poor could charge the state for the cost of the child's upkeep and apprentice the child to its former master. In 1809, 40 percent of the state treasurer's expenditures went for the maintenance of abandoned slave children. In 1811 this part of the law was repealed.

The New Jersey Society for Promoting the Gradual Abolition of Slavery request leave . . . to present before the legislature their . . . testimony in favor of the law now depending for the gradual extinction of slavery in this state.

New Jersey Society for Promoting the Gradual Abolition of Slavery, "To the Legislative Council and General Assembly of the State of New Jersey," n.d., NJSL. Reprinted by permission of the New Jersey Department of Education, Division of the State Library.
"An Act for the Gradual Abolition of Slavery" (passed February 15, 1804), Acts of the Twenty-eighth General Assembly of the State of New Jersey, *Laws of New Jersey, 1800–1807*, 251–254.

The principle of hereditary bondage can no longer be defended in a land of freedom and by a people distinguished for reason and humanity. And few . . . will plead for it on the ground of private property. Even those who hold by purchase . . . cannot in candor but acknowledge that to enslave children to the latest posterity for the cost of the parent, and that too after the father and mother have worn out their lives in servitude for the price paid, is a satisfaction vastly disproportionate.

It is alleged that to emancipate those now living . . . would be to violate private rights. . . . But as respects those who may in future be born this objection does not apply. . . . The time has arrived when the united voice of reason and policy require that they should be admitted to the common blessings of liberty and not come into existence only to labor for others, . . . to be bought and sold . . . and transmit the same wretched inheritance to their posterity. The obvious way to effect this great and necessary end will be to declare that all born after the passage of the law shall at some given age be free men and free women and their children wholly free.

Surely years and years of servitude will compensate sufficiently the master for the cares and expenses of childhood. How little indeed is really expended upon the first period of their infancy? Nurtured by the mother, . . . uneducated, and almost unheeded, they arrive at the age of usefulness at an imperceptible cost. Few of them but at seven and ten years old begin to earn their subsistence. . . . Will not servitude until twenty-one fully repay the expenses of infancy? It may be alleged that cases of particular hardship will happen. Some parents may have proved a burden and some children, from accident or disease, continue so for many years; but these instances will be rare and the inequality be greatly overbalanced in the general operation of the liberal term of twenty-one years' service. What extensive regulation ever takes place without producing some individual losses? Legislators must often act without respect to these on the wide scale of public utility. . . . They indeed will cease to act at all if a few possible or probable disadvantages of a private nature must deter them from the execution of measures calculated for the good of the whole.

If . . . perpetual slavery is politically wrong and morally a departure from the great laws of nature and humanity, certainly this question of profit and loss may be adjusted. Shall that forever stand in the way of emancipation? Will nothing short of the servitude of children to the end of time satisfy the owner for the . . . value of the parent . . . ? We ask . . . for no law to touch property in possession, however acquired; neither for the disannulling of that by which twelve thousand human beings are doomed to die as they were born: . . . vassals in a land of freedom. We supplicate you for the unborn. These have not been bought and when they come into possession let a fair equivalent in personal service satisfy the possessor for the care and cost of their infancy. A period will then be fixed after which it may be said that in New Jersey no man is born a slave.

It is not credible that prejudice or personal interest can much longer hold out against a claim like this, . . . a claim advocated by the natural feelings of the human heart and acknowledged by Americans in their act of independence, as among the most undeniable rights of man. . . . We . . . hope that the propitious moment has come, . . . when an assembly of enlightened legislators, acting on the principles of eternal justice and in conformity with their Christian characters will resolve to . . . proclaim liberty to the captives. . . . Thus will it be your praise to have blotted from your country perhaps its greatest crime.

The Gradual Abolition Act of 1804

Be it enacted by the Council and General Assembly of this State . . . that every child born of a slave within this state, after the fourth day of July next, shall be free; but shall remain the servant of the owner of his or her mother, and the executors, administrators or assigns of such owner . . . and shall continue in such service, if a male, until the age of twenty-five years and if a female, until the age of twenty-one years.

And be it enacted that every person being an inhabitant of this state, who shall be entitled to the service of a child born as aforesaid . . . shall, within nine months after the birth of such child, cause to be delivered to the clerk of the county whereof such person shall be an inhabitant, a certificate in writing, containing the . . . name, age, and sex of the child so born . . . and the clerk of such county shall receive from said person twelve cents for every child so registered; and if any person shall neglect to deliver such certificate to the said clerk within said nine months, such person shall . . . pay for every such offence, five dollars, and the further sum of one dollar for every month such person shall neglect to deliver the same. . . .

The person entitled to the service of any child born, as aforesaid, may nevertheless, within one year after the birth of such child, elect to abandon such right; in which case a notification of such abandonment . . . shall be filed with the clerk of the township or . . . county in which such person shall reside. But every child so abandoned shall be maintained by such person until such child arrives to the age of one year, and thereafter shall be considered as a pauper of such township or county, and liable to be bound out[1] by the trustees or overseer of the poor in the same manner as other poor children are directed to be bound out. . . . Such child, . . . until it shall be bound out, shall be maintained by the trustees or overseer of the poor of such county or township, as the case may be, at the expense of this state, . . . and every person who shall omit to notify such abandonment as aforesaid, shall be considered as having elected to retain the service of such child and be liable for its maintenance until the period to which its servitude is limited.

1. Binding out was a system whereby orphaned or neglected children were put in foster homes in a manner somewhat similar to indentured servitude and also to the apprenticeship system. The child stayed with his or her foster family for an agreed-upon term. During this time the child performed duties in return for room and board. Localities generally had "overseers of the poor" who administered the arrangement and paid the foster care providers for their charges' upkeep.

A Shoemaker, Three Plows, and an Eagle (1806)

Although small in size, this image has great symbolic value. Drawn by an unknown artist, it decorated an 1806 map of Newark prepared by Charles Basham of the Newark Academy. (The school is still in operation, although now located in Livingston.)

By combining the elements that he did, the artist tied together a number of themes. First, he suggested the local and national prominence of shoemaking. In Newark it dominated the economy: one Newarker in three was employed in the making of shoes. Nationally, boot- and shoemaking was the largest industry in the country in the decades before the Civil War.

At the time of this drawing, shoemaking was primarily a household industry. The master shoemaker generally supervised production in a small workshed behind his cottage. Goods were made on custom order or sold in batches to a nearby shopkeeper. A few younger journeymen shoemakers worked under the master's supervision. Expecting someday to become masters themselves, they already owned the tools they brought to the master's shop. In return for their labor they received wages, room, board, and clothing. The shoemaker's wife and daughters often worked (in the cottage, not in the shop with the men) as hand stitchers, sewing the upper part of the shoe to the sole. Younger sons were apprentices either to their father or to a nearby craftsman at this or another trade, someday to become journeymen and eventually master craftsmen.

Moreover, by seating the shoemaker next to the three plows of the state symbol, our artist connected the artisan and the farmer, the twin pillars of republican society. As self-sufficient property owners, both were expected to contribute to building a democratic society based on political and economic independence, personal liberty, private property, and a free market.

The federal eagle further suggested the connection between these two virtuous livelihoods and the new nation. Abundance and freedom in a society of artisans and farmers were the fruits of the war for independence.

"A Foe in Disguise Is More Dangerous Than an Open Enemy": An Advocate of Sending African Americans to Africa (1824)

The American Colonization Society was formed in 1817 by a New Jerseyan, Presbyterian minister Robert Finley of Basking Ridge. The colonization idea was a conservative corollary to the antislavery movement. Colonizationists assumed that blacks were inferior to whites. Their program was to remove the threat to white society that they believed free blacks represented by resettling them in Africa.

In 1822 the Society established Monrovia (later renamed Liberia) in West Africa as a refuge for free blacks, whose transportation and settlement the society arranged. Over the next forty years approximately twelve thousand African Americans settled in Liberia. The group had wide support among northern whites; it also had three main sources of opposition. Among whites, slavery advocates opposed colonization because it was a form of abolitionism, while abolitionists rejected its racism. By far the most meaningful opposition, however, came from free blacks who considered themselves Americans.

The following excerpt comes from a speech delivered in July 1824 by James S. Green at a meeting held in Princeton to consider forming a New Jersey chapter of the American Colonization Society. (See document 36.)

Let us consider how New Jersey is interested in this plan of colonization. Will its adoption improve our situation? . . .

We find by the census of 1820 that the black population of New Jersey is more than twenty thousand. What a mass of ignorance, misery, and depravity is here mingled with every portion of our population, and threatening the whole with a moral and political pestilence. . . . This enormous mass of . . . deadly pollution will . . . be ultimately taken out of her territory if the plan of the Colonization Society be adopted. This is the special concern . . . which the state of New Jersey has in this great national affair. . . .

"Proceedings of a Meeting Held at Princeton, July 14, 1824, to form a Society in the State of New Jersey to cooperate with the American Colonization Society," 1824, Rutgers. Reprinted by permission of the Department of Special Collections and University Archives, Rutgers University Libraries.

Here is a host of individuals shut out by education or prejudice from all social intercourse with the whites; entertaining no natural feelings of sympathy or kindness towards us; utter outcasts from all the highest privileges of free men. . . .

By the policy and habits of the country, the blacks are completely excluded from every post of honor and profit; they are denied all alliance with the whites, either in business or by marriage; they are almost shut out from every employment of a liberal character. . . . By such means you destroy all the usual incentives to industry. . . . A freed Negro, who must always be a proscribed individual, is . . . sunk below the level of the community around him. . . .

We have upon our statute book a law which by a slow but certain process is ultimately to emancipate the whole black population of our state. . . . Look forward for twenty years to come and recollect that your black population will then all be free—no longer under the chains of slavery. . . . You will then have, without exaggeration, a black population amounting to at least twenty-five thousand individuals, and every one of them excluded by your laws from all participation in the government—made to bear a portion of its burdens and yet allowed no part in the election of those who impose burdens. This, it may be recollected, was the very ground of our complaint against Great Britain, which brought on the War of our Independence. There is intelligence enough among the blacks to be fully appraised of this fact and . . . it will not fail to be urged. . . .

There are those . . . in the state who . . . would remove the whole of these objections and obstacles at once by admitting the blacks to a full and perfect participation of all the immunities, privileges, and honors of the white population. . . . I seriously doubt whether there are three white persons in the state who would really and truly act upon this plan. Nay, I seriously doubt whether there is one white father or mother in New Jersey who would be willing that a son or a daughter should contract marriage with the best-educated Negro, male or female, that now exists. And what do you think . . . of a black governor, a black chief justice, a black member of Congress, a black member of the legislature, a black Justice of the Peace, or even a black lawyer. I appeal to you . . . whether the very naming of these things does not excite feelings which demonstrate that they could not, at least for a long time to come, be realized among us. . . . Call it folly to be frightened by the word black; prejudice to hate a black skin, . . . to separate this race so widely from ourselves. I admit it all. But still the fact is so and you cannot help it. You must put the blacks by themselves and they must make a society of their own, if they are to be real freemen. Humanity, as well as justice, calls for this. For among the whites of this country they will be treated for some generations to come, if not forever, as inferior beings. . . .

Nothing short of an actual removal of the blacks from among us will furnish relief to a dreadful disease which slavery has brought on the body politic. Preventives and sedatives and alternatives will not do. Nothing but total amputation will effect a cure.

Liberty and Justice for All

NOTABLE EVENTS

1830	Baltimore and Ohio Railroad begins operation; Camden and Amboy Railroad and Delaware and Raritan Canal chartered
1831	McCormick reaper invented
1833	First railroad in New Jersey, the Camden and Amboy, begins operation
1834	Mill women strike at Lowell, Massachusetts
1837	Mount Holyoke, first women's college in nation, opens
1839–1843	Depression
1843	North American Phalanx opens near Red Bank
1844	First message sent by telegraph; new state constitution abolishes property qualification for voting
1846	Wilmot Proviso
1848	Women's Rights Convention, Seneca Falls, New York; regularly scheduled steamship passage between Liverpool and New York City
1849	California gold rush
1850	Hawthorne, *The Scarlet Letter*; Compromise of 1850
1851	Maine adopts prohibition
1854	William Lloyd Garrison burns a copy of the United States Constitution at an antislavery meeting
1857	Dred Scott case; economic depression; mass meeting of unemployed men held in Newark
1858	Lincoln-Douglas debates
1860	Lincoln elected president; South Carolina secedes from Union
1861	First federal income tax; Confederacy established; first New Jersey regiments depart for battle
1863	Paper dress patterns introduced; Emancipation Proclamation issued; draft riots in New York City
1865	Lee surrenders at Appomattox; Lincoln assassinated; Thirteenth Amendment ratified; Ku Klux Klan organized
1866	New Jersey State Board of Education created
1867	Alaska Purchase
1868	Typewriter patented

1868　President Andrew Johnson impeachment proceedings; Fourteenth Amendment ratified

1869　Transcontinental railroad completed; Rutgers defeats Princeton in first ever intercollegiate football game

Selected New Jersey Population Statistics, 1830–1860

Year	1830	1840	1850	1860
Population (× 1,000)	321	373	490	672
% Female	49.2	49.6	49.8	50.1
Race				
% White	93.5	94.1	95.1	96.3
% Black	6.5	5.9	4.9	3.7
% Urban	5.6	10.7	17.6	32.7
People per square mile	43.3	50.3	66.0	90.6
N.J. % of U.S. population	2.5	2.2	2.1	2.1

"Fathers, Protectors, and Friends": The Lenape's Last Appeal (1832)

Historians differ over when to end the story of the Lenape in New Jersey. Some put the beginning of the end as early as the last third of the seventeenth century, just as the English arrived. There can be little doubt that the following excerpt represents some kind of ending. It comes from a letter sent to the legislature by a Delaware Indian named Bartholomew Calvin, who was writing on behalf of a group of forty Delawares residing in New Jersey. The group was claiming that they held fishing and hunting rights to undeveloped land under the terms of the Treaty of Crosswicks.[1] Calvin, then seventy-six, had been raised at the Brotherton Reservation. He was a graduate of the College of New Jersey and a Revolutionary War veteran.

The legislature, in what they termed an "act of beneficence, not justice," gave the Indians two thousand dollars.

My Brethren—I am old and weak and poor, and therefore a fit representative of my people. You are young and strong and rich, and therefore fit representatives of your people. But let me beg you for a moment to lay aside the recollections of your strength and of our weakness, that your minds may be prepared to examine with candor the subject of our claims.

Our tradition informs us, and I believe it corresponds with your records, that the right of fishing in all the rivers and bays south of the Raritan, and of hunting in all unenclosed lands, was never relinquished, but on the contrary, was expressly reserved in our last treaty held at Crosswicks in 1758.

Having myself been one of the parties to the sale, . . . I know that these rights were not sold or parted with.

We now offer to sell these privileges to the state of New Jersey. They were once of great value to us, and we apprehend that neither time or distance, nor the non-use of our rights, has at all affected them, but that the courts here would consider our claims valid were

1. In February 1758 at a meeting at Crosswicks in Burlington County, representatives of the provincial government and representatives of the Indians met to resolve remaining land-claim conflicts and to develop a procedure for handling future land sales. The meeting led to the establishment of the Brotherton reservation. (See document 15.)

John W. Barber and Henry Howe, *Historical Collections of New Jersey* (New Haven, 1869), 510–511.

we to exercise them ourselves, or delegate them to others. It is not, however, our wish thus to excite litigation. We consider the state legislature the proper purchaser, and throw ourselves upon its benevolence and magnanimity, trusting that feelings of justice and liberality will induce you to give us what you deem a compensation.

We have ever looked up to the leading characters of the United States (and to the leading characters of this state in particular) as our fathers, protectors, and friends. We now look up to you as such, and humbly beg that you will look upon us with that eye of pity, as we have reason to think our poor untutored forefathers looked upon yours, when they first arrived upon our then extensive but uncultivated dominions and sold them their lands, in many instances, for trifles.

"No Incorporations": Citizens Oppose Charters for New Businesses (1836)

The years after 1815 witnessed extraordinary economic change. Roads, canals, and early railroads were built; manufacturing changed in scale from the small shop to the small factory. Goods were bought and sold over ever-widening distances. These changes, which we call the market revolution, had enormous social impact; all aspects of life were touched, from the workplace to the home.

To many observers these changes seemed to be the fulfillment of the American revolutionary dream. Increased wealth would bring prosperity and independence to all. Other people, such as the Monmouth County residents whose petition to the legislature is excerpted here, feared the market revolution was creating greater inequality and new forms of dependency rather than enabling all to achieve economic independence.

Petitions such as this were very common in this period. Their authors often had different reasons for being uneasy about this kind of economic development. Sometimes they were artisans in danger of being reduced to wage labor. Often they were merchants, investors, or farmers who simply could not get such charters for themselves and who therefore resented a system that restricted their opportunities because political favoritism determined who got the charters.

In either case the authors fell back upon the political language of American republicanism that had animated debate over the meaning of the American Revolution. (See documents 23 and 24.)

All acts of incorporation are . . . exclusive privileges granted to a few in derogation of the rights of the mass of the people. . . . They . . . subvert the fundamental principles of any republican government. Being desirous to preserve that equality necessary to perpetuate a government like our own, based upon principles of republicanism, . . . your petitioners . . . view the numerous petitions for acts of incorporation now before your honorable bodies with the utmost distrust and alarm. . . . They recognize in them a[n] . . . extension, of that inequality of rights and privileges which already exists to an alarming extent among the people of this, as well as other, states of this union. . . .

"Memorial to the Honorable, the Legislative Council and General Assembly of the State of New Jersey," *Votes and Proceedings of the Sixtieth General Assembly of the State of New Jersey* (1836), 204–209.

They view the incorporation of railroad companies . . . as antirepublican and unwarranted by the spirit of that instrument upon which our national independence was established. Not only because they, like all other corporations, enjoy by special legislation certain exclusive, or monopoly, privileges which no other class of our citizens can enjoy, and thus beget a power that may be wielded for the most corrupt purposes; but also because they, by their charters, are permitted to take possession of, and use for their own private purposes, any property through which they may think it expedient to run their road, whether the owner give his consent or not. And thus exercise a right which few, if any, of the despots of Europe could exercise.

It matters not whether those companies find it necessary to exercise this right. . . . It is enough to know that they are vested with such a right and that they have derived it from that department of our government which, in the opinion of your petitioners, was instituted to protect the equal rights of all its citizens to their property, as well as to their lives and sacred liberty.[1] . . .

Incorporated manufacturing companies . . . become monopolizers of trade, the inevitable consequences of which are: first to paralyze and eventually to annihilate individual enterprise in the mechanic arts; compel mechanics in comfortable business, who have spent years in acquiring a knowledge of their profession (and who, of course, know no other) to abandon their vocation and . . . become operatives in the mammoth factories of their incorporated competitors; blast the fair prospects of worthy, amiable, and respectable families; and finally turn all those streams of wealth, of which manufacturing is the fountain, into one broad channel which thus is made to empty itself directly into the pockets of a privileged few. . . .

Numerous facts in the history of American chartered banking might be adduced to prove the inequality it creates, the uncertainty in business which it produces, and the innumerable mischievous consequences to which it undeniably leads. . . .

Your petitioners have only to contrast the innumerable failures that now burden the history of events every two or three years . . . with those that occurred previous to the introduction of chartered banking into this country.

In those days men advanced with a slow but steady pace to wealth. But now some avail themselves of the lottery of speculation . . .

1. According to republican political thought the legislature was the key branch of government. It was given more power than the executive branch in these years; its members were expected to be socially representative of their consituents; and it was to act in the interests of the common good.

greatly dependent on paper-money banking and become suddenly rich while others . . . risk their all and become as suddenly poor. . . .

Aside from titles of nobility, no legislative grants are so repugnant to our present admirable form of government . . . nor so productive of those aristocratic distinctions which are most peculiarly adapted to the perversion of the patriotic intentions of our venerated forefathers as acts of incorporation. . . . If the public good require a railroad, a canal or any other internal improvement, the public, i.e., the state, should construct and own the same. . . .

Any incorporation, by throwing a mantle of protection around a few individuals of which the great mass of the people are . . . deprived, is incompatible with . . . the fundamental principles upon which the American government is based.

Entertaining no doubts, therefore, as to the nature and tendency of incorporation; and relying with implicit confidence upon the wisdom and patriotism of your honorable bodies, your petitioners must earnestly entreat your honorable bodies to refrain from granting any act or acts of incorporation, for any purpose or purposes under any pretence whatever, during your present term.

"The Ornament of Youth": A Schoolgirl's Needlework Sampler (c. 1837)

In the early decades of the nineteenth century a growing number of young girls attended private schools, often called female academies, or seminaries. These institutions trained their students to win husbands and to take their places in households as mothers responsible for raising the country's next generation. The curriculums in these academies featured modern languages, music, literature, history, and geography: refined subjects, the knowledge of which developed one's character. Masculine subjects such as mathematics, theology, Greek, and the natural sciences were avoided. In addition, "feminine" activites such as sewing and fancy needlework were stressed. This kind of education reinforced in two ways the notion that a woman had no place in the man's world of business. First, it elevated the domestic sphere from a duty to a fulfilling pursuit. Simultaneously, it denied women the education that might have equipped them to find a place in the men's world of affairs.

Sampler is not a precise term—it means a piece of needlework, often signed and dated, that displays a variety of stitches and designs. Around 1830 a particular form of sampler was very popular, often occupying an important part of the curriculum for girls from nine or ten into the early teenage years. This kind of sampler is well represented by the piece illustrated here, stitched by Eure Ann Titus, probably at Eliza A. Rue's school in Pennington, sometime around 1837.

Eure Ann's sampler combined three popular elements: a sentimental slogan, a family tree, and much decorative detail. The slogan, although probably chosen by Mistress Rue or another adult, suggests the primarily ornamental place of education in a girl's life. Schooling was an adornment for a young girl. It enhanced her desirability as a prospective bride and mother. Although she could read and write, she did not learn how to function in a man's world or to do anything outside the home.

The decorative border—a basket of fruit and a frieze of grape leaves and clusters—employed symbols of abundance and comfort common in Pennsylvania and New Jersey samplers. It also displayed the child's proficiency at stitching.

The samplers were more than advertisements of genteel handiwork skills,

---

however. Often, they became prized possessions, important emblems of self-expression. Frequently, they were hung on walls, particularly when other decorative articles were scarce.

The genealogical information, like the elaborate borders, displayed the artist's needlework. But it did something else, too. It reminded the artist that, fine needlework skills notwithstanding, her identity was established principally through her family.

"Hearts Which Yearn for Africa"?: Samuel Cornish Rejects the Colonization Plan (1840)

The author of the lengthy pamphlet excerpted here was Samuel E. Cornish, an abolitionist and writer who lived in Essex County between 1838 and 1845; he ministered to the Negro Presbyterian Church in Newark. This essay, which Cornish coauthored with Theodore S. Wright, dismissed the plan of the American Colonization Society on a number of grounds, only two of which are reflected in this excerpt.

Cornish believed that the future of African Americans lay in the United States, and he vigorously supported efforts to improve the circumstances of northern blacks. The other complaint expressed in this excerpt is an issue that recurs over the centuries: white reformers, even well-intentioned ones, have frequently denied African Americans their own voice on matters in which they were directly interested. (See document 28.)

The undersigned colored citizens . . . have not been inattentive to the course of the colonization meetings. . . . As the sole object of these meetings was to act on the interest of the colored people, it is a matter of course that we should feel . . . anxious about their results. And this the more especially as none of [us] were invited to take part in them, and they have been carried on without any reference whatever to [our] wishes or opinions. Shut out from these meetings where it would seem altogether essential that our views should be fully known, our natural recourse is to the press. . . .

It is not our intention at this time to enter on the relations of the colonization scheme to the multiplied interests of our country. We propose limiting ourselves . . . to the effect of the scheme on the colored people of the free states. . . .

Mr. Butler[1] asserted that the colonization project was received with

---

1. This probably refers to Benjamin F. Butler (1795–1858), who was a leading northern Democrat. A law partner of Martin Van Buren, he served as attorney general under Andrew Jackson and later was U.S. attorney for the Southern District of New York. Butler, like Lincoln and many other prominent northerners, supported colonization in theory if not in practice. The northerners' argument

---

Samuel E. Cornish and Theodore S. Wright, *The Colonization Scheme Considered, in its Rejection by the Colored People* (Newark, 1840). Reprinted by permission of the New Jersey Historical Society.

great delight by the colored people, for whom it was set on foot. . . . If this had been said of southern slaves . . . there would probably have been no one to dissent from the opinion. But so far as it was intended to apply to the free colored people of the South, and to the colored inhabitants of the free states, we cannot . . . find sufficient grounds for excusing, much less justifying, Mr. Butler for saying, "the free colored people have hearts which yearn for Africa." . . .

The Colonization Society was scarcely known to have been organized before its object was protested against. . . . The largest meeting ever yet held of the colored people of the free States—the number being computed at 3,000—came together in Philadelphia, to consider the Colonization scheme. . . . There was not a single voice in that vast assembly which was not raised for its decisive, thorough condemnation.

Meetings of a similar kind were held in . . . all the cities and in most of the large towns throughout the free states. The abhorrence which was generally expressed of the whole scheme proved that those to whose acceptance it was offered regarded it but as little more merciful than death. . . .

The colonization scheme was set on foot . . . by slaveholders with the view . . . of perpetuating their system of slavery undisturbed.[2] From the first, no very high expectations seem to have been entertained that an enterprise so unnecessary, so unnatural . . . would commend itself strongly to that class of the community to which it purported solely to be addressed. But little reliance appears to have been placed on obtaining their voluntary consent to exchange, for the fens and morasses of barbarous and heathen Africa, this, the country of their fathers for generations and of their own nativity: where land was abundant and cheap; where labor was in demand and its rewards sure; where education could be obtained, albeit . . . with difficulty; where the common ordinances of religion . . . were established; . . . and where . . . they might yet live in hope that the dark cloud of slavery which had so long obscured the free principles asserted by our governments would one day pass away and permit these principles to shine in all their warmth . . . if not on themselves, on no very distant generation of their descendants. The benefits proposed to the

---

generally was that blacks could never become full members of American society because of their inherent inferiorities and because of white racism; thus, the only long-term solution to the problem posed by the end of slavery was to enable blacks to return to Africa.

2. Cornish and Wright are wrong here. The colonization movement was led by those who wanted to end slavery but believed that the races were fundamentally incompatible.

free colored people by a removal . . . involved the necessity, to a great extent, of breaking up their domestic relations—relations singularly dear to them, because of the sweet and (we speak from experience) enduring consolations they afforded in seasons of persecution and distress. . . . So far as the Society depended on the voluntary consent of the colored people, it might as well have been dissolved. . . .

You may say that seeing the colored people cannot, as a class, rise to an equality with the community around them, much less to honors and distinctions, and that they cannot be happy here, we merely act on the popular prejudice with a single view to their happiness. Whilst we by no means draw in question the sincerity of this declaration, we yet beg leave to say that the body of the colored people of this country who are free . . . consider . . . that their happiness has been committed to their own keeping; and that . . . they deem themselves reasonably well qualified, on the score of intelligence, to judge what will most promote it. After mature consideration, they decided against the colonization scheme as eminently hostile to their happiness. The working of the scheme for twenty years has served but to confirm them in the soundness of their decision. . . .

We ask you . . . whether you ought to persist in a scheme which nourishes an unreasonable and unchristian prejudice; which persuades legislators to continue their unjust enactments against us; . . . which affects us with the feeling that our condition is unstable and prevents us from making systematic effort for our improvement or for the advancement of our own usefulness and happiness and that of our families.

The White Flag of Temperance: A Song (1842)

In the early nineteenth century Americans drank about three times more alcohol per person than they drink today. The temperance movement was a reaction against this high level of alcohol consumption. Like other reform movements of the day, temperance emerged from a revival of Protestant evangelicalism known as the Second Great Awakening. Adherents hoped to purify society by removing individual sin. Temperance advocates urged individuals to abstain from hard liquor and drink wine and beer in moderation.

The movement peaked in the 1840s, when it turned away from efforts to persuade individuals to make moral choices that would benefit themselves and their society. Instead, its radical wing began urging state governments to provide the moral leadership that, they felt, the churches no longer could. Led by Maine, fifteen states (New Jersey not among them) prohibited the sale of all intoxicating beverages in the 1850s. Most of these laws were later repealed or overruled by the courts.

The prohibition idea appealed to many members of the new Republican party, but they didn't want it to compete with the primary issue that brought the party into being: opposition to the expansion of slavery. By keeping prohibition out of the party platform the Republicans hoped to attract drinkers as well as those who opposed the movement because they believed religious groups, not government, should take the lead on moral issues.

The words to the following song were distributed at a Fourth of July "Temperance and Sabbath Day" celebration in Marksboro, now part of Blairstown, Warren County. A number of temperance themes are reflected in it.

Tune—Star-Spangled Banner

Rouse freemen, arouse, for action prepare,
Rush forth to retrieve your fond homes from invasion,
Your breasts as of yore, to the battle make bare;
But conquer by power of moral persuasion,
With manly resolve, let each one declare,
The yoke of intemperance, he never will bear;
Fling out the white flag, let it float in the gale,
Till temperance, all over our land shall prevail.

"Temperance and Sabbath Day School Celebration in Marksboro," 1842. Rutgers. Reprinted by permission of the Department of Special Collections and University Archives, Rutgers University Libraries.

See parents unite, and children combine,
To wipe off the scourge that degrades our fair nation;
Their "lives, sacred honor, and fortunes," resign,
To rescue their country from base degradation.
Devolution's pure streams, incessantly rise,
From woman's kind bosom, to God in the skies;
To lead on to conquest, the hosts of the free,
And save the "asylum of sweet liberty."

Our cause still goes on, we'll be undismayed;
The fountains of mis'ry will soon cease their flowing,
While Heaven directs us, we'll not be afraid,
For cold water armies to millions are growing:
In Israel's God, we'll still put our trust,
And boldly march onward; "our cause it is just,"
Soon the white flag of temperance "in triumph shall wave,
O'er the land of the free and the home of the brave."

A View of Dover, c. 1844

Had coffee tables been popular in the 1840s, John Warner Barber and Henry Howe might today be thought of as the authors of one of New Jersey's earliest books for placing on them. Following a pattern Barber had established in previous books on New York, Connecticut, and Massachusetts, he and his younger associate traveled the state, interviewing inhabitants, collecting facts, and drawing what they saw. They were striving to "interest the feelings, refresh the memory, and instruct the mind." The woodcut of Dover reproduced in this collection is representative of the 120 illustrations found in Barber and Howe's Historical Collections of New Jersey: Past and Present, *all of which were rendered from their field drawings. In a sense they were pre-photography documentarians.*

At the time of this work Dover was a village in Randolph Township; it had about four hundred inhabitants, two churches, a school, and a post office. Principally an iron-manufacturing center, Dover sported two rolling mills, a forge, a foundry, and some small shops that turned out rivets, nails, and spikes. There were also other tradesmen in the village, as in virtually all others: blacksmiths, wheelwrights, and saddle-, cabinet-, and shoemakers.

The most striking feature of the illustration is probably the plumes of smoke pouring out of the ten stacks that are visible. What are the illustrators trying to say? How may all this smoke be reconciled with Barber and Howe's documentary approach and with their favorable description of Dover as set in "a beautiful valley enclosed by mountains of a romantic character"? What we see today as pollution was not seen by them as a negative. Perhaps it even added to the setting by representing a busy and industrious community whose residents are joined through their work.

There is something else notable about this illustration. Dover, about ten miles northwest of Morristown, is not in the center of New Jersey's industrial corridor; it is far from it. How is this to be explained? In the first phase of the industrial revolution, factories were located near sources of power (usually water) and natural resources that could provide fuel and supplies. Only later, decades after this illustration was made, was the strong connection established between factories and cities. It took improvements in transportation and the technology of manufacturing to broaden the market for a factory's goods and make big cities the best location for manufacturers.

John W. Barber and Henry Howe, *Historical Collections of New Jersey* (New Haven, 1869), 400.

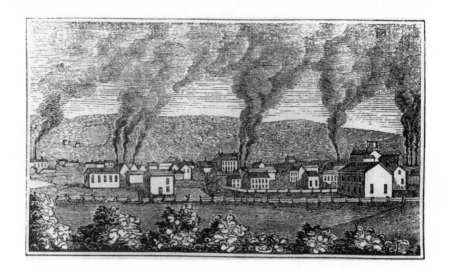

"Shall New Jersey Be Last?": Dorothea Dix Calls for a Hospital for the Mentally Ill (1845)

Dorothea Dix was one of the most forceful reformers our nation has known. A former teacher, Dix adopted the cause of the mentally ill after she taught a Sunday school class in a Massachusetts jail where mentally ill women were kept among criminals.

New Jersey was the fourth state in which Dix campaigned, the first where prior to her arrival the state government had made no provision whatsoever for the care of the mentally ill. Her work in New Jersey followed a pattern she used elsewhere. First she carefully investigated conditions in the various jails, prisons, poorhouses, and poor farms around the state. Then Dix sent a memorial to the state legislature, which is excerpted below.

She presented evidence of the shameful conditions she had observed and she called on the legislature to build a hospital for the mentally ill. Her argument was both fiscal and moral, as have been the arguments of many reformers since. A hospital for the mentally ill administered on the most advanced principles of the day was the humane thing to do, according to Dix. It would also be cheaper in the long run.

Dix's campaign was successful. Ultimately she helped design the hospital that the legislature authorized. When it opened in 1848, New Jersey became the last state in the Northeast to provide systematic care to the mentally ill. Nonetheless, Dix was proud of her accomplishment. She visited the facility often over the years, referring to it as her "first-born child," because the new hospital was the first built entirely as a result of her effort. In 1881 she retired to its grounds, where she lived until her death in 1887.

I come to solicit your attention to the condition and necessities of . . . the insane poor in the State of New Jersey. . . .

I do not come here to quicken your generous impulses and move you to emotion by showing the existence of terrible abuses. . . . I come to ask justice of the legislature of New Jersey for those who, in the providence of God, are incapable of pleading their own cause. . . . Be patient with me, it is for your own citizens I plead. It is for help-

---

Dorothea Dix, "Memorial to the Members of the Senate and General Assembly of the State of New Jersey," 1845, NJSL. Reprinted by permission of the New Jersey Department of Education, Division of the State Library.

less, friendless men and women in your very midst I ask succor, . . . the foul air of whose dreary cells still oppresses my breath, the clanking of whose heavy chains still sounds upon my ear. Have pity upon them. . . . Their grievous, forlorn estate may be shared by yourselves or your children. A solemn responsibility is intrusted to you. . . . It is for you to surround these unfortunate beings with such protecting influences as their incapacity for self-care demands, and to guard against the aggravation of like evils and miseries for the future.

Within the last few months I have traversed a considerable portion of your state, and have found in jails and poorhouses, and wandering at will over the country, large numbers of insane and idiotic persons whose irresponsibility and imbecility render them objects of deep commiseration. These, whether the subjects of public bounty or of private charity, are . . . left to exposures and sufferings at once pitiable and revolting. . . .

A cursory survey of the state has exhibited so many patients distributed in the state prison, the county jails, the poorhouse[s] . . . as to prove that your pecuniary interest is united with the plea of humanity, to urge you to immediate action on the subject. . . . It is certainly difficult to comprehend why New Jersey, with ample means, unembarrassed by state debts and prosperous in all her public relations . . . should fail to take an honorable . . . position in the establishment of such state institutions as the wants of her citizens require. . . .

The [Salem] County poorhouse is . . . near Sharptown. . . . There are here, beside several epileptics and persons of infirm minds, eight insane. One woman of middle age has been crazy seventeen years. Two of the patients were in chains; one man, very crazy for nearly thirty years, has been out of his small apartment but "ten times for more than nineteen years." He is considered very dangerous. . . . No appropriate care can be rendered here to lessen . . . the terrible horrors of madness. . . .

In a basement room . . . lay, upon a small bed, a feeble, aged man whose few gray locks fell tangled about his pillow. As we entered, he addressed one present saying, "I am all broken up, all broken up. . . . The mind, the mind is going; almost gone." . . . This feeble, depressed old man—a pauper, helpless, lonely and yet conscious of surrounding circumstances and not now wholly oblivious of the past, . . . who was he? . . . In his young and vigorous years he filled various places of honor and trust among you. . . . He was for many years a member of the legislature. . . . He became insane. . . . In time he was . . . removed to the poorhouse. . . . He is withering away in an obscure room of a county poorhouse, receiving his share of that care and attention that must be divided and subdivided among the hundred feeble, infirm and disabled inmates. For such men . . . is no hospital needed? . . .

In Piscataway . . . one violent madman was chained in an outbuilding which has been constructed for the purpose a few hundred yards from the principal dwelling. This consisted of one strong dark room; a stove had been placed upon one side as remote from the chained man as possible, to guard from the dangers of his firing the building. . . . The room was cold and damp and . . . entirely bare of all furniture: dark and dull and utterly comfortless. The madman chained, naked except a straitjacket laced so as to impede the motion of the arms and hands, exposed and filthy, now raging like an imprisoned tiger . . . now uttering the foulest, vilest language; for a moment soothed into quietness, then like a demon writhing and raving. . . .

Insanity is a malady which requires treatment appropriate to its peculiar and varied forms. The most skillful physicians in general practice are among the first to recommend their patients to hospital treatment. . . . If this care is needed for the rich, for those whose homes abound in every luxury which wealth can purchase, . . . how much more is it needed for those who are brought low by poverty and are destitute of friends, for those who find refuge under this calamitous disease only in jails and poorhouses or, perchance, in the cells of a state penitentiary?

But suppose the jail to afford comfortable apartments, decently furnished, and to be directed by an intelligent and humane keeper— advantages not frequently brought together. What then? Is not a jail built to detain criminals, bad persons who willingly and wilfully transgressing the civil and social laws are for these offenses for a time imprisoned? Where is the propriety, where the justice of bringing under the same condemnation persons not guilty of crime, but laboring under disease? . . . It is more than time this unchristian abuse would cease. . . .

The disposition to annoy and distress insane and imbecile persons is not confined to our jails, it is exhibited in the poorhouses. . . . If prisons are unfit for the insane . . . poorhouses are certainly not less so. . . .

Most of the sufferings and neglects to which I have found the insane exposed have not been the result of hard-hearted brutality, but of ignorance, of want of qualification for discharging those duties. . . . Many have truly believed that an insane man or woman was no better than a mere brute. . . . They have not supposed them susceptible of emotions of pain or pleasure, capable of being controlled through kind influences, or of being restored through any cares they could bestow. . . .

It is said that the establishment of hospitals involves great expense, that it is much cheaper to maintain the insane elsewhere. Is it also computed at what actual cost these are supported in the state penitentiary, in county jails, in poorhouses, and in families; what sums are consumed by their uncontrolled habits of destructiveness, what are lost by their crimes when under frenzied impulses they fire buildings, take human life, and make wreck of all social and domestic peace and happiness. . . .

On the ground of a discreet economy alone it is wise to establish a state hospital in New Jersey. But I will not dishonor you by urging this suit on the money-saving principle. I will not unman and unchristianize you by urging other incentives to prompt and liberal action than those which humanity presents. I am sure it is not a parsimonious spirit which has delayed this work here. I perceive the liberal appropriation of money to sustain the poorhouses and to fill the many channels of public and private charity. Evidences of a kindly benevolence reach me continually in provision for the poor and needy and in care of the distressed. The insane and idiots alone have been too long insufficiently provided for. . . .

The delay of providing suitable asylums for the insane produces miseries to individuals and evils to society, inappreciable . . . except by those who have given time to the examination of the subject and who have witnessed the appalling degradation of these wretched sufferers in the poorhouses and jails and penitentiaries of our land. Shall New Jersey be last of "the thirteen sisters" to respond to the claims of humanity and the demands of justice?

Religion and Republicanism: New Jersey's Fugitive Slave Policy (c. 1846)

The problem of what to do about runaway slaves was an important part of the wedge that split the northern and the southern states into camps whose differences could not be settled by compromise. The issue went back to the federal Constitution, which specified that slaves who escaped to a free state remained slaves, vulnerable to recapture. In 1793 Congress allowed slave owners to seize their escaped slaves in any state and take them to a state or federal court to establish ownership. Early in the nineteenth century several northern states passed what were known as personal-liberty laws, whose purpose was to prevent the kidnapping of free blacks. New Jersey additionally provided for a jury trial to establish the legal status of the individual.

In 1842 the U.S. Supreme Court ruled that enforcement of the fugitive slave clause in the Constitution was entirely a federal matter. This led a number of northern states to pass new personal-liberty laws forbidding state officials from aiding in the recapture of slaves and prohibiting the use of state or local jails. These, in turn, led to southern calls for federal legislation on the fugitive slave question, which were answered with the Fugitive Slave Act of 1850.

The petition excerpted here calls on the New Jersey legislature to enact such a law, a call it did not meet. In addition, in the last decade before the Civil War, New Jersey was alone among northeastern states in creating no legal problems for traveling slave owners who brought their slaves into the state.

Your petitioners, citizens of New Jersey, . . . respectfully pray that you will . . . pass a law prohibiting all state officers and citizens from . . . aiding in the arrest of . . . fugitives in the State of New Jersey, except under the mandate of the United States marshal or other officers of the general government. . . .

The Constitution and laws of the United States empower the master to arrest his slaves anywhere in the Union by the aid of the officers of the general government, and this we think is sufficient without obliging or allowing any citizen of this State to aid in such arrest.

"Petition to the Legislature of the State of New Jersey," n.d., Rutgers. Reprinted by permission of the Department of Special Collections and University Archives, Rutgers University Libraries.

We ask you to pass a prohibitory statute saying that no such officer or citizen shall participate in said arrest, nor shall any state court have jurisdiction in such case, nor any jail be used to detain such fugitive, because the powers of the general government are sufficient for the master. . . . If no such statute exist prohibiting our officers or citizens under penalties from said participation, then malicious and avaricious persons, from hatred or the hope of reward, will become informers against peaceable and innocent colored people, to the ruin and breaking up of families and not infrequently the enslavement of free colored persons, of which many instances could be cited.

The people of New Jersey have abolished slavery in their domain, thereby declaring it wrong. . . . They should not become its voluntary supporters elsewhere, beyond what the Constitution of the United States requires.

It is objected to such legislation as we propose that it virtually prohibits the master from recovering his slave and violates his constitutional right to reclaim him. To this we reply that the master can, or should, have no other than constitutional right and has that whether we legislate or not.

He may take his slave where he can find him, or apply to the United States District Court, which upon proper evidence shall require the marshal to arrest said slave or slaves and bring him or them before said court or district judge, who shall decide upon the validity of the master's claim. . . .

We respectfully suggest that if the United States government has not jails or places of security for persons thus arrested—charged with no crime but an effort to regain their freedom, which New Jersey has declared to be the right of all men—that the general government should provide such places . . . and not use our jails or prisons for purposes which New Jersey will not allow in the case of her own citizens.

As we only ask of your honorable body to be exonerated from any farther participation in the monstrous enormity of slavery than the Constitution of the United States requires . . . but which humanity and the conscientious feelings of at least 100,000 persons in New Jersey appear to demand, we renew our request for your compliance with our petition.

We further pray your honorable body to repeal the last section . . . of the Act for the Abolition of Slavery[1] . . . which allows any slaveholder to move into New Jersey with his slaves. We think it an unnec-

1. This law, approved April 18, 1846, allowed nonresidents traveling with a reasonable number of "personal or household slaves" to enter and leave New Jersey with their property.

essary sanction of the ruinous and shocking system of slavery and makes our legislation inconsistent with itself and with the enlightened policy of the state.

If the master bring his slaves here we wish him to have no more than constitutional guarantees for their possession. If our sister states will maintain the blight of slavery upon them, we earnestly and solemnly protest in the name of our religion and our republicanism against being obliged to aid them. . . .

We wish every man guiltless of crime to be free when he enters New Jersey.

"Learning Cannot Be Disunited from Religion": A Letter on the Public School System (1848)

Of the many pre–Civil War efforts to improve American society, none was more far-reaching than the movement to open common schools, as they were called—schools for the children of the common man. In New Jersey the campaign began in the early 1820s when a group calling itself the Friends of Education began advocating more and better schools and better legislation on the issue. The group's efforts were opposed by a complex coalition that consisted of people without children who did not want to pay taxes; religious interests who feared competition with their own schools; Catholics who opposed the schools' Protestant orientation; working people who depended on their children's incomes; and conservatives who thought it was a waste of money to try to educate the masses.

Lucius Q. C. Elmer of Bridgeton took up many of these issues in the letter excerpted here, which he wrote to Governor Daniel Haines, himself an advocate of expanding and improving the schools. Elmer was a leading public figure—a former state assemblyman and U.S. congressman before he wrote this letter, the state's attorney general and a member of the state supreme court after it.

The issues he raised were heatedly debated in Elmer's day. Many of them remain with us.

The great importance of general education in a republic like ours is acknowledged by all. . . . Every year witnesses new efforts . . . to perfect a system of public schools free to all and worthy [of] the support of all. . . . The private efforts of the citizen cannot be safely relied on to provide a competent education for all the children in any community. Upon this point there is general concurrence of opinion. But whether the government ought to undertake this duty, or to what extent it may safely and advantageously interfere, are questions of great moment upon which there is a great diversity of sentiment. . . .

A large and influential denomination of Christians . . . has come out in decided reprobation of the whole system of public schools, and commenced an effort to substitute . . . parochial schools, "in which

---

Lucius Q. C. Elmer, "To The Governor of New Jersey," February 1, 1848, NJSL. Reprinted by permission of the New Jersey Department of Education, Division of the State Library.

the usual branches of a sound elementary education are taught; with the addition of daily religious instruction from the Bible under the superintendence of a Christian teacher."[1] . . .

Any system of education of which religious truth and duty do not constitute an essential and prominent feature is of very doubtful utility, if not positively pernicious. . . . Being myself . . . one of the directors of a public school established under the laws of this state where an attempt is making . . . to teach the usual branches of a sound elementary education with the addition of daily religious instruction from the Bible, under the superintendence of Christian teachers; and which is not only free to all . . . children of a suitable age, but the advantages of which are eagerly sought by all, from the children of our wealthiest to those of our poorest citizens, . . . I am persuaded there is no real incompatibility between a system of state schools and the general introduction of sound religious instruction. . . .

Adjusting a system of schools, established by authority of law and supported by taxation, as to afford sound religious instruction without interfering with the conscientious scruples, or at least the deep-rooted prejudices, of the many sects prevailing among us is exceedingly difficult. . . . It is also true that the disposition to get rid of these difficulties by excluding religious instruction altogether . . . has manifested itself so strongly on many occasions, as to account for . . . the effort to adopt another plan. But the true question is: can more good be accomplished by adhering to the system of public schools . . . than by abandoning it? . . .

How far the state should go in the establishment and control of public schools is a question of great importance. . . . By many it has been taken for granted that the government should not only contribute funds . . . but that it should regulate the kind of instruction to be given. . . . The attempt to do this, although productive of good in many respects, is liable to so great abuse that I think it ought to be entirely abandoned. . . .

But because it is conceded that the state ought to establish and support schools, and that these schools ought to teach religious duties in conjunction with letters and science, it by no means follows that the state ought to prescribe the mode in which this duty shall be performed. . . . Let this duty be left in the hands of the teachers and of those who employ them. . . . Leave them full liberty to do as their consciences dictate. . . .

Few will . . . insist that the state should be called on to prescribe

---

1. Elmer is referring to the Catholics, whose efforts to establish parochial schools in New Jersey were very strong.

any particular course of religious instruction. The great difficulty of doing this without interfering with the conscientious scruples of many worthy citizens would probably prevent the attempt. . . . Very many, however, seem to think that to protect these scruples the government should go to the other extreme and absolutely prohibit religious instruction in the public schools. . . . These persons forget that this will not less interfere with the consciences of those who believe that moral should always accompany intellectual culture and that the Bible contains the only true standard of morals. They forget, too, that those of this belief comprise the great body of the community. Although our Constitution very properly declares that there shall be no establishment of one religious sect in preference to another, that no religious test shall be required, and that no person shall be denied the enjoyment of any civil right merely on account of his religious principles, yet it does by no means proscribe religion. On the contrary it expressly recognizes a God and our accountability to him. . . . The Christian religion is the religion of most of the people. Upon this principle the public business, as a general rule, ceases on Sunday and our legislative bodies invite Christian ministers to pray for a divine blessing on their labors. . . .

As our laws now are, the inhabitants of the different school districts in the state have full liberty . . . to regulate the public schools as they deem best. . . . This freedom from control by a central power of any kind . . . I trust will be most scrupulously maintained. . . . Let Christians of all denominations heartily unite in the great work of imparting to our youth Christian instruction in our public schools and let this great principle of leaving every district to perfect freedom be steadily maintained and I do not fear the result. . . . Each district will thus be left, as in New Jersey it now is left, to be governed by the majority. . . . In some cases, probably, the majority will discard religious instruction altogether and in some what is taught will be grossly erroneous. But so it will be on any plan that can be devised. . . . It will no doubt happen in some cases that individuals will even be compelled to contribute to the support of schools they cannot with a good conscience allow their children to enter. . . . Such, or similar difficulties, beset every system of government. Taxes are constantly raised and applied by government to objects to which some of those who contribute are most conscientiously opposed. . . . The small minority who cannot thus be satisfied must be left free to promote their peculiar views in their own way, wherever they are found in sufficient numbers to make it practicable. This is their right.

"Germans Assaulted Indiscriminately": Ethnic Violence in Hoboken (1851)

Neither the Germans involved in the episode described here, nor the "Short Boys" and their allies on the other side were all from New Jersey. Many had come from New York for the day. But it is fitting that this melee between participants at a Sunday picnic and a group of nativist[1] ruffians took place in Hoboken, because in 1880 the United States Census called Hoboken the "most German city" in the country.

The German population of New Jersey had just begun to grow rapidly at the time of the fracas described. A number of well-educated refugees who fled the unsuccessful revolution of 1848 had arrived, and these were joined by a larger stream of immigrants, mostly workers, craftsmen, and farmers from southwestern Germany. A million Germans came to the United States in the 1850s. In New Jersey the German-born population in 1860 was three times its 1850 size.

Yesterday was . . . the holiday of Pentecost[2]—a day which in Germany is commemorated by festivals in the woods. A large number of Germans, ten to twelve thousand in all, perhaps, crossed to Hoboken . . . where they . . . had leased for the day the cricket ground, some distance from the village. . . . Here, under the trees, stands for the sale of beer and refreshments were erected, beside a platform for the orators of the day and a band of music which accompanied them. All parties present seemed to enjoy themselves, and the beer, especially, flowed in torrents from the barrels on tap down hundreds of thirsty throats.

Everything passed off peaceably till toward the close of the afternoon, when some difficulties occurred through the presence of a gang of rowdies . . . known by the title of "The short boys." These scamps . . . soon created a disturbance at the scene of the festival. . . . They were armed, and evidently came for the purpose of assault, as

1. Someone generally hostile to immigrants. Although nativism has been persistent in American history, it was especially intense in the years before the Civil War when it was directed at Irish and German immigrants in particular.
2. The seventh Sunday after Easter, commemorating the descent of the Holy Spirit on the apostles.

New York Herald Tribune, May 27, 1851. Reprinted in Richard Hofstadter and Michael Wallace, eds., *American Violence: A Documentary History* (New York: Alfred A. Knopf, 1970), 310–312.

they commenced, without provocation, to insult the females, over-throw the refreshment tables, and destroy the property of the ven-dors. . . . The Germans . . . had determined, at first, to avoid a collision on account of the number of ladies and children who were present, but these outrages were not to be tolerated and the offenders were driven off. . . . A regular fight commenced. . . .

The rowdies retreated toward the village, followed by the Ger-mans, and a sort of running fight was kept up for the whole distance. The Turnverein (Society of Gymnasts)[3] took an active part in the con-flict and were marked out as special subjects of resentment. On reach-ing the village the rowdies were reinforced by . . . a gang of boys from fourteen to sixteen years of age. Toward evening they assembled be-fore the gates of the ferry and prevented the Germans coming in from the festival from reaching the boat. For more than an hour they shut off all communication. About half-past six the procession, consisting of the Turnverein . . . and other associations, accompanied by large numbers of Germans with their families, came in from the woods. . . . The front of the procession . . . was assailed by a shower of stones. . . . The procession halted and the Turners, taking the lead, advanced against the mob, for the purpose of clearing a way to the ferry boat. A violent fight then commenced, which lasted with little intermission for two hours. The rowdies were armed with guns, pistols, swords, clubs and slingshots, and after the first attack the Germans entered the German beer-houses in the neighborhood and armed themselves. Two are known to be killed. . . .

Previous to the arrival of the procession, all the returning Germans were assaulted indiscriminately, some of them being knocked down while walking with ladies. Sometimes they were asked if they were Germans before being struck and one who replied in the affirmative to the question whether he was a Turner immediately received a mus-ket ball in his side. It is said that the house of a German named Beiner was attacked and the furniture demolished. A great number of per-sons were severely, and some mortally, injured. Many were stabbed in different parts of the body, or beaten with stones. One man had his head shockingly cut by a large pole, the end of which was covered with spikes. The fight was one of the most brutal . . . which ever occurred in this vicinity. The sheriff of the county was early on the ground, endeavoring to quell the riot. He . . . ordered out the military from Jersey City. . . .

The number of arrests made was near forty, a large portion of

3. An organization that combined gymnastics and politics. Turnvereins flour-ished in the United States among the immigrants of 1848, combining liberal, even socialist, politics with self-defense.

whom were Germans. They were bound hand and foot, and sent to the county jail at Bergen. The militia remained on guard till half-past 11 o'clock, when everything appeared to be quiet and they left. . . . It is impossible precisely to ascertain the number of killed and wounded. There are certainly four of the former and probably fifty of the latter, some of whom will not recover. Twelve or fifteen of the rowdies were badly injured.

"The Union in Jeopardy": A Fourth of July Speech (1851)

Robert F. Stockton, the author of this speech, was one of the most notable figures in New Jersey history. During a distinguished navy career he saw action in the War of 1812 and the Mexican War. In the latter conflict he commanded the capture of Southern California. The town of Stockton, California, commemorates his role. His navy service culminated in a term as secretary of the navy; while in that office he abolished the practice of flogging midshipmen.

Stockton was a leading figure in the American Colonization Society, which sought to return African Americans to their native continent. (See documents 28 and 32.)

Following a two-year term in the United States Senate, Stockton became the president of the Delaware and Raritan Canal Company. In that position he exerted a great influence on the affairs of the state.

In the speech excerpted here Stockton was as prescient as he was racist. He linked three of the common themes of political discourse of the day: treatment of the Indians, slavery, and the manifest destiny[1] of the United States to spread across the continent. Stockton, unwilling to limit national expansion to North America, argued that the country's growth would end unless the Union was preserved along the lines of the Constitution, which, of course, had sanctioned slavery.

On the 4th of July, 1776, the Declaration of Independence was signed by our patriotic forefathers and delivered into the hands of the people. . . .

That was . . . no small candle lit under a bushel. It was a great fire built on the top of a mountain to show the way that the great Anglo-American family were taking to God and liberty. It has been burning brighter and brighter, till it has illumined this continent from the Atlantic to the Pacific Oceans and I hope it will . . . ascend higher and higher until it lightens up the dark cavern of Tierra del Fuego,[2] and redeems even the Patagonian[3] wanderer to liberty and civilization.

1. The belief that God ordained white America to expand its institutions across the continent.
2. A group of islands at the southern tip of South America.
3. Patagonia is a region in southern Argentina and Chile, sometimes thought to include Tierra del Fuego.

"Address Delivered at Elizabethtown, July 4, 1851." Reprinted in *A Sketch of the Life of Robert F. Stockton* (New York: Derby and Jackson, 1856), 79–84.

I congratulate you, fellow-citizens . . . that we are permitted once more to celebrate this anniversary under the broad banner of the Union. . . . I have lived for the Union, the whole Union, and nothing but the Union. I can remember nothing before the Union, and I desire to know nothing and to remember nothing after it shall be dissolved. . . .

But we have fallen upon evil times. At the North, a fanaticism . . . is at work . . . in the vain and delusive expectation of . . . the equality of the white and black races of men. At the South, the watch-fires of the Revolution have been rekindled in the preparation for the defense of their homes. . . . The men of the South are preparing for war in the hope of redressing their wrongs and avenging their insults by an appeal to the sword. . . .

Our forefathers left Europe to . . . avoid religious persecution and despotic power and to establish freedom of religion and civil liberty. . . . The sufferings and hardships arising from the climate and the want of necessary supplies were not the only difficulties with which our fathers had to contend; but those which grew out of their contact with the aborigines of the country were more hazardous and distressing. I will not dwell upon the conflicts between the white and the red man. The story of the Indian is too sad and too well known to make it necessary or agreeable to dwell on the subject. But I must remind you that the race is fast wasting away before the march of civilization. . . . The advancement of civil and religious liberty is so important to the happiness of the human race that no considerations connected with the temporary misfortunes of any portion of the human family can be permitted to interfere with its progress. . . .

Amalgamation with the white race was utterly impracticable. . . . The only question seemed to be which of the two races should suffer most. . . . While we may shed a tear of sorrow at the sufferings of the Indian, or on the ashes of his wigwam, we may at the same time thank our God that He has thus made us the instruments to forward His purposes toward our race. . . .

When our fathers felt themselves strong enough to assert their right to all those privileges of free and independent men, which by a common heritage they had derived from their ancestors, . . . they published to the world that declaration of their principles which you have just heard read. . . . Now, in violation of every rule of fair criticism, there are persons who say that the practice of our government is inconsistent with the principles of the declaration, because, while that instrument proclaims that all men are born free and equal, we keep in bondage a portion of the human family. It is an error to say that the general expression of a sentiment contained in an instrument of that kind is to control the sense of that instrument. It must be taken as a whole, and any single or isolated passage must be construed by the obvious intent and meaning of the instrument itself. It is quite obvious that the general expression alluded to is applicable only to men in their national and not in their individual character. . . .

Fellow citizens . . . the Union [is] in jeopardy. . . . Unless the aggression of the northern and eastern agitators be arrested . . . a dissolution of the Union is . . . probable. . . .

If such a calamity should occur, I hope that New Jersey . . . will unite, for better or worse, with those who are willing to abide by and respect . . . the Constitution. . . . I have no doubt that in such an event the northwestern states would unite with New Jersey, Pennsylvania, and the South. The South is their common customer; there is their market. The republic so constituted would have no natural repugnance to the spread of civilization and reformed religion over that portion of the continent which seems now to be but imperfectly subjected to their influence. . . . Already has the Anglo-Saxon avalanche descended the western slope of the Rocky Mountains to the Pacific shores. Hitherto the impulse has been westward and westward chiefly has been the march of empire. . . . It . . . must naturally soon take another and more southern direction.

I am only stating what I consider the law which governs the progress of the Anglo-Saxon race. I will not . . . defend what I believe to be the inevitable destiny of my country and my race. . . . I feel assured that my country, if she remains united in all her integral parts, will, within fifty years, acquire more wealth and power than any sovereign potentate or dominion which now sways or ever before swayed any portion of the destiny of mankind. . . . Let us not . . . prevent the peaceable progress of our countrymen over a continent which Providence seems to have designed for their occupation and civilization.

The position which would practically limit the republic at the south, . . . I cannot approve. That position is assumed under the plausible idea of limiting the area of slavery. The assumption that would not permit the admission of a state into the Union without a restriction on slavery is an aggression on the south which finds no warrant in the Constitution. We have as much right to say that the population of a State shall be all Protestants or all Catholics as to prescribe the kind of labor to be employed by its people. We have as much right to force slavery upon a state as to interdict it. . . . The Constitution . . . nowhere gives authority to Congress to prescribe to an emigrant going to the public lands what kind of property he shall take with him or what kind of property he shall not take with him. . . .

I deny that the government (or Congress, or the North) have any right to say that a state asking to be admitted into the Union shall be refused admission unless she discards from her borders a portion of the property of fifteen sister states. . . . Whether the evils of slavery are such as the abolitionists represent them to be, no considerations connected with those evils . . . will warrant a violation of the . . . Constitution. The Constitution is neutral on the subject of slavery. To make it aggressive or defensive is to violate it. The Union can only be preserved by a strict adherence to the Constitution. If that be violated, the bonds of the Union are broken and the aggrieved parties will seek redress and compensation without regard to its obligations.

In conclusion fellow-citizens I will express the hope that . . . in all coming time the stripes and stars our patriot fathers followed to victory or death may wave, as they wave today, over a united people.

"Escaped from the Confinement of the Needle": The North American Phalanx (1853–1855)

During the first half of the nineteenth century, the number of self-employed craftsmen and farmers declined while the number of wage earners increased. Americans were thus trading the status of independent producer for that of dependent wage laborer. This trade was resisted in many ways, however. One way was the development of experimental communities based on collective ownership of property and emphasizing cooperation over competition. Some participants were motivated by abstract utopian principles; some were seeking an alternative to the world of wage labor.

Mary Paul, the author of the letters to her father excerpted here, was born in northern Vermont in 1830. She was a domestic servant, a worker in the textile mills of Lowell, Massachusetts, and a self-employed coat maker before she moved, in 1854, to the North American Phalanx[1] near Red Bank (Monmouth County). After she left the Phalanx upon its collapse in 1855, Paul worked as a housekeeper in New Hampshire, where her widowed father was living. In 1857 Paul married the son of her former boardinghouse keeper in Lowell. She and her husband moved to Lynn, Massachusetts, where Paul bore two children before her father died and the correspondence that provided the basis for this information ended.

The North American Phalanx was the largest and most successful of the nearly thirty utopian communities established according to the principles of French socialist Charles Fourier (1772–1837), who believed that men and women would do best when living in collectives no larger than twenty-five hundred people.

Brattleboro, November 27, 1853

I have a plan for myself which I am going to lay before you and see what you think of it. When I was at Manchester last spring my friend[s] . . . were talking of going to New Jersey to live and proposed that I should go with them. . . . The people among whom they are

---

1. *Phalanx* comes from a Greek word meaning "line of battle." As used here it suggests members of a group working in close association with one another.

Reprinted in Thomas Dublin, ed., *Farm to Factory: Women's Letters, 1830–1860* (New York: Columbia University Press, 1981), 98–123. Copyright © 1981 by Columbia University Press. Used by permission.

going are Associationists. The name will give you something of an idea of their principles. There [are] about 125 persons in all that live there, and the association is called the "North American Phalanx." . . . The advantage that will arise from my going there will be that I can get better pay without working as hard as at any other place. The price for work there being nine cents an hour, and the number of hours for a days work, ten. Besides I should not be confined to one kind of work, but could . . . have the privilege of doing anything that is done there—housework, if I choose, and that without degrading myself, which is more than I could do anywhere else. . . .

At the Phalanx . . . all work, . . . and all are paid alike. Both men and women have the same pay for the same work. There is no such word as aristocracy there unless there is real (not pretended) superiority. . . . The members can live as cheaply as they choose, as they pay only for what they eat, and no profit on that, most of the provision being raised on the grounds. One can join them with or without funds and can leave at anytime they choose. . . .

A woman gets much better paid there than elsewhere, but it is not so with a man, though he is not meanly paid by any means. There is more equality in such things according to the work, not the sex. You know that men often get more than double the pay for doing the same work that women do. . . . Their principles are just what I would like to see carried into practice, and they are, as far as means will allow, at the Phalanx. Another advantage from living there is this: the members can have privileges of education free of expense to themselves alone, the extent of this education must of course depend on the means of the society. . . . I wish you to let me know what you think of my plans. If you have any real objection or if you would rather I would not go so far away, let me know and I will cheerfully give up the idea of going.

Brattleboro, December 18, 1853

I was glad to find from your letter that you approve my plans in regard to going to New Jersey. I have not heard anything definite about my going since I wrote you. I am hoping to know something very soon . . . .

If I thought I could make a decent living at Claremont I would come back there, but I have tried to my satisfaction and must work where I can get more pay.

North American Phalanx, N.J., May 7, 1854

We arrived here . . . and were kindly received. . . . We have been very busy all the week putting things to rights. Have not done much work beside our own. I have worked about two hours each day for the Phalanx, three quarters in sweeping, one and a quarter in the dining hall, cleaning and laying the tables. Tomorrow I am going to begin sewing, which will add three hours each day to my work. On ironing days I shall iron one, two, or three hours just as I like. . . . The place is very pleasant and the people remarkably kind. Upon the whole I think that I may like it very well. . . .

Take care of yourself and don't work too hard. I wish that you could be here. I think you might find enough at your work to keep you busy as many hours in a day as you would want to work. There are a few here who work at one kind of business all the time, but it is from choice.

Phalanx, October 2, 1854

I am getting along very well here, better than I should at sewing. I have averaged about six hours work per day through the month of September. I do not yet know how much I shall have for it, but I find I can live here easier and work but half the time than away from here and work all the time. Besides I am convinced that the work I do is better for my health than sewing. I have not done any sewing of any consequence and shall not be likely to have a great deal to do beside my own and there is always enough of that. . . .

When I wrote you before I think peaches were the go but they are all gone and forgotten now I expect. The sweet potatoes are being gathered now. They raise a great many here and we have plenty of them to eat. Three weeks ago yesterday the mill was burned to the ground. This was a great loss to the Association and puts them back in all their work as well as their plans. . . . There were several kinds of business carried on (beside the milling) in the building, and the tools connected with them belonged to individuals. Some of the losses are heavy.

Phalanx, March 3, 1855

I did not wish to write until I had something definite to say respecting my prospects here. . . . The loss of the mill involved the Association in difficulties from which it would be hard to extricate it. . . . This Association is most certainly in the very last stage. I am sorry to say it but there appears to be no hope and a year at the farthest will terminate the existence of the North American Phalanx, in all probability. I do not know how long I can stay here but I shall not leave until I am obliged to do. The life here has many attractions and advantages which no other life can have and, imperfect as it is, I have already seen enough to convince me that Association is the true life. And although all the attempts that have ever yet been made towards it have been failures, inasmuch as they have passed away (but they have all left their mark) my faith in the principles is as strong as ever, stronger if possible. There is a better day coming for the world. . . .

Don't be worried about me, Father, for I am certainly more comfortable here than I could be anywhere else. I suppose when I leave here I shall have to take up sewing again, as that seems to be the only thing open to me. I flattered myself that I had fairly escaped from the confinement of the needle, but I shall have to return to it after all. Well I expect it will be all for the best . . . Give my love to everybody that cares for me.

Phalanx, April 12, 1855

A good many of the members have already gone away and others are preparing to leave.

From your last letter I perceive you have a very erroneous idea of affairs here. You say the place . . . seems to be in the hands of capitalists who have lost their courage when the hard times came. In this you are wrong. To be sure a good many of the stockholders are rich men, but the man who holds two thousand dollars of stock has no more control than the one who only has one hundred. . . . It is true that many have lost their courage in the hard times but it is no more the rich man than the poor one. . . .

I know many will exult in the downfall of this place, but each are shortsighted. Charles Fourier's doctrines, although they may contain many absurd ideas, have enough of truth in them to keep them alive until the world shall be ready for them.

Phalanx, June 11, 1855

I don't know but you will think I am strayed away or stolen, it is so long since I have written you, but I assure you I am safe and sound. . . . The weather . . . has been cool all the spring. We have had but a few really warm days as yet. . . . Everything is in good condition, potatoes are in blossom . . . strawberries ripened late but we are having them . . . in great abundance.

Yesterday two thousand baskets (measuring half a pint each) were sent to market. . . . I have all the strawberries I want to eat and it is the first time in my life that I was ever so favored. I went out one day and picked twenty baskets, but made myself almost sick by doing it. . . . I don't know how long I can stay here. . . . Where I shall go and when I go away is more than I can guess.

"Equality, Liberty, and Prosperity": The Workingmen's Union of Trenton (1858)

The 1850s witnessed an increase in labor organization. During the preceding decades many workshops had been turned into small factories. Where once the boundaries between master and journeymen had been porous, the barrier between owner and worker was growing harder to cross. When skilled workers joined together they sought more than the improvement of their immediate job situations. The labor movement before the Civil War spoke in terms of all producers, not just wage workers, and it called for a just society, often invoking the republican ideals of the American Revolution to advocate an egalitarian society based on a hard-working, virtuous, independent citizenry.

This excerpt from a platform of the Workingmen's Union of Trenton is illustrative of labor organizations of the day. Its authors take up taxation, the tariff, public-school funding, political corruption, and other themes. They do not deal with wage rates, working hours, or working conditions, although these were issues that organized labor was fighting over.

Whereas the working classes, though they have produced all the wealth and blessings of civilized society, have never enjoyed equal social and political privileges with those that work not and yet consume the labor of others;

And whereas the idle and the vicious . . . secure the election of persons to make our laws and to execute them who have no sympathy with or regard for our interests, therefore:

Resolved, that in order to secure our rights and protect our interests it is necessary that we should have organization and united action. The producing classes have the intellectual and physical strength to control the legislation of the world and yet for the want of systematic united action have been controlled and oppressed in all countries and ages.

Resolved, that we will unite in a permanent organization and demand from our rulers the passage of laws to secure the following just and reasonable objects.

"Platform and Constitution of the Workingmen's Union of the City of Trenton," Trenton, 1858, Rutgers. Reprinted by permission of the Department of Special Collections and University Archives, Rutgers University Libraries.

Nationally: That the burdens of taxation shall be lightened by discharging all persons drawing pay from the government who are not performing active necessary duties. Swarms of office holders are being multiplied, who eat out our substance and who perform little or no public service, but manage to control the political action of the people and thus abridge their liberties and rights. . . .

The revenue laws should be revised and the duties assessed only on such goods as come in competition with our domestic manufactures. Duties thus assessed . . . would give important protection to our industrial interests and secure employment to thousands now out of work and out of the means of subsistence. This . . . would not only give important relief to the laboring masses but it would lessen the burdens of taxation. . . .

The government lands should be withheld from the hands of speculators and sold only to actual settlers, in limited quantities, at cost. Railroad companies and monopolists are fast absorbing the uncultivated lands which, of right, should belong to those that cultivate them; and thus they are destroying the common heritage and closing up the only safe asylum for the laboring millions from the hand of oppression.

In state: Taxation should be lightened by discharging all unnecessary officers, by cutting off the fees of all salaried officers. . . . The revenues of the state derived from chartered companies, as they are the price of special privileges and belong to the people, should be appropriated to the support of the common schools of the state, and as education is a primary want of a free people, these schools should be extended until knowledge shall be as free as the air we breathe.

As working men cannot afford to pay the expenses of litigation out of their earnings, the laws . . . should be so altered as to enable them to get their pay for their work without being subject to repeated delays and appeals so numerous as to compel them to submit to any terms that may be dictated to them, however oppressive or unjust. . . .

A radical change in the judiciary of the state is demanded by the interests of all. Interminable litigation may be kept up by anyone who has the money to pay for it, and the poor man may be robbed at any time of all that he has by a rich prosecutor. . . .

Justice through our courts should be made sure and cheap, without eternal litigation. . . . We desire the enactment of such laws as may be necessary to secure to us, and all our fellow citizens, equality, justice, and prosperity. . . .

The object to be attained by this Association shall be the establishment and maintenance of a pure Democratic-Republican government, under which all may enjoy equality, liberty, and prosperity. Some of the specific measures shall be. . . .

That the army and navy shall be republicanized by opening the path of promotion to those that enter as common soldiers and sailors and by the discharge of all idlers.

That the state expenditures shall be curtailed by the abolition of all unnecessary offices. . . .

That a more direct responsibility of the office holders to the people shall be established.

The Sense of Justice in All Good Men: Feminist Tax Resistance (1858)

The author of this brief letter was a new mother, recently arrived in New Jersey when she took the dramatic step described below. But Lucy Stone was already a prominent figure in the women's rights movement. A graduate of Oberlin College and a well-known antislavery activist, Stone did not take her husband's name upon marrying Henry Blackwell in 1855; she called herself Mrs. Stone. For many years thereafter a married woman who retained her premarital surname was known as a "Lucy Stoner."

In 1867 Stone helped found the New Jersey Woman Suffrage Association. She was its president in 1868 and its moving force until she and her family left New Jersey for Stone's native Massachusetts in 1870. After she left, the woman suffrage campaign in New Jersey was relatively inactive for twenty years.

Shortly before she sent this letter Stone gave a speech to a women's rights convention in which she linked women's lack of the right to vote to the colonists' "no taxation without representation" cause. Her act was designed to dramatize this point. In later years Stone added many planks to her argument for granting women the right to vote, but in this tax protest she was simply trying to call attention to an injustice.

The result of Stone's tax resistance was that some of the Blackwell/Stone family property was confiscated and sold at auction to pay the delinquent tax bill, but family friends bought most of it at the auction and returned it.

Orange, N.J.

Mr. Mandeville, Tax Collector, Sir:

Enclosed I return my tax bill, without paying it. My reason for doing so is that women suffer taxation and yet have no representation, which is not only unjust to one half of the adult population, but is contrary to our theory of government. For years some women have been paying their taxes under protest but still taxes are imposed and representation is not granted. The only course now left us is to refuse to pay the tax. We know well what the immediate result of this refusal must be.

But we believe that when the attention of men is called to the wide

Reprinted in Felice Gordon, *After Winning: The Legacy of the New Jersey Suffragists, 1920–1947* (New Brunswick: Rutgers University Press, 1986), 6, 7.

difference between their theory of government and its practices in this particular, they cannot fail to see the mistake they now make by imposing taxes on women, while they refuse them the right of suffrage, and that the sense of justice which is in all good men, will lead them to correct it. Then shall we cheerfully pay our taxes—not till then.

"Join Our Destiny with the South": Former Governor Price Champions the Confederacy (1861)

During the winter of 1860–1861 the likelihood grew that force would be necessary to keep the South in the Union. Most New Jerseyans, Democrats and Republicans alike, favored compromise to avoid conflict. The terms of compromise that Democrats proposed favored the South more than did Republican suggestions because opposition to the extension of slavery was the basic issue dividing Democrats and Republicans.

The author of the letter excerpted here, Rodman M. Price, was the Democratic governor of New Jersey between 1854 and 1857. He wrote the letter in response to having been asked about New Jersey's interest in the event of southern secession. Price, who had headed Stephen A. Douglas's presidential campaign in New Jersey, gave an answer that was popular with the state's merchants and manufacturers. But it was so unpopular elsewhere that it contributed to Republican victories in municipal elections held around the state shortly after its publication.

Price was a delegate to the Washington Peace Conference of 1861, which futilely sought to avert the war. Throughout the war he was a prominent member of the peace faction of the Democratic party, members of which came to be known as Copperheads.

If we . . . remain with the North, separated from those who have, heretofore, consumed our manufactured articles and given employment to a large portion of our labor, . . . our commerce will cease, European competition will be invited to southern markets, our people be compelled to seek employment elsewhere, our state becoming depopulated and impoverished. . . . These are the prospective results of remaining with the present northern confederacy. Whereas to join our destiny with the South will be to continue our trade and intercourse—our prosperity, progress, and happiness—uninterrupted and, perhaps, in an augmented degree.

Who is he that would advise New Jersey to pursue the path of desolation when one of prosperity is open before her, without any sacrifice of principle or honor, and without difficulty or danger;

Reprinted in Charles M. Knapp, *New Jersey Politics During the Period of the Civil War and Reconstruction* (Geneva, N.Y.: W. F. Humphrey, 1924), 53, 54.

besides being the course and policy, in my judgment, most likely to reunite all the states under the glorious "Stars and Stripes"?

The action of our State will prove influential . . . upon the adjoining great states of Pennsylvania and New York; and I am confident that the people of those states, whose interests are identical with our own to a considerable degree, will, when they elect, choose also to cast their lot with the South. . . .

It takes little discernment to see that one policy will enrich us and the other impoverish us. Knowing our rights and interests we dare maintain them. The Delaware River only separates us from the State of Delaware. . . . A portion of our state extends south of Mason and Dixon's line and south of Washington city. The Constitution made at Montgomery has many modifications and amendments desired by the people of this state, and none they would not prefer to disunion.

We believe that slavery is no sin; "that slavery—subordination to the superior race—is his [the African-American's] natural and normal condition."[1] . . . It is, in my opinion, the only basis upon which the country can be saved; and, as the issue between the North and the South . . . [the question of territorial rights] was . . . nothing to us, let us, then, save the country. Let us do that which is most likely to reunite the states speedily and peacefully.

1. Here Price is quoting the Confederate Constitution.

"Brave Volunteers of New Jersey": A Civil War Song (1861)

Although New Jersey was politically divided throughout the war, the men of New Jersey responded courageously to the call to defend the Union. Altogether about 88,000 sons of New Jersey served in the Union forces, well above the 78,248 called for during the course of the conflict. Notably, a draft was never held in the state.

New Jersey paid a heavy price for its defense of the Union. Sixty-three hundred New Jerseyans, by one estimate, gave their lives to the cause. Many times this number were injured.

The following song reflects New Jersey's prompt response to the call for a military effort to keep the southern states in the Union. The term Jersey Blue *was first used to refer to the hardy troops from New Jersey whom Colonel Peter Schuyler commanded during the Seven Years' War. It was revived during the War for Independence and again by former Governor Richard Howell during the Whiskey Rebellion of 1793; the troops Howell led fought against farmers from western Pennsylvania who refused to pay a tax on whiskey that they distilled.*

Tune—"The Red, White, and Blue"

The brave volunteers of New Jersey,
  All patriots, noble and true;
Aroused at the call of our country,
  We'll stand by the red, white, and blue,
To tyrants we can never give in;
  Rebellion shall have its just due,
For union and liberty live, in
  The hearts of the true Jersey Blue.

Bold treason, uprising, is striving
  To pluck the bright stars from the blue;
And freedom's last hope is surviving
  Maintained by the swords of the true—
Shall liberty languish and perish,
  Because we are not brave, or true?

Theophilus Townsend Price, "The True Jersey Blue," 1861, Rutgers. Reprinted by permission of the Department of Special Collections and University Archives, Rutgers University Libraries.

Oh no! in our bosoms we cherish
    The fame of the true Jersey Blue.

Our fathers of old, long before us
    Won, and left a proud name for their sons,
Their spirits are hovering o'er us,
    Their blood in their children still runs—
Oh long may we share in, and merit
    The glory to patriots due;
We'll maintain the proud name we inherit
    Long, long live the true Jersey Blue.

No party nor clan shall divide us,
    The Union we'll place above all—
The laws of our land must still guide us
    United we'll stand, or we'll fall—
And long may the blessings of heaven
    Descend on the brave and the true;
Three cheers for the union be given,
    And three for the true Jersey Blue.

The Devil in Their Hearts: A Republican Congressional Candidate (1862)

Joseph P. Bradley did not win election to Congress as a result of the campaign in Hudson County during which he gave the speech excerpted here. He did not even come close. It was hopeless for a supporter of the Lincoln administration to have won such an election in largely Democratic Hudson County.

But this was not the end of Bradley's public career. After the Civil War, President Ulysses S. Grant nominated him to the United States Supreme Court, where he served as an associate justice from 1870 until his death in 1892.

A Rutgers College graduate and a corporate lawyer, Bradley was a Whig before the Republican party emerged. He urged compromise between the North and the South until the attack on Fort Sumter turned him into a unionist because he believed secession was treason. Bradley was also a champion of the Thirteenth Amendment to the Constitution, which abolished slavery. He wanted to punish the disloyal states, and thus he argued that only a majority vote of the states that had not seceded was necessary for the amendment's ratification.

In the year 1788 . . . the question was shall we adopt the noble Constitution under which we live, which should constitute us one country, one nation, one people, bound up to one destiny. Now the question is whether we shall remain so. . . .

We are divided: rent and torn by civil war and engaged in a terrible struggle to save the nation from destruction, to preserve our institutions and vindicate the authority of the Constitution. . . .

Who are the authors of this wicked rebellion which has been excited in the southern states against this glorious government? How did it arise? Many say the North are the authors of it. . . .

I do not justify the intemperate language used by some northern fanatics. I never did justify it; I have always thought it wrong in principle. I am speaking the sentiments of all conservative men. . . . We were always willing to concede to the South all their just rights—the entire control and regulation of their own affairs. The Constitution gives us no power to meddle with them, no more than it gives them

Charles Bradley, ed., *Miscellaneous Writings of the Late Joseph P. Bradley* (Newark: L. J. Hardham, 1901).

power to meddle with us. The Constitution was founded on the idea that the states should regulate their own affairs.

We have also been always willing to concede to them a fair proportion of the new territory which should be acquired by our common treasure and common arms.[1] And if there were men at the North who disputed these rights, they were few in number and did not represent the general feelings of the North. No, gentlemen, it was no invasion of southern rights by the North that produced this wicked rebellion. Never, never. It was the devil in the hearts of the southern ringleaders—the determination if they could not rule to ruin. That was the cause. . . .

In view of this great effort to war against and destroy our government, what is the duty of the government? . . . To put down the rebellion, cost what it may. That's the great principle which animates us today. That's the pole star of our political principles. The rebellion must be put down. Nothing else must be thought of. . . . The Union must and shall be preserved. You may talk of mistakes, of official acts which are not strictly according to law—about violating this or that clause of the Constitution. It may be so. If so, we can punish them for it after a while. But for the present, I repeat it, we have nothing to do but to put down the rebellion, and hold up the President's hands whilst he is trying to do it. . . .

I have seen in a speech made not far from this place the sentiment that we must be kind and conciliating to our southern "brethren"; that we must not deal harshly with them. . . .

Up to the time that the rebellion became a fact, I could endorse that sentiment with all my heart. I could go with any man, or set of men, in effecting a compromise with the South. . . . But when they became rebels and refused compromise and flung conciliation in our face and endeavored to destroy our country, they were my brethren no longer. . . . If they come in and submit to the authority of the Constitution, I can then again hail them as brothers; but not till then. Until then they are enemies, and to be dealt with as enemies. The plea that we cannot do this or that in a war against them is absurd. We might as well say we couldn't do such things in a war against England or France. . . .

The Constitution has in it powers relating to war, and for the suppression of insurrection and rebellion. . . . We have the power to take the same steps to put them down as we have to carry on a foreign

1. The overarching political issue of the decade before the Civil War was whether slavery would be allowed to expand into the territories. This question changed slavery from a problem about which compromises were possible into one that created the "house divided against itself," in Lincoln's famous evocation of the biblical phrase, that "cannot stand."

war, and in the exercise of those powers we are just as much within the Constitution as we are in returning their fugitive slaves in time of peace. . . .

It is not for me, gentlemen, to discuss this or that particular measure of the Administration. It is not for me to sit in judgment in matters of such minor importance. If the line of authority has been overstepped we must not stop now to punish the guilty. Now we must put down the rebellion, and restore the authority of the Constitution and laws. . . .

I deprecate party politics in a time like this. I would say to all patriotic men of every party, let us unite in this great and holy cause until peace shall be restored on the only basis on which it can permanently stand—the unity of the whole country under the old Constitution and the old flag.

Fight Secessionism in the Field, Abolitionism at the Ballot Box: The Democratic Party (1862)

New Jersey was probably the most racially conservative state in the North. Although the proportion of African Americans in its population was roughly twice that of any other free state, among northern states before the war only in New Jersey did the courts fail to rule that slavery was inconsistent with the state constitution.

The basis of the state's strong support of the war effort was principally to restore the Union, as the other documents in this section suggest. The state Democrats used the slogan "The Constitution as it is, the Union as it was."

When President Lincoln announced the Emancipation Proclamation,[1] Democratic reaction was fierce. The following excerpt comes from a position paper issued by the leadership of the party.

The Democratic State Central Committee . . . disclaim[s] the doctrine of secession upon which the southern states have placed themselves. It is a political heresy which finds no place in the Constitution and is subversive of the principles of our government. . . . The rebellion must be put down—the rightful power of the government must be restored. The Democratic party is conservative; it stands . . . for the Union, the Constitution, and the enforcement of the laws. . . . We yield to no one in attachment and devotion to the Union. . . . Our sons, our brothers, and friends are now in the field ready to fight and die in defence of their country; and many of us mourn the loss of those who have already fallen in the contest. . . .

But there are mighty questions in connection with this war which are now agitating the public mind very deeply. . . . For what purpose is it now waged, and how, and upon what principles, should it be conducted, and when should it cease? . . .

1. President Lincoln announced in September 1862 that all slaves in states still in rebellion would be set free on January 1, 1863. On that day he issued the final proclamation, following through on his September promise. The final proclamation exempted the four border states and parts of three Confederate states controlled by the Union army because these states were not in rebellion against the United States.

"Address of the New Jersey Democratic State Central Committee to the Voters of the State," 1862, Rutgers. Reprinted by permission of the Department of Special Collections and University Archives, Rutgers University Libraries.

The sole purpose of the war, as asserted by Congress and approved by the administration, is to suppress rebellion, establish the authority of the Constitution, and restore the Union. This being accomplished the war is to cease. . . . It was to be a war not against states but against the rebellious people of the states, to bring them back to their rightful allegiance. It could have no other legitimate object.

But . . . efforts have been made to turn the war from its avowed and just purpose and make it an abolition war—a war for general emancipation. . . .

We regret, but are not surprised, that such efforts have been made. . . . We have in our midst a party who are bent upon this purpose. They do not wish to see the war ended or the Union restored on the principles of the Constitution. They insist that it shall be so prosecuted as that emancipation shall be a necessary consequence—slavery must be abolished. This, as we all know, is not a new idea. We have long had fanatics in the North who have denounced slavery in the states as a national sin, and the Constitution of the United States, which recognizes it, as a covenant with darkness and infamy. At first these were looked upon as agitators and disturbers of the national peace. . . . Friends of the Union and of order everywhere avoided them. Yet they persevered. . . . They took hold of the . . . radical spirit which always exists in a greater or less degree in a free government and turned it to their benefit. . . .

Since the breaking out of this rebellion they have become more bold and confident in their purposes, . . . until at length the President . . . issued his proclamation decreeing freedom to slaves after the 1st of January, 1863, unless the rebel states should before that time return to their allegiance.

The joy with which this proclamation was received by the radicals . . . was almost unbounded. . . . Is there not reason to fear that . . . the war is to be carried on for other purposes than the restoration of the Union? But you are told that emancipation is not an object of the war, that it is only a means adopted to crush the rebellion and restore peace to the country. . . .

As such a means it is simply unconstitutional. No power to free slaves in the South has been given to the Executive. . . . Nor can it be justified as a war power. . . . There is no power of that kind which can justify the President as the military head of the nation to blot out of existence the institutions of whole states, and destroy the private property of the innocent people of those states along with the guilty, . . . upon the plea that such property and institutions help to sustain the rebellion.

There is no necessity for the exercise of any such war power or for any violation of the Constitution. We believe this rebellion can be subdued by constitutional means faithfully and honestly applied. . . .

And there are strong reasons . . . against the policy of this measure. It is offensive to the border slave states who, amid divisions, . . . are striving manfully to sustain the Union. If the proclamation is of any avail, and the rebellion subdued, of what value is their property? They ask that while standing by the Union they shall not be stricken down themselves. . . .

And what is to become of these three or four millions of colored persons suddenly emancipated and let loose upon the country? If they remain in the South they can only secure their actual freedom by force—by a servile insurrection, which, if once commenced would sweep over the land. . . . If they should escape to the North it would be ruinous to free labor and we should be loaded with intolerable burdens. . . .

It is alleged by some that we are opposing the government and creating divisions in the loyal states and thus giving aid and comfort to the enemy. This is a singular charge against Jerseymen. Why, during the whole period of this rebellion, New Jersey has been a loyal state and she has been a Democratic state. The Democrats and conservatives in the state were earnest in their efforts to prevent a civil war. But when the blow was struck at Sumter and war came, the State of New Jersey was among the first to offer her support to the government. Her troops were among the foremost in the field and she has promptly met every demand. And was this the work of Republicans alone? They will not say it was, and if they should the very stones would cry out against them. . . .

While we fight secessionism in the field, we must fight abolitionism and radicals at the ballot box.

The Union Is the Only Guarantee: Soldiers Protest the Peace Resolutions (1863)

The Eleventh Regiment of New Jersey Volunteers was recruited in the middle of 1862. Its members saw action at such famous battles as Fredericksburg, Chancellorsville, and Gettysburg. Of the original enrollment of 979, a quarter died and about 360 were wounded.

In the document excerpted here the officers of this regiment protest a resolution that the state legislature passed calling for immediate peace talks.

Whereas the legislature of our native state . . . has sought to tarnish its high honor and bring upon it disgrace by the passage of resolutions tending to a dishonorable peace with armed rebels seeking to destroy our great and beneficent government, the best ever designed for the happiness of the many; and

Whereas we her sons, members of the Eleventh Regiment New-Jersey volunteers, citizens representing every section of the state, have left our homes to endure the fatigues, privations, and dangers incident to a soldier's life in order to maintain our republic in its integrity, willing to sacrifice our lives to that object . . . deeming it due to ourselves that the voice of those who offer their all in their country's cause, be heard when weak and wicked men seek its dishonor; therefore

Resolved, that the union of the states is the only guarantee for the preservation of our liberty and independence and that the war for the maintenance of that union commands now, as it ever has done, our best efforts and our heartfelt sympathy.

Resolved, that we consider . . . the so-called Peace Resolutions, as wicked, weak, and cowardly, tending to aid by their sympathy the rebels seeking to destroy the republic.

Resolved, that we regard as traitors alike the foe in arms and the secret enemies of our government who at home foment disaffection and strive to destroy confidence in our legally chosen rulers.

Resolved, that the reports spread broadcast throughout the North . . . that the army of which we esteem it a high honor to form a part, is

Reprinted in Earl Schenck Miers, ed., *New Jersey and the Civil War* (Princeton: D. Van Nostrand, 1964), 106–108.

demoralized and clamorous for peace on any terms are the lying ut-
terances of traitorous tongues and do base injustice to our able comrades who have never faltered in the great work, and are not only
willing but anxious to follow their gallant and chivalric leader against
the strongholds of the enemy.

Resolved, that we put forth every effort, endure every fatigue, and
shrink from no danger until, under the gracious guidance of a kind
Providence, every armed rebel shall be conquered and traitors at
home shall quake with fear as the proud emblem of our national independence shall assert its power from north to south and crush be-
neath its powerful folds all who dared to assail its honor, doubly
hallowed by the memory of the patriot dead.

Organized and Armed to Resist the Draft (1863)

In July 1863 mobs of Irish working people attacked the draft office, the homes and offices of prominent Republicans, and the African-American citizens of New York City. Lasting three days, the New York draft riot, an event of complex causes, was the worst civil disorder in American history.

The underlying cause was the issue of conscription. The North had initially hoped to avoid a draft, raising its army through volunteers. Even when it was instituted, the draft's purpose was probably as much to stimulate voluntary enlistment as to raise a conscripted fighting force. Altogether about 8 percent of the Union soldiers were draftees, or their purchased substitutes. In New Jersey, the quotas were exceeded, so a draft was never held.

The author of this excerpted letter to Secretary of State William H. Seward[1] was Martin Ryerson, a prominent banker from Sussex County.

I have learned this week much in relation to the state of affairs in New Jersey concerning the draft, which I deem it my duty to communicate through you to the government, to the end that we may be spared the horrors of the New York riots. . . .

In . . . cities and towns along the railroads and in the mining districts there are large numbers of Irish, and I am convinced that they are organized . . . to resist the draft, many of them armed. . . . I know that in this . . . county and the adjacent county of Morris, among the iron and zinc mines they are organized and armed. In this town several loyal citizens . . . have been threatened with personal violence and the destruction of their houses and stores. To produce this state of things, our Copperhead leaders have been . . . inflaming in every possible way the prejudices and passions of the people, and preparing their minds for an uprising. . . .

The minds of the poor, even of Republicans, are terribly inflamed

---

1. William H. Seward, Lincoln's secretary of state, is credited with deft diplomacy that kept European nations from entering the war on the side of the Confederacy. He coined the often-used phrase "irrepressible conflict" to describe the coming of the war. Seward is probably most famous for advocating the 1867 purchase of Alaska from Russia for $7 million.

Robert N. Scott, ed., *The War of the Rebellion: A Compilation of the Official Records of the Union and Confederate Armies*, ser. 1, vol. 27, pt. 3 (Washington, D.C.: U.S. War Department, 1889), 935–937.

by the three-hundred-dollar clause in the enrolling act,[2] the objections to which certainly have much force. A rich man, who without this might have had to pay one or two thousand dollars, or more, for a substitute, can now get off for three hundred dollars, and the poor . . . say they ought to have been left to make their own bargains, for they could have procured substitutes for less than three hundred dollars. You can readily perceive how demagogues use this to inflame the poorer and ignorant classes. The clause was well meant, but in my judgment is an unfortunate mistake.

Should the attempt be made at this juncture to enforce the draft in New Jersey, you may be sure it will be met by a widespread and organized resistance. The police force of the state is of very little account and we have but few organized regiments or companies of militia, and some of them are mainly composed of Copperheads. And, what is worse, while our governor[3] . . . earnestly desires the suppression of the rebellion, yet he lacks the nerve and decision necessary for such a crisis and is so hampered by party ties and associations that he could not be relied on to do his whole duty. . . . I am convinced that in this county we cannot now enforce the draft, and the attempt would result in sad scenes of havoc and bloodshed, and am persuaded that the same is true of many other counties. . . .

I earnestly desire the enforcement of the draft, as well for its present absolute necessity to crush speedily the rebellion as to settle for all time that we have a government capable of defending itself . . . but in view of the present state of affairs, I would respectfully, but most earnestly, solicit that for the present the draft be suspended in New Jersey until it is first thoroughly enforced in New York.

2. The Enrollment Act of 1863 made every able-bodied male citizen (as well as aliens who had filed for naturalization) between the ages of eighteen and forty-five eligible for the draft. The law permitted a conscript to pay a fee that exempted him from the particular draft call in which he had been selected, but not from future calls. Three hundred dollars was more than half the average yearly wage of an unskilled worker.
3. Joel Parker, a moderate Democrat, supported the war to return the rebellious states to the Union, but opposed the Lincoln administration's handling of the war.

Black Troops Performed with Dignity: General Sickles on Postwar New Jersey (1865)

The recipient of the letter excerpted below was Brigadier General Hugh Judson Kilpatrick, active in the centrist wing of the state Democratic party.[1] His correspondent, Major General Daniel Ephraim Sickles,[2] was one of the most renowned Civil War generals. In an effort to heal internal rifts between moderates and Copperheads, Kilpatrick invited Sickles to address the New Jersey Democrats. Sickles declined the invitation, but he raised a number of important issues: the factions within Democratic ranks; New Jersey's opposition to the Thirteenth Amendment to the United States Constitution; and the role of black troops in the war.

My Dear Kilpatrick. . . .

Before the war you and I were among those who exerted themselves to put the Democratic party of New Jersey in power. I believe the masses of the Democracy[3] of New Jersey are today as patriotic as any of our countrymen; but the controlling leaders have managed to put the state in an attitude of obstinate and persistent hostility to the Union sentiment of the nation. In New York the Democratic state convention has recently declared that . . . "they cordially support President Johnson . . . in all such constitutional measures as he may inaugurate to harmonize the country and restore and cement the union of the states." As I understand it, this is precisely the ground you occupy in New Jersey. . . .

The party in power in New Jersey might learn a good deal from South Carolina, Mississippi, and Alabama. In these States, when

1. Kilpatrick was a West Point graduate and a cavalry commander. He was the first regular army officer wounded in action during the war. His recklessness in combat earned him the nickname Kilcavalry.
2. Sickles was a prominent New York Democrat whose early support for Lincoln earned him his military commission. He lost a leg in the Battle of Gettysburg, but is probably most notable because before the war he shot his wife's lover (the son of "Star-Spangled Banner" composer Francis Scott Key) and was acquitted of all charges on the grounds that he was defending his home.
3. The Democratic party.

"Democrats Will You Read This? General Sickles on the New Jersey Democrats," n.d., Rutgers. Reprinted by permission of the Department of Special Collections and University Archives, Rutgers University Libraries.

slavery was found dead, it was decently buried. . . . New Jersey refuses her assent to an amendment of the federal constitution abolishing slavery. Is this Democratic?[4] . . .

When I read the so-called Democratic platform of New Jersey for 1865, I find there an effort to screen the rebels from their treason by casting the blame of the rebellion on the northern majority which elected the lamented Lincoln. I find there a long and not very novel lecture about . . . the right of the states to do as they please. . . . In one breath the administration of President Johnson is condemned for arresting northern traitors and for refusing to pardon defiant southern rebels.

The truth is, I do not believe the authors of the New Jersey Democratic platform . . . regard the rebels as having lost either rights or consideration by their treason. Neither the rebellion nor its authors are denounced. No one is denounced except the government that put the rebellion down. These are not the real sentiments of the New Jersey Democracy. . . . I rejoice to see you charging through them, as, under Pleasanton,[5] you broke the enemy's lines at Brandy Station, and as you afterwards drove the flying foe before you to his hiding place behind the fortifications of Richmond.[6]

I would not have you suppose, my dear General, that I am not duly grateful for the kind offer of "sympathy" tendered by the Democratic Convention of New Jersey to the officers and soldiers engaged in the late war. I presume that they are sorry for us that we did not keep out of the war as they did, and, of course, we ought to seize with avidity that compliment to white courage and white patriotism paid to us at the expense of the black troops.

"The credit of the victories won by the Union Armies are due alone to the white officers and soldiers." This quotation from the seventh resolution is as generous as it is grammatical. You and I know, as all our comrades know, that the exclusion of the black troops from a fair share of praise is as unjust as it is mean. They performed their duty with courage and fidelity and zeal.[7] They have proved their fitness to

4. The New Jersey legislature, under Democratic control, rejected the Thirteenth Amendment. When Republicans controlled it briefly, this decision was reversed.
5. Major General Alfred Pleasanton commanded the cavalry at the battle of Brandy Station (June 1863), the largest cavalry engagement of the war. Although technically a defeat, this battle demonstrated that northern horse-mounted troops were a match for their Confederate counterparts.
6. Kilpatrick's military fame stemmed from a daring and nearly successful raid he led in 1864 on Richmond, the Confederate capital.
7. At the outset of the war the Lincoln administration refused to use black troops because it feared losing the border states. But after the Emancipation Proclamation, black soldiers were recruited in large numbers. Altogether, nearly 200,000

enjoy the freedom which their valor helped to win. If, as the Copperheads say, the war was waged for emancipation, is it not right that the race which was to be enfranchised should share the peril of the conflict? If, as we say, the war was prosecuted to defend the Union and Constitution of our fathers need the Copperheads complain that Negroes took their places in the ranks?

African Americans served in the Union army and navy; they fought in every theater of operations and sustained far higher casualties than white troops, because some Confederate commanders ordered their men to kill black troops whom they had captured rather than hold them as prisoners of war.

Vacation at Long Branch (1869)

The idea of a vacation as we know it is approximately 150 years old. It began when wealthy easterners started frequenting spas and resorts on the Atlantic coast, in the Catskill Mountains, and elsewhere. Cape May, which promoted the restorative powers of sea breezes and ocean bathing, was similar to other early retreats in beginning as a health resort.

Around the Civil War a growing number of salaried, white-collar workers were receiving a week or more of paid vacation annually. The steady nature of their work enabled these people to plan their time and budget for a family trip. In addition, the expanding railroad network brought more vacation spots within reach of more people. The New Jersey shore, so close to both Philadelphia and New York, sprouted many beach communities that attracted nearby city dwellers for a few weeks' stay each summer.

Many different types of resort developed. Some, such as Long Branch, depicted here, were for the rich and famous and those who liked to hobnob with them; others were more modest. Still others had a religious orientation. Ocean Grove, for example, was a Methodist camp meeting.

This picture is a mechanical reproduction of a drawing by noted artist Winslow Homer, whose initials are etched in the sand. Published in the summer of 1869 in Appleton's Journal, *it depicts a scene at the shore in Long Branch. In it one can see two different images of femininity that were in conflict with one another in the years immediately after the Civil War. The ideal antebellum young woman was expected to be pale, fragile, innocent, and submissive. Among these women, extremely white skin was considered beautiful; they stayed out of the sun or wore hats and carried parasols to shield themselves from its darkening rays. They did not participate publicly in any strenuous physical activity. Such women are represented by the corseted pair on the left, wearing clinging skirts with bustles at the rear, the fashion of the day. The latest fashions were generally on display at these hotels and resorts.*

In the center of the image, in mid-range, four women are seen in bathing attire. Two are sitting in the water at the edge of the tide. One is standing in the water leaning forward as if to observe something, and another, in a form-fitting suit (demure by our standards, revealing by those of her day) is ankle deep in the water. She appears to be stretching or exercising. What she is doing is far less strenuous than the activity of the men behind her in the surf, but it is physical, active, and public nonetheless: a departure from the norm of the day. These women, it may be argued, represent the emerging ideal—

Appleton's Journal, August 21, 1869, art supplement.

women who are heartier, bolder, less modest, and freer to enjoy the sun.

The foreground figure is the puzzle. Is she opening her parasol to shade herself? Is she, thereby, choosing the older and more demure style of female frailty and genteel whiteness? Or is she closing it, symbolically rejecting Victorian constraints and expressing a new freedom for women? Perhaps she plans to sit in the sand with her feet in the water, joining those women of her day who were demanding freedom to express publicly glimmers of sensuality.

Capital and Labor?

NOTABLE EVENTS

1870   Fifteenth Amendment ratified; Atlantic City builds its first boardwalk

1871   Statewide systems of free public schools established; Stevens Institute of Technology founded

1873   Panic of 1873; Singer sewing machine factory opens in Elizabeth

1874   Barbed wire patented; school attendance made complusory in New Jersey

1876   Custer's last stand; National (baseball) League founded; Women's rights advocates disrupt the Centennial Exposition in Philadelphia; Mark Twain's *Adventures of Huckleberry Finn* banned by the Denver Public Library; Standard Oil Company opens a refinery in Bayonne

1877   Nationwide railroad strikes; Prudential Insurance Company founded

1879   Edison's incandescent light bulb patented

1882   Roselle becomes first New Jersey town fully lit by electricity

1883   Time zones standardized; Agricultural Experiment Station opens in New Brunswick

1885   Johnson brothers open bandage factory in New Brunswick

1886   American Federation of Labor organized

1888   Poem "Casey at the Bat" published

1889   First All-American football team selected

1890   Sherman Anti-Trust Act; first execution by electricity

1891   Game of basketball invented

1892   Ellis Island immigration station opens

1893   World's Columbian Exposition, Chicago

1894   Pullman strike; Coxey's "Army" of unemployed men marches on Washington; New Jersey Federation of Women's Clubs founded

1895   Stephen Crane publishes *The Red Badge of Courage*; Mary Philbrook becomes the first woman in New Jersey admitted to the bar

1896   *Plessy* v. *Ferguson* case decided by the United States Supreme Court

1898   Spanish-American War

1900	Congress unseats polygamous Representative Brigham Roberts of Utah
1903	W.E.B. DuBois publishes *The Souls of Black Folk*; first (baseball) World Series
1906	Pure Food and Drug Act passed; great San Francisco earthquake
1907	First comic strip runs in a daily newspaper (in San Francisco)
1908	First railroad tunnel opens under the Hudson River
1909	National Associaton for the Advancement of Colored People founded

Selected New Jersey Population Statistics, 1870–1900

Year	1870	1880	1890	1900
Population (× 1,000)	906	1,131	1,445	1,884
% Female	50.3	50.5	50.1	50.0
Race				
% White	96.6	96.6	96.7	96.2
% Black	3.4	3.4	3.3	3.7
% Urban	43.7	54.4	62.6	70.5
People per square mile	122.2	152.5	194.8	254.0
N.J. % of U.S. population	2.3	2.3	2.3	2.5

"First-Class Female" or "Inferior Male": Hiring Women Teachers (1870)

In the middle of the nineteenth century the notion that a woman's influence was best exerted at home dominated public discussion of where and how women should work. Teaching was considered an acceptable occupation for women because it was consistent with a woman's genteel and nurturing temperament. In the 1850s teaching became a major vocation for unmarried women. In many cases it was a woman's only alternative to employment in a factory.

After the Civil War most teachers in northern cities were single women. Men were rejecting teaching because of its low pay. By the beginning of the twentieth century perhaps two-thirds of public school teachers were women. In the Northeast the figure may have been 90 percent. These female teachers were generally paid between half and two-thirds as much as their remaining male counterparts.

Underpaying women teachers was possible because so few other opportunities were available to educated women. The feminization of teaching had important consequences for the development of public education. For instance, the availability at bargain rates of a large supply of women teachers made possible the rapid spread of tax-supported secondary education.

In the following passage, Ellis A. Apgar, who was New Jersey's first commissioner of public instruction (the equivalent of today's commissioner of education), addresses some of these issues. (See document 37.)

Since last year there has been a decrease of twenty-six in the number of male teachers employed in the state and an increase of two hundred and thirty-five in the number of females employed. This . . . has been going on for several years past and . . . the time is not far distant when we must depend almost entirely upon female teachers to educate our children. Nor is this fact to be deplored. . . . Those schools which are under the exclusive charge of females compare favorably, both in discipline and scholarship, with those taught by male teachers. The willingness of women to work for low wages has, undoubtedly, induced trustees to engage them more exclusively, but at the same time it must be admitted by all that the schools of the present day are superior to those of former times. A female teacher who

Report of the State Board of Education and State Superintendent of Public Instruction for the School Year Ending August 31, 1870 (Trenton, 1870), 39–41.

can be employed for from four hundred to six hundred dollars per year, the wages usually paid in our rural districts, is far more likely to succeed and do justice to a school than the male who can be employed for the same amount. For that sum a first-class female can usually be employed, but a male teacher who has no higher ambition than to teach for such wages is not likely to be rated better than second or third class, and whatever difference there may be in the opinions entertained respecting the comparative merits between first-class females and first-class males, there can be no question but that a first class female is more to be desired in our schools than an inferior male. Notwithstanding this fact, there are hundreds of districts throughout the state which are still pursuing the blind policy of employing such males as they can get for these wages in preference to the excellent females who can be obtained for a similar amount.

Workman Today, Capitalist Tomorrow: A Vision of Industrial Harmony (1872)

The occasion for the speech excerpted here was the opening of a large exhibition of the industries of Newark in late summer 1872. The orator, Theodore Runyon, was a Mexican War general and a Civil War mayor of Newark. Runyon may be excused his optimism because Newark, like other factory cities, was prospering in the years after the Civil War. Approximately one-quarter of the population was employed in about a thousand factories, which on average had thirty hands who were earning five hundred dollars per year, working a ten-hour day.

Runyon probably was thinking of a larger context than Newark's seemingly rosy future. A year before Newark's industrial exposition, workers in Paris had taken over the city for a period. In the United States the years immediately after the Civil War witnessed a large upsurge in the activity of trade unions demanding an eight-hour day. This movement, which seemed to be suggesting that wage labor was a permanent status for American workers, and whose strike tactics were growing increasingly militant, challenged Runyon's picture of a well-ordered city of hard-working craftsmen, any of whom could someday become employers themselves. Additionally, as other documents in this collection suggest, the conditions of work and terms of employment in New Jersey factories were less satisfactory than Runyon suggests.

Runyon could not have known about the event that did most to undermine his vision. Roughly thirteen months after the trade show, an economic depression began that ruined thousands of businesses and threw out of work more than a million employees. (See documents 53 and 54.)

The industries of a people are their best and most valuable possession. Whatever may be the natural resources of a country . . . they are not to be compared in worth with that intelligent self-denying toil and industry which of themselves create wealth, and which of themselves can make a people great. . . .

Especially is it true that our industries are our best possessions in this country, where development is the order of the day . . . where the workingman is also the citizen with a voice in the management of

Theodore Runyon, *An Address Delivered at the Newark Opera House, May 22, 1872 on the Inauguration of a Popular Movement in that City for the Erection of a Statue to Seth Boyden. Also, An Address Delivered on the Opening of the Newark Industrial Exhibition, August 20, 1872* (Newark: Ward & Tichnor, 1880).

the affairs of the government equal to that of the wealthiest capitalist or the greatest landholder; and where the road, not only to opulence but also to whatever influence and position his merits may entitle him, lies open before him; and where the success of the employer is not, as it is in other countries, wrought out by the distress of his operatives. Here the capitalist of today was the workman of yesterday who worked out by his own industry and ability the fortune he enjoys. . . .

The people never fail to regard it as one of the chief duties and purposes of government to secure to them all reasonable protection in their trade and business interests. And as the design and result of such attention on the part of government is to secure to the artisan higher compensation for his labor and skill, it follows that it necessarily attaches the people to their government, and binds their affections to their institutions. . . . Comparison of their happier lot with that of those similarly situated in other lands, the contrast of their bright future with the dark and dismal hopelessness of the operatives in other countries . . . not only makes our workmen satisfied with the government under which they live, but bind[s] them to it by the strong cord of self-interest. Not so, however, with the ill-paid workman. . . . He is discontented. He may be troublesome. He cannot long retain respect for institutions under which with his best efforts his wife and children starve before his eyes. He cannot long endure a government which condemns him and his to a hopeless servitude.

The fact that the workman of today . . . may be the capitalist and employer of tomorrow—that he who receives wages today may be the dispenser of wages tomorrow—that the workman of our country is no laborer in the sense in which the term is used elsewhere as indicating a permanent condition in life, but is a citizen politically . . . equal to any, asking nothing of charity or pity, but only that which is his right, and which it is to the public advantage to concede, invests our industrial interests with an importance and dignity which those of no other country can claim.

DOCUMENT 53

Wan Faces and Stunted Minds: Child Labor (1884)

The last quarter of the nineteenth century saw a tremendous expansion of industry. New Jersey factories began making everything from steel and machines to drugs, packaged foods, and household products. More and more New Jerseyans made their livelihoods in these plants, where the hours were long and the conditions often miserable. The wages of an unskilled worker were not high enough to support his family, so he was often joined in the work force by other members of the family—women and children. Perhaps one child in six between the ages of ten and fifteen held a job during the last third of the nineteenth century.

Gradually, sentiment developed that government should regulate the industrial order. One of the first issues to attract reformers' attention was the plight of children in the factories. In 1883 New Jersey created the position of inspector of factories and workshops; the inspector's job was to report on compliance with legislation passed that year to set conditions under which children could be employed in factories.

The excerpt here comes from the second report to the legislature of Mr. L. T. Fell, the inspector.

The examinations we have made in the leading districts of the State dishearten and distress. . . . The number of children who are being reared in ignorance, fitted for injuring society, in whom the natural feelings are destroyed and who forget all the good they have ever learned, whose homes are too often habitations of wretchedness and who seem to have no hope is appalling. The condition of these children appeals to all who desire to save society from lawlessness and ruin and who prefer prevention to punishment. The children of the toiling poor are not naturally disorderly or lawless. They were not born thieves, liars, prostitutes, or murderers. They are as capable of good as the children who are more favored, and, with proper care and protection and nurture, they would make honest, honorable, and intelligent citizens. With their wan faces and dwarfed forms and stunted minds these little ones of our State outstretch their arms and appealingly implore the lawmakers of New Jersey to afford them the . . . protection which they so much need. . . .

Second Annual Report of the Inspector of Factories and Workshops of the State of New Jersey (Trenton, 1884), 14–25.

The average age at which these children went to work was nine years. As a rule they had been sent to school about their sixth or seventh year and taken away about two years later for the purpose of being put to work. All of them had been accustomed to work ten hours a day and many of them thirteen and more hours a day through overtime. . . . Children who had been set to work at an early age were, as a rule, delicate, puny, and ignorant; they knew the least, having forgotten the little they had been taught before going to work. The most healthy and intelligent were those who had attended school till their thirteenth or fourteenth year. . . . The average weekly wages of the children examined would not amount to two dollars. . . . The work at which some of the children are engaged is, in very many cases, dangerous to life and limb and is suited only for persons of mature years. . . . Some employers send agents to Castle Garden[1] in New York City to hunt up poor Europeans with children who cannot speak the English language, the object being, of course, to get the labor of parents and children at a nominal price and to bring both into competition with our own citizens. . . .

There is no exaggeration in saying that three-fourths of the work-children know absolutely nothing. . . . Not two percent know anything about grammar or have ever been taught any. . . . The vast majority could not spell words of more than one syllable and very many could not spell at all. About ten percent could answer questions in simple multiplication. Of the remaining ninety percent the majority could not add up the smallest numbers. At least ninety percent know absolutely nothing about simple geographical and historical questions. The number able to read and write in a distinguishable way was shockingly small and very many could neither read nor write even their own names. Very few of these children, the large majority of whom were born in the United States, ever heard of George Washington. . . . Over ninety-five percent never heard of the Revolutionary War, Abraham Lincoln, the Civil War, Governor Abbett,[2] or President Arthur.[3] At least sixty percent never heard of the United States or of Europe. At least thirty percent could not name the city in which they lived and quite a number only knew the name of the street where they housed. Many who had heard of the United States could not say where they were. Some said they were in Europe. . . . Many big girls and boys were unable to say whether New

---

1. Immigration depot administered by New York State from 1855 to 1890. It was located at the bottom of Manhattan Island.
2. Leon Abbett, Democratic governor of New Jersey, 1884–1887; 1890–1893.
3. Chester A. Arthur, Republican president of the United States, 1881–1885.

Jersey was in North or South America. Girls were found in Jersey City and Newark who never heard of New York City. . . . Ninety-five percent could answer no questions about other states or cities of the United States. Children . . . in some cases never heard the name of their native country, and others could not locate them.

Denied the Rights of Citizens: Conditions at Oxford Furnace (1892)

Controlling the expanding industrial economy of the late nineteenth century was like trying to tame a wild animal. Businessmen tried a variety of means to increase profitability in a difficult environment. They introduced new equipment. They opposed craft workers who attempted to control their workplace. They demanded long hours of their employees. They lowered wages. They issued their own paper money, called scrip. Many employers, particularly mine owners, insisted that their employees shop only at company-owned stores, which charged inflated prices.

Conditions at the Oxford Iron and Nail Company in Warren County, once one of the largest nail manufactories in the country but in 1892 not profitable, were so bad that the pro-business state legislature reluctantly appointed a committee to investigate. Their report is excerpted below. The committee recommended that the state create the post of an inspector of mines and that the legislature enact a law requiring biweekly payments in cash.

We find that the puddlers[1] employed by the Oxford Iron and Nail Company, numbering nearly one hundred, were requested to make six heats per day requiring thirteen hours of continuous labor and that they justly refused to comply with the demand made upon them, for the reason that it was a physical impossibility for them to perform such laborious service for so many hours, except at a sacrifice of health as well as causing permanent injury to their constitutions and thus affecting not only the employees themselves but the helpless ones dependent upon them for support and maintenance. . . .

The committee is of the opinion that their refusal was . . . just and right. . . . The company closed its doors against them, refusing to permit them to continue their work as before, throwing not only the puddlers and their helpers out of employment at the beginning of winter, but also the employees engaged in the manufacturing departments of the company. . . .

Many of the employees . . . working at the furnace . . . did not

1. Skilled workers whose hot, heavy task consisted of tending pig iron in a furnace as it softened and was rid of carbon and other impurities before it could be shaped into whatever forms were desired. At Oxford the molten iron was to be rolled into nails.

Journal of the Forty-eighth Senate of the State of New Jersey (1892), 203–206.

receive full compensation for the labor performed by them. . . . They received pay for twenty-five hundred pounds of iron while the daily product of one employee frequently exceeded twenty-six and twenty-seven hundred pounds and if, as was frequently the case, the daily product was less than twenty-five hundred pounds, a reduction was made by the company. This grievance of the employees was undisputed. . . . The puddlers at Oxford did not receive the compensation to which they were equitably and justly entitled. . . .

The committee feels . . . that in many instances the employees have been directly, or indirectly, intimidated and thus denied the rights which, as free citizens, they were entitled to enjoy without restraint and that their objection to this interference with their vested rights brought about discharges from employment without just or reasonable cause.

Another . . . serious grievance . . . was the company's neglect of the men engaged in mining. . . . Necessary and proper precaution was not taken to protect the lives of the workmen employed in the mines and as a consequence many were killed or injured. . . .

A serious and very important grievance of many employees . . . was based upon the arbitrary detention of the wages due to them. . . . The wages of many of the employees were so long retained after they became due that they were of necessity compelled to purchase upon credit at the store of the company, and in many instances were thus compelled to pay excessive prices for the common necessaries of life. . . . During a year's service they would receive but a pittance in actual cash, the company deducting the store account and rent out of the first money earned and ofttimes delivering empty envelopes to the employees on an alleged pay day. . . .

An employee working the entire month of January would not receive a settlement at the store or elsewhere until the twenty-fifth of the following month. . . . A payment in cash, every two weeks, would greatly relieve them, and permit them to rent houses and purchase goods where they could be secured to the best advantage. Payment not later than two weeks seemed to be the desire of all the witnesses appearing before the committee, with the exception of those directly interested in the Company.

"Rare Opportunities": The Trenton Business College (1893)

In addition to the growing industrial work force of mostly immigrant factory hands, there were other developments in the labor force of the late nineteenth century. The new factories needed a multitude of bookkeepers and clerks to keep records and manage correspondence. They also needed office managers, salesmen, purchasing managers: a host of occupations that required new skills such as using typewriters and adding machines. In 1900 about a quarter of the work force was employed in these "service" occupations.

Operations such as the Trenton Business College[1] sprang up in many cities to offer the training necessary to take advantage of these new opportunities. The college may even have benefited from the serious economic downturn that began in the year it prepared this advertisement, because at weak moments in the business cycle many people turn to retraining for renewed opportunity.

There are other aspects of note in this item. Advertising itself was a new profession, closely linked to the rise of the mass production industries and the white-collar workers who supported them. The disclaimer included in the text suggests that the public may have had a healthy skepticism toward advertisers' claims. This may be because in the late nineteenth century the vast majority of advertisements that readers would have seen were for patent medicines.

This advertisement appeared in a booklet published to celebrate the unveiling of a monument commemorating the Revolutionary War Battle of Trenton.

---

1. The Trenton Business College, founded in 1865, is the forerunner of Rider University, now located in Lawrence Township, Mercer County.

Trenton Battle Monument Association, Program for the Dedication of the Trenton Battle Monument (1893), 24.

The Trenton Business College

and School of Shorthand and Typewriting

offers rare opportunities to young men and women who wish to prepare for business

THE COURSE OF TRAINING INCLUDES

Book Keeping

Business Practice

Spelling and

Language

Penmanship

TRENTON BUSINESS COLLEGE.

Arithmetic

Rapid Calculation

Invoicing

Correspondence

Commercial Law

ALL TAUGHT BY SPECIALISTS OF LONG EXPERIENCE

We invite you to enroll on the merits of what we have done and are still doing. Our graduates are in demand and are filling the best positions in this and other communities

It sometimes occurs that advertisements are not supported by facts

We invite you to call and see for yourself what we are doing

The Peach Exchange in Pittstown (1901)

Peaches had been shipped by rail from New Jersey to nearby cities for around forty years when this photograph was published in 1901. The crop of 1900 was worth more than a million dollars.

Although peaches were grown in all parts of the state, Hunterdon County was the center of the region in which peaches were grown for sale to a wide market. In 1890 there were 4.4 million adult peach trees in New Jersey, 2 million of them in Hunterdon County. The San Jose scale (an insect that attacks fruit trees) arrived around 1895, however, and took its toll. In 1900 there were only 2.75 million peach trees bearing fruit in New Jersey.

As New Jersey's peach crop recovered, the center of peach growing moved to southern New Jersey, where late frosts—to which the Hunterdon County harvest had been vulnerable—were less common. In addition, the application of commercial fertilizers allowed peaches to grow where previously they had not done well.

Franklin Dye, ed., *New Jersey Handbook* (Trenton: State Board of Agriculture, 1901), 38.

"A Square Deal": Progressives and Taxes (c. 1905)

This campaign poster was probably prepared by Alden Freeman, the force behind the scenes of the Citizen's Union, an important progressive organization based in suburban Essex County.

Despite significant opposition—this advertisement was refused by the Montclair Times and by the Public Service Corporation for display in its trolley cars—Assemblyman Everett Colby was elected to the state senate, where he became one of the leading figures in New Jersey progessivism. During Colby's first year in office a bill that required somewhat more equal taxation of railroad property was passed and signed into law by Governor Edward C. Stokes.

Equal taxation of railroad property was a key issue for Colby and other progressives because tax disparities were a serious problem for northern cities such as Newark and Jersey City. Much of their most valuable land was in the hands of railroads, which paid taxes on a schedule more liberal than other taxpayers used: less than a quarter of the usual property tax. To make matters worse, the tax on so-called main stem property (the most valuable real estate) was collected by the state, which returned none of what it collected to the municipalities through which the main stems ran. Local taxes were paid on other property used directly for railroad purposes, but at a low rate—about two-thirds that of other property owners. Only railroad-owned property not used for railroad purposes paid taxes at full local rates.

Legislation allowing municipalities to tax railroads at full local rates, while valuable to northern cities, would have cost the state money. South Jersey did not support the idea because that region had little to gain and would have to help make up the lost revenue. South Jersey's opposition was lessened when the revenue the new tax measure raised was dedicated to public schools.

Alden Freeman, *A Year in Politics: A Record with Suggestions to Civic Workers* (n.p., n.d.), 16.

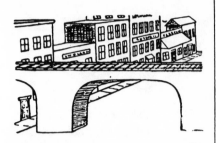 

This Railroad Main Stem	This Taxpayer's House
Was elevated at a cost to Newark of	Was Erected With
$1,500,000	**The Money of the Owner.**
and the taxpayers will have to raise	The City of Newark Contributed
$75,000 a Year for Thirty Years,	**NOT ONE CENT**
To Pay the Principal and Interest on This Debt.	To the Erection of This House.

This Property	This Property
Improved by the Taxpayers, Pays Tax at the Rate of	Improved by the Owner, Pays Tax at the Rate of
$5 PER $1,000.	**$22.70 PER $1,00'')**
of Valuation.	of Valuation.

Major Lentz And the County Committee Indorse the Law Which Fixes this Rate. **Everett Colby** Favors a Law to Compel Railroads to Pay the Same Rate that the Citizen pays

A Square Deal Between the Corporations and the People.

"A Traitor State": Raking New Jersey Muck (1906)

The following selection is from The Struggle for Self-Government, *the second major book of Lincoln Steffens, a leading muckraker.* Muckraker *was the term applied to a group of journalists who emerged in the early twentieth century and were committed to exposing the corruption that they believed had infected American life. The name was coined by President Theodore Roosevelt in the year* Struggle *was published.*

The antitrust movement, which provides the background to Steffens's chapter on New Jersey, excerpted here, developed from a sense on the part of many Americans that economic and political life were out of their control. A society that valued independent entrepreneurs and self-sufficient producers was threatened by large corporations that concentrated economic power into a few hands. Of course such concentration was often necessary to achieve efficient mass production of products such as light bulbs or automobiles, but it was a challenge to American ideals nonetheless.

The New Jersey legislature had created such loose general incorporation laws that businesses from around the country, regardless of where their operations were located, were incorporating in New Jersey, paying to the state treasury fees that might otherwise have come from taxes. The national impact of the policy is symbolized by the incorporation of Standard Oil of New Jersey (the forerunner of Exxon), the first enterprise in American history capitalized at over $1 billion.

Steffens focused on the issue of what makes good citizenship. Is it right, he asked, for the voters of one place to think only of themselves while ignoring the needs of others? This is a variation of a larger question about the nature of civil society which has been debated for thousands of years. There are those who argue that the pursuit of self-interest is what makes a society work; and there are those whom we might call communitarians who argue that the naked pursuit of self-interest without its subordination to the larger, general good is corruption.

Every loyal citizen of the United States owes New Jersey a grudge. . . . This state doubly betrays us. The corrupt government of Illinois

Lincoln Steffens, *The Struggle for Self-Government, Being an Attempt to Trace American Political Corruption to Its Sources in Six States of the United States with a Dedication to the Czar* (New York: McClure, Phillips, 1906), 209–211, 269–270, 280–281, 286, 290, 292–294.

sold out its people to its own grafters; the organized grafters of Missouri, Wisconsin, and Rhode Island sold . . . their states to bigger grafters outside. . . . The offense which commands our special attention, however, and lifts this state into national distinction, is this: New Jersey is selling out the rest of us.

New Jersey charters the trusts.[1] Now, I am not "antitrust," and I have no words to waste upon an economic discussion of the charter-granting function of government, state or national. Citizenship is my theme . . . the effect on the nation as a whole of the failure of any part—ward, town, county, or state—to do its full duty. And the point to fix in mind at present is that when, a few years ago, the American people were disposed to take up . . . the common great trust problem, some of the American people seized it and settled it alone; when the states united were considering whether to maintain the system of competition, which was called the "life of trade," some of the states declared for monopolies; when the United States was contriving to curb the growth of overwhelming combinations of capital, New Jersey . . . sold to the corporations a general law which was a general license to grow, combine, and overwhelm as they would, not in Jersey alone, but anywhere in the United States. Maybe this was wise, but that isn't why Jersey did it. She not only licensed companies to do in other states what those states would not license; she licensed them to do in those other states what she would not let them do in Jersey. No, our sister state was not prompted by any abstract consideration of right and wisdom. New Jersey sold us out for money. She passed her miscellaneous incorporation acts for revenue. And she gets the revenue. Her citizens pay no direct state tax. The corporations pay all the expenses of the state and more. It was "good business." But it was bribery, the bribery of a whole state; and it was treason. If there is such a thing as treason by a state, then New Jersey is a traitor state. . . .

Let's see if that is too strong a term. . . . In 1891 . . . the people of the United States were antitrust. We may have been foolish, we may have been wrong; but in the period from 1887 to 1894 our thinkers were proposing, our legislators were legislating, and our courts were deciding to check the growth of great combinations of capital which threatened competition in trade.

That was the time when New Jersey said to the trusts: "Come to us. We'll let you do anything. You needn't stay here. Pay us for them and we'll give you letters of marque[2] to sail out into the other states and do

1. Trusts were large-scale, monopolistic business combinations.
2. Letters of marque represent permission granted to agents of one government to attack the ships of another and seize their property.

business as you please. The other states have made your business a crime; we'll license you to break their laws. We'll sell out the whole United States to you and cheap." . . .

It was in this spirit that, in 1894, when the Great White Spirit Company wanted to run a distillery in Massachusetts, and couldn't do it as a Massachusetts company because Massachusetts law forbade the organization of domestic companies for distilling purposes, New Jersey provided the charter. Massachusetts had not thought to provide against "foreign corporations," so New Jersey set that distillery right down on the banks of the Charles River, and there it stayed until insolvency closed it. . . .

Jersey is a state in business. The businessmen who govern her have turned her into a great commercial concern. Does it pay?

Her main line has paid well so far. The miscellaneous corporations, which netted her $707,000 in 1896, paid . . . in 1903, $2,177,297.81. Her debt was wiped out. She is famous for her schools. She has the finest roads in the country; one-third of the macadam roads in the United States are in New Jersey. But listen to her new governor, Edward C. Stokes. . . . "Of the entire income of the government, not a penny was contributed directly by the people. . . . The state is caring for the blind, the feebleminded, and the insane, supporting our prisoners and reformatories, educating the younger generations, developing a magnificent road system, maintaining the state government and courts of justice, all of which would be a burden upon the taxpayer except for our present fiscal policy." . . .

Many of us envy Jersey. She is making money at the expense of the rest of us; she is trafficking in treason; but Delaware, Maryland, West Virginia, South Dakota, and Maine are seeking by still greater liberality to get the trusts to come to them, and New York, Rhode Island, Massachusetts, and others would like to—because they think it pays. That is the American attitude. And the great American question is: Does it pay?

Let us go back to Jersey. Does it really pay her? Has she good government?. . . .

The trouble there is that such citizenship as they have is mean, narrow, local. Jersey, in the mind of the average Jerseyman, is a group of counties, and his concern . . . is with the petty evils of his own sordid surroundings. My concern is for the other states that Jersey is selling out, my interest is in the story of the troubles she has caused me and you, not in the troubles of Jerseymen. . . .

The thing to do is . . . all the counties should get together, pledge their own legislators not only to represent their own county, but the wishes of good citizens in all counties. . . . These same citizens should see to it that this legislature should, first, send to the Senate senators who would represent you and me,[3] and second, pass no bills that would betray the will and injure the business of the United States. But, no, the local spirit of Jersey is the spirit of counties, cities, and states all over the country. It is the home-rule sentiment which says: "Give us good government and to hell with the rest." And that, again, is the American spirit.

If our national government is corrupt, it is because Jersey and other states, being corrupt, send their Keans[4] and Drydens[5] to the senate, and their Gardners[6] and McDermotts[7] to the house to misrepresent all of us. And if Jersey and the other states are corrupt it is because their Jersey Cities and their Hudson and Essex counties, being corrupt, send their graduates in corruption to the state legislature to misrepresent all the counties. Jersey men can't see it so, but this is the truth: Jersey's policy toward the trusts, which is the cause of so much trouble to all the rest of us, is the cause of the trouble of all the counties of Jersey. The corruption of those counties is the foundation of the "good" state government that sells us out for fees, which, turned back into the counties to relieve them of taxes, act upon the character of Jersey's citizens like bribes: they keep Jerseymen contented with a state government which represents, not you and me and them, but corrupt special business interests, at home and abroad.

3. Before 1911 U.S. senators from New Jersey were chosen by the state legislature, rather than elected directly by the voters. In 1913 the U.S. Constitution was amended to require direct election of senators in all states in the Union.
4. U.S. Senator John Kean, Republican from Elizabeth, served from 1899 to 1911.
5. U.S. Senator John F. Dryden, Republican from Newark, served from 1902 to 1907.
6. Congressman John J. Gardner, Republican from Egg Harbor, served from 1892 to 1913.
7. Congressman Allan L. McDermott, Democrat from Jersey City, served from 1901 to 1907.

"The Forman's Vulgar Advances": Sexual Harassment in Vineland (1907)

Approximately half of the Jewish immigrants who worked in industry were employed as garment workers. Such laborers usually worked sixty hours a week in a factory, more if they sewed at home.

The following letter was published in the New York–based, Yiddish-language newspaper The Forward. *In 1906 its editor, Abraham Cahan, established an advice column that quickly became the paper's most popular feature. Called "A Bintel Brief" (literally, "a bundle of letters"), it helped eastern European Jewish immigrants face the difficulties of life in their new country.*

The letters provide an important source of information about the lives of these immigrants. This one introduces a number of themes beyond the obvious one of sexual harassment, which was relatively commonplace in the garment trade. Bosses, foremen, and male co-workers were all known to take advantage of young women in the shops. How weak was the young woman's position in such a circumstance is suggested by the feeble answer provided to this writer. Generally speaking, the answers to "Bintel Brief" letters were thoughtful and, if not always practical, written in a way that suggested the editor identified with the writer and was sensitive to the problem at hand.

I am one of those unfortunate girls thrown by fate into a dark and dismal shop and I need your counsel.

Along with my parents, sisters, and brothers I came from Russian Poland where I had been well educated. But because of the terrible things going on in Russia we were forced to emigrate to America. I am now seventeen years old, but I look younger and they say I am attractive.

A relative talked us into moving to Vineland, New Jersey, and here in this small town I went to work in a shop. In this shop there is a foreman who is an exploiter and he sets prices on the work. He figures it out so that the wages are very low. He insults and reviles the workers; he fires them and then takes them back. And worse than all of this, in spite of the fact that he has a wife and several children he often allows himself to "have fun" with some of the working girls. It was my bad luck to be one of the girls that he tried to make advances to. And woe to any girl who doesn't willingly accept them.

Though my few hard-earned dollars mean a lot to my family of eight souls, I didn't want to accept the foreman's vulgar advances. He started to pick on me, said my work was no good and when I proved to him he was wrong, he started to shout at me in the vilest language. He insulted me in Yiddish—and then in English, so the American workers could understand too. Then, as if the devil were after me, I ran home.

I am left without a job. Can you imagine my circumstances and that of my parents who depend on my earnings? The girls in the shop were very upset over the foreman's vulgarity but they don't want him to throw them out, so they are afraid to be witnesses against him. What can be done about this? I beg you to answer me.

ANSWER: Such a scoundrel should be taught a lesson that could be an example to others. The girl [should] bring out into the open the whole story about the foreman, because there in the small town it shouldn't be difficult to have him thrown out of the shop and for her to get her job back.

"A Menace and Detriment": Farmers Against the Automobile (1908)

There was little organized resistance to the coming of the automobile, despite the profound changes it brought to American life. The idea that the horseless carriage was an improvement over its horse-drawn counterpart was widely accepted by about 1903. Farmers were slowest to concede this. In 1905 the National Patrons of Husbandry, the parent organization of the group represented in the excerpt below, officially called on its members to accept the automobile.

Although the authors of the following document say the car "has come to stay," their tone suggests they may not have taken this to heart. Their point of view might be summarized like this: We have seen the future and we don't like it.

The odds were, of course, heavily stacked against opponents of the automobile. In 1905 there were 3,640 motor vehicles registered in New Jersey. In the year of this resolution, Henry Ford introduced the Model T, his "car for the great multitude," and William C. Durant founded General Motors. In 1910 there were 16,520 cars registered in New Jersey.

Whereas a new mode of conveyance has within a few years been introduced upon our public roads; and

Whereas it is now generally accepted as a fact that this new mode of carriage has come to stay; . . . and

Whereas automobiles are a great menace and detriment to safe, pleasant, and unobstructed travel . . . with horse vehicles, rendering it especially unsafe for women and children; and

Whereas we are convinced that the casualties . . . caused by the automobile . . . are so great in number that they should be placed in the same class as the steam railroad cars as to safety, which are carefully guarded and restricted by our laws; and

Whereas, notwithstanding their great danger, . . . these automobiles are today running upon our roads practically (as to right of way at least) under the same laws and restrictions that applied to horse vehicles when there was no other mode of conveyance and each and every one made use of the roads under equal conditions, and was required by law to give half of the road; and

---

Reprinted in Harry B. Weiss, *The New Jersey State Grange Patrons of Husbandry, 1873–1954* (Trenton: New Jersey State Grange, 1955), 126.

Whereas . . . automobile clubs representing a great deal of wealth and influence . . . intend coming to our legislature to remove, rather than increase, any restrictions that may now be upon their entire freedom in the use of our roads;

Therefore be it resolved that it is the sense of this Marl Ridge[1] Grange[2] . . . that a law should be enacted . . . to compel the automobiles to give the right of way on our country roads. Viz: the entire middle of the road wherever possible since they are an automaton entirely under control, as their advocates claim, while the horses are often unmanageable; and

Resolved that their speed over our roads shall invariably be limited to a rate at which they can be completely controlled within fifty yards, which rate . . . must not exceed twenty miles per hour.

Resolved that a more stringent law should be enforced to punish anyone found running or taking part in running or controlling an automobile when apparently under the influence of intoxicants.

1. There are lots of places in New Jersey with "marl" in their names. The marl belt runs from Monmouth County southwest to Salem County. I could not determine where this one was.
2. An organization of farmers.

War, Depression, War

NOTABLE EVENTS

1913   First moving assembly line begins; forward pass used in college football; Paterson Silk Strike

1914   Panama Canal opens; First World War begins; U.S. troops invade Mexico; Margaret Sanger arrested for distributing birth control information; E. R. Burroughs publishes *Tarzan of the Apes*

1917   Russian Revolution; U.S. enters First World War; race riot in East Saint Louis, Illinois; German property seized at New Jersey docks

1918   Daylight savings time introduced; flu epidemic; New Jersey College for Women (Douglass College) opens

1919   Eighteenth (Prohibition) Amendment to the U.S. Constitution ratified; Palmer Raids; American Legion founded

1920   Nineteenth (women's suffrage) Amendment to the U.S. Constitution ratified; first commercial radio broadcast

1921   Immigration quotas established; short skirts become popular; world's second radio station (WJZ) begins operation in Newark

1922   Mussolini comes to power in Italy

1923   *Time* magazine started; Equal Rights Amendment introduced; electric razor patented

1925   Scopes trial

1926   Passaic textile strike; suspension bridge opens between Camden and Philadelphia

1927   Sacco and Vanzetti executed; Charles Lindbergh flies across the Atlantic; Babe Ruth hits sixty home runs; first sound movie; Holland Tunnel under Hudson River opens to vehicular traffic

1928   Stock market soars; first Mickey Mouse cartoons

1929   Air mail service begins at Newark Airport; stock market crashes; Great Depression begins

1931   "Star-Spangled Banner" becomes national anthem; Japan seizes Manchuria; George Washington Bridge opens

1932   Franklin Delano Roosevelt (FDR) elected president

1933   Hitler comes to power in Germany; Prohibition repealed; Pulaski Skyway dedicated; Einstein arrives in Princeton

1935	Works Progress Administration (WPA); National Labor Relations Act; Congress of Industrial Organizations (CIO) established
1936	*Gone With the Wind* becomes best-selling book in United States history; state capitol occupied by unemployed protesters
1937	United Auto Workers (UAW) sit-down strikes
1939	Second World War begins
1940	Selective Service Act; nylon stockings introduced
1941	Germany attacks Russia; Japan bombs Pearl Harbor; U.S. enters Second World War
1942	Japanese-Americans interned
1943	Race riots in Harlem, Detroit, and elsewhere
1945	FDR dies; Germany surrrenders; atomic bombs dropped on Hiroshima and Nagasaki; Japan surrenders; United Nations founded
1947	Marshall Plan announced; third New Jersey state constitution approved; New Jersey National Guard integrated
1949	"Bikini" bathing suit introduced; Communist victory in China

Selected New Jersey Population Statistics, 1910–1940

Year	1910	1920	1930	1940
Population (× 1,000)	2,537	3,156	4,041	4,160
% Female	49.3	49.6	49.8	50.3
Race				
% White	96.4	96.2	94.7	94.5
% Black	3.5	3.7	5.2	5.5
% Urban	76.4	79.9	82.6	81.6
People per square mile	342.1	425.5	544.9	560.9
N.J. % of U.S. population	2.8	3.0	3.3	3.1

Put Fairness in the Saddle Again: Governor Wilson's Inaugural Address (1911)

Woodrow Wilson was governor of New Jersey for only two years, but he is one of the leading figures in state history nonetheless. He was the president of Princeton University before he was elected governor and, later, president of the United States. During his term as governor he engineered legislation that catapulted New Jersey from laggard to leader in progressive reform. He pushed through laws that regulated public utilities, created a workmen's compensation system, and subjected local elections to impartial scrutiny.

The following excerpt comes from the address Wilson delivered to the legislature upon his inauguration as governor in January 1911. In it Wilson articulated two of the main assumptions that lay at the heart of political progressivism. Progessives such as Wilson believed that government could and should try to keep the playing field level. Even more basically, for Wilson and his associates it was an axiom that as history unfolded, humanity progressed.

I assume the great office of governor of the state with unaffected diffidence. Many great men have made this office illustrious. A long tradition of honorable public service connects each incumbent of it with the generation of men who set up our governments here in free America to give men perpetual assurance of liberty and justice and opportunity. . . .

The whole world has changed within the lifetime of men not yet in their thirties; the world of business, and therefore the world of society, and the world of politics. The organization and movement of business are new and upon a novel scale. Business has changed so rapidly that for a long time we were confused, alarmed, bewildered, in a sort of terror of the things we had ourselves raised up. . . .

Corporations are no longer hobgoblins which have sprung at us out of some mysterious ambush, nor yet unholy inventions of rascally rich men, . . . but merely organizations of a perfectly intelligible sort which the law has licensed for the convenience of extensive busi-

Arthur Link, ed., *The Papers of Woodrow Wilson* (Princeton: Princeton University Press, 1976). 22:345–354. Copyright © 1976 by Princeton University Press. Used with permission.

nesses; organizations which have proved very useful but which have for the time being slipped out of the control of the very law that gave them leave to be and that can make or unmake them at pleasure. We have now to set ourselves to control them soberly but effectively, and to bring them thoroughly within the regulation of the law.

There is a great opportunity here for wise regulation. Wise adjustment will mean the removal of half the difficulties that now beset us in our search for justice and equality and fair chances of fortune for the individuals who make up our modern society. . . .

No wise man will say . . . that he . . . knows how to frame the entire body of law that will be necessary to square business with the general interest, and put right and fairness and public spirit in the saddle again in all the transactions of our new society; but some things are plain enough and upon these we can act.

In the first place it is plain that our laws with regard to the relations of employer and employee are in many respects wholly antiquated and impossible. They were framed for another age, which nobody now living remembers. . . . The employer is now generally a corporation or huge company of some kind; the employee is one of hundreds or of thousands brought together, not by individual masters whom they know and with whom they have personal relations. . . .

Workingmen are marshalled in great numbers for the performance of a multitude of particular tasks under a common discipline. They generally use dangerous and powerful machinery, over whose repair and renewal they have no control. New rules must be devised with regard to . . . their obligations to their employers and their responsibilities to one another. New rules must be devised for their protection, for their compensation when injured, for their support when disabled. . . .

There is something very new and very big and very complex about these new relations of capital and labor. A new economic society has sprung up, and we must effect a new set of adjustments. We must not pit power against weakness. The employer is generally, in our day, as I have said, not an individual but a powerful group of individuals, and yet the workingman is still, under our existing law, an individual when dealing with his employer in case of accident, for example, . . . as well as in every contractual relationship. We must have a workingman's compensation act which will not put upon him the burden of fighting powerful composite employers to obtain his rights, but which will give him his rights without suit, directly, and without contest, by automatic operation of law, as if of a law of insurance.[1]

1. Under a "workingman's compensation" law, a worker injured or sickened as a result of his job would receive his medical expenses and a fixed income until he

This is the first adjustment needed because it affects the rights, the happiness, the lives and fortunes of the largest number and because it is the adjustment for which justice cries loudest and with the most direct appeal, to our hearts as well as to our consciences.

But there is regulation needed which lies back of that and is much more fundamental. The composite employer himself needs to have his character and powers overhauled, his constitution and rights reconsidered, readjusted to the fundamental and abiding interest of society. If I may speak very plainly, we are much too free with grants of charters to corporations in New Jersey. A corporation exists, not of natural right but only by license of law; and the law, if we look at the matter in good conscience, is responsible for what it creates. . . . It cannot righteously allow the setting up of a business which has no sound basis or which follows methods which in any way outrage justice or fair dealing or the principles of honest industry. . . .

A modern corporation . . . is in no proper sense an intimate or private concern. It is not set up on the risk and adventure of a few persons—the persons who originated it, manage it, carry it to failure or success. On the contrary, it is set up at what may be called the common risk. It is a risk and adventure in which the public are invited to share, and the hundreds, perhaps thousands, who subscribe to the stock do in fact share in it, often times without sharing also, in any effectual manner, in the control and development of the business in which their risk is taken. Moreover, these modern enterprises . . . conduct business transactions whose scope and influence are as wide as whole regions of the Union, often as wide as the nation itself. They affect sometimes the lives and fortunes of whole communities, dominate prices, determine land values, make and unmake markets, develop or check the growth of city and of countryside. If law is at liberty to adjust the general conditions of society itself, it is at liberty to control these great instrumentalities which nowadays, in so large part, determine the character of society. Wherever we can find what the common interest is in respect of them we shall find a solid enough basis for law, for reform. . . .

The great matter of conservation seems to me like a part of the same subject. The safeguarding of our water supply, the purification of our streams in order to maintain them as sources of life, and their protection against those who would divert them or diminish their volume for private profit, the maintenance of such woodlands as are left us and the reforestation of bare tracts more suited for forest than for field, the sanitation of great urban districts such as cover the northern

---

recovered. In turn, the worker would be precluded from suing the employer. Such a law exists in New Jersey today.

portions of our state by thorough systems of drainage and of refuse disposal; the protection of the public health and the facilitation of urban and suburban life—these are all . . . part of the one great task of adjustment which has fallen to our generation. Our business is to adjust right to right, interest to interest, and to systematize right and convenience, individual rights and corporate privileges, upon the single basis of . . . the common good for whose safeguarding and maintenance government is intended.[2] . . .

We are servants of the people, of the whole people. Their interest should be our constant study. We should pursue it without fear or favor. Our reward will be . . . the satisfaction of furthering large ends, large purposes, of being an intimate part of that slow but constant and ever hopeful force of liberty and of enlightenment that is lifting mankind from age to age to new levels of progress and achievement. . . . We shall have been instruments of humanity, men whose thought was not for themselves but for the true and lasting comfort and happiness of men everywhere. It is not the foolish ardor of . . . radical reform that I urge upon you, but merely the tasks that are evident and pressing, the things we have knowledge and guidance enough to do . . . with confidence and energy. I merely point out the present business of progressive and serviceable government, the next stage on the journey of duty. The path is as inviting as it is plain. Shall we hesitate to tread it?

2. As proposed by Wilson and other Progressives, the purpose of conservation proposals was to save natural resources for future use by the public and businesses. Today New Jersey's conservation laws are enforced by the Department of Environmental Protection and Energy, created in 1970.

"Fierce Every Way": The Paterson Silk Mills (1913)

The Paterson Silk Strike of 1913 is the most famous event in the history of New Jersey labor. It lasted six months, involved twenty-five thousand workers, and shut down the textile mills of the city. The Industrial Workers of the World (IWW) played an important role in the strike, organizing a strike committee with representatives from each mill. Leading IWW figures such as Carlo Tresca, Bill Haywood, and Elizabeth Gurley Flynn advised the strike committee.

A pageant to raise money for the strike was organized by the writer John Reed. It was held at Madison Square Garden to great critical acclaim, but it raised little money.

Teresa Cobianci, a ribbon weaver influenced by Elizabeth Gurley Flynn, was fifteen when she gave this interview to The Masses, *a radical magazine. Cobianci was overly optimistic in her assessment of the strike. It ended with virtually no gains for the workers who had been demanding an eight-hour day for a minimum pay of twelve dollars per day and a return to tending only one or two looms per employee.*

I came [to America] when I was four, with my mother and my brother, but I went back when I was eight. . . .

I do not like this country. My mother did not like this country either. . . . When we came to America she went to work in the silk mills. She got consumption. . . . Some days the workers would bring her home fainting from the mills. She would tell people, "Only for my children, I would like to die." . . .

One day she told father, . . . "I want to go back to Italy to die." . . . She took my brother and me and went back to her father in Caserta. In a few months my mother died. . . .

My brother and I lived four years with our grandfather. I went to school three hours in the morning. I had a governess, too. She taught me music and embroidery, and would take me out in the hills in the afternoon. It was not like here. . . .

Then when I was twelve, my father came for my little brother and me. . . . Over here I went to school for a year, . . . but my father he kept talking about the day when I shall go to work. His wages had

Inis Weed and Louise Carey, eds., "I Make Cheap Silk," *The Masses* 5, no. 2 (November 1913):7– 10.

been cut a little at a time, so he received only half so much as when he first come. And my stepmother, she said, "Yes, Teresa will soon be able to go to the mills." The summer I was thirteen my father he said, "Now you must go," and he fixed it up. . . . I cried, but I went to work. . . .

Bamford's is not a good place to work. . . . It's fierce every way. The air is bad. The windows are nailed down. The little panes that turn are never opened in winter. . . . In summer they are not open unless you ask. The floor is so rough great splinters stick into your shoes. It is very dirty too. . . .

When I started weaving ribbon my father and Mr. Bamford they made a contract over me for one year. . . . All the other weavers are young like me and work on contract. . . .

Every pay we girls get only half. The mill holds back the other half until we've worked a year. . . .

Most of the girls go before the year is up. They rather lose the money than stay and be treated so mean. The bosses they holler and curse at you so. The superintendent and forelady, they aren't so bad, but they have to holler when the bosses come round. . . .

By and by I got so I felt sick. Every week I would have to go home two or three afternoons. It was such a pain in the pit of my stomach. The doctor said it was because I hurry so. . . .

I was on the stairs one day eating my lunch. One of those big wheels with fire hose around came loose and fell on my head. And I don't know nothing after that for the whole afternoon. But they tell me I had fits. No, they didn't call the doctor—not on your life. . . . My father called the doctor. He said I should stay home a while and not go back to the mill until I felt good again. The top of my head hurt all the time but I went back to work after five days. My father he had been on strike nine months and we needed the money. . . .

I hate to go back to that mill. . . . I hate always to be fined and screamed at. Maybe a girl wastes a little silk. If they do not know who did it, they fine everyone. . . . They steal our hooks and scissors from us and then we have to buy them back again for thirty-five cents. Then we must clean up the mill Saturdays after twelve. . . . We do not get paid for it. They take it out of our holiday.

I want always to go back to Italy, but since the strike I am more happy here. . . . We are all together. We stand solid. My father he says there will always be bosses. I say, "Yes? Then we shall be the bosses."

Yes, I am still a Catholic. These days I feel different. You go to confess and the priest he tries to find out all about the strike and he scolds us that we belong to the union. I like IWW better than God. God, he don't talk for me like IWW. . . .

For me [the strike] has paid me. I get twenty-five percent increase in my wages. All of us at Bamford's get a raise, and no more children in the mill. . . . Nor do they holler at us so.

The labor inspector, he is on the job, too, since the strike. . . . There are guards on the dangerous machinery. There are . . . fire alarms. . . .

I don't know [if this will last]. If it don't, we strike again.

"The Social Order of an American Town": Randolph Bourne on Bloomfield (1913)

Until his life was cut short by influenza during the epidemic of 1918,[1] Randolph Bourne was one of the best essayists of his generation, renowned for his assaults on hypocrisy.

The Atlantic Monthly *published the description of his native Bloomfield (Essex County), excerpted here, not long after Bourne's graduation from Columbia University. It provided the basis of the thesis he later submitted for a master's degree in sociology.*

One can imagine the mixture of emotions that Bloomfield's town fathers must have felt over this controversial piece. On the one hand, a native son had published an article in a distinguished national magazine; on the other, he painted an unflattering picture of the city.

Bourne's description of Bloomfield is, of course, open to argument, but the issues he raised were important. He questioned whether locally owned firms were better than companies owned by outsiders. He described relations among three distinct social classes and identified three particular areas where these classes differed.

Lowest in the social scale is, of course, the factory class. The town has . . . a woolen mill which is the most beautiful example of paternal feudalism that can be found. The present owner inherited it from his father, who had inherited it from his. He lives in a big house overlooking the mill pond and personally visits the office every day. The mill employs hundreds of men, women, and children, and one would say . . . they were fortunate to be so singularly free from absentee capitalism. The owner is one of the most respected men in the community, head of the Board of Education, president of the local bank. And yet . . . [it] does not seem as if his employees are one whit better off than if they were working for a soulless corporation. The hours are the maximum allowed by law, the ages of the children the minimum, and there is much night work. . . .

1. This epidemic killed more than half a million Americans, most of whom died in the last months of 1918. The disease was especially dangerous to young adults. Roughly two-thirds of its victims were between the ages of twenty and forty.

Randolph Bourne, "The Social Order of an American Town," *The Atlantic Monthly* 111 (February 1913):227–236.

The employees of the mill are . . . men who have worked there for fifty years—their sons and daughters joining them as fast as they grow up—steady, self-respecting men who have perhaps saved enough to buy a little cottage near the mill. Then there are the younger men and women, mostly drifters, who stay in a factory until they are "laid off" in a season of depression and then move about until they find work somewhere else. Lastly there is the horde of Italian and Polish . . . children who pour out of the mill-gates at night when the whistle blows and whom one hears running past again in the morning before seven. . . .

The town can already boast a Polish quarter and an Italian quarter, the former . . . superior in prosperity and attractiveness . . . possessing a vigorous community life of its own. The Italian quarter is typical enough of the struggles of too many of our immigrants. It can hardly be possible that these people have left anything worse in the old country than this collection of indescribable hovels, . . . this network of unpaved streets and small gardens and ashes and filth. . . . Their American neighbors . . . are filled with an almost childlike faith in the temporary nature of this misery. These people are in America now . . . and will soon be making money and building themselves comfortable homes. Meanwhile all that can be done is to surround them with the amenities of civilization and wait.

The most impressive thing about the working class, on the whole, is the profound oblivion of the rest of the population to them. . . . The town . . . seems to have a whole class living in it but not of it, quite apart and detached from the currents of its life.

The psychology of this working class is different from that of the other classes. The prevailing tone is apathy. There is no discontent or envy of the well-to-do, but neither is there that restless eagerness to better their position and that confidence in their ultimate prosperity which the American spirit is supposed to instill into a man. . . . They are chiefly concerned in holding their jobs and escaping the horrors of unemployment—in making both ends meet. . . .

The rest of the people, while they comprise two distinct classes, are much more homogeneous. They . . . diverge only on aspects of manners and social qualifications. There is first the ruling class, in their case really hereditary, consisting of the direct descendants of the early settlers and of the men who built the old church in 1789. The old church has been the stronghold of their power; it preceded the town and gave the old families a political preeminence which . . . has never been seriously questioned. These families still own much of the land of the town and their power and influence shows itself in a thousand ways. Their members are elders and trustees of the old church, officers of the banks, honorary members of committees for patriotic celebrations. No local enterprise can be started without their assent. . . . New schools, parks, fire houses, . . . all these questions are settled finally according to the effect they will have on the pockets and interests of this ruling class.

And yet, strange to say, their activity is seldom direct. They work rather through that great indispensable middle class that makes up the third division of the townspeople. It is hard to define what separates these from the ruling class. Many of the families have lived in the town for many years; many of them are wealthy; many of them have profitable businesses. . . . In most of the affairs of the town, this class seems to act as the agents of the ruling class. The members of this class are the real backbone of the town's life. They organize the board of trade, . . . inaugurate and carry through the celebrations, do the political campaigning, . . . keep the civic machinery running. But little of what they do seems to be carried through on their own prestige. It is always with the advice and consent of the bigger men. . . .

The difference between the ruling class and the middle class . . . shows itself in . . . church matters, in recreation and business. . . .

Church lines follow . . . social lines. The aristocracy is centered in the old church, staunchly Presbyterian. Its . . . affairs are in these aristocratic hands as absolutely as they were in the hands of the great-grandfathers who built the church. . . . The middle class . . . strongholds are the Baptist and Methodist churches. . . . The church means much more to these middle-class people than it does to the aristocracy. The services are conducted with greater ardor, and attended with much more regularity. . . . There is a Catholic church, but it confines its ministrations strictly to the working class. . . . Any entrance of its priest into public affairs is looked upon with the deepest suspicion.

In business matters the line between the two classes is equally sharp. The members of the ruling class hold, as a rule, business positions of considerable importance in the neighboring city [Newark], while the middle class is largely engaged in local trade, or in smaller positions in the city. There is a certain slight social stigma that attaches itself to a young man who takes up work in town. . . . There is a distinct social prejudice, also, on the part of the ruling class against anything that savors of mechanical labor, and this is another point of divergence from the middle class, who are less squeamish. . . . The differences between the classes are differences of taste and business position, and not in the least of industry and ability.

Lastly, the two classes diverge in the way they amuse themselves . . . It looks as if the middle class contrived to have a better time of it than the aristocracy. The most striking institution of the former is the lodge—Masons and Odd Fellows and Elks and Woodmen. The class membership of these fraternal organizations is very evident. Of all the institutions of the town, the lodge is the most definitely middle-class. No member of the ruling class or the factory class can be found within the ranks. . . . The ruling class has only a near-by country club to compensate it. . . . In comparison with the busy social . . . life of the middle class, that of the aristocracy appears almost tame. . . .

The ruling class . . . recently alienated their middle-class following by a proposal to annex the town to the neighboring city. . . . They are sincerely puzzled and pained at the indignant outcry against the merging of the town with a corrupt, machine-ridden city. They say it . . . will raise the value of real estate and they cannot see the exquisite naiveté which is lent to this argument by the fact that they themselves own most of the real estate in the town. . . .

The social spirit of this ruling class seems to consist in the delusion that its own personal interests are identical with those of the community at large. . . .

In command of the Board of Education, they kept school facilities at the lowest possible point for years, until an iconoclastic superintendent aroused public sentiment and forced the erection of new buildings. The ruling class in command of the old church does nothing to extend its work beyond the traditional services and societies, although there is crying need for social work among the foreign population of the town.

Vote for the Woman Suffrage Amendment (c. 1915)

In October 1915 the voters of New Jersey rejected an amendment to the state constitution that would have given New Jersey women the right to vote. This defeat, along with others the suffragists endured that fall, led to the abandonment of efforts to win women the right to vote by proceeding state by state. The movement gradually unified around a campaign to win a change in the federal Constititution.

The excerpts here come from five circulars that the New Jersey Woman Suffrage Association prepared, probably during the unsuccessful 1915 campaign to win passage of a women's suffrage amendment to the state constitution. The arguments they used reflect the main thrusts of the debate in this day. One theme was that of justice and equality: in a true democracy women deserved the same rights as men. The other was that of women's differences: since women had different talents and social roles, they needed representation at the polls.

Who Represents Her?

If a woman is responsible for an accident, if she defaults on her contracts, if she slanders her neighbors is any man arrested, sued [or] bound over to keep the peace?

If a woman steals from her employer does her father, husband, brother, or son serve out her term in prison?

If a woman kills somebody what man represents her in the prisoner's dock during her trial? What man represents her in the electric chair if she is convicted?

If a widow or unmarried woman fails to pay her taxes is the property of a male relative or the man next door sold to satisfy the debt to the state? . . .

Why is it that the only place in the world where man wants to represent woman is at the polls?

True Democracy

We believe that:

"Governments derive their just powers from the consent of the governed." . . .

Alice Paul Centennial Foundation, Mount Laurel, New Jersey. Reprinted by permission of the Alice Paul Centennial Foundation.

A democracy is a "government of the people, by the people, and for the people." . . .

Women are people and are governed. . . .

No state can be a true democracy in which one-half the people are denied the right to vote. . . .

Women need the vote for the same reasons that men need it. . . . Because laws regulate a woman's life and the lives of her children, and because they tax her property . . . she should have the right to share in the making of the laws. . . .

Isn't It True?

Isn't it true that:

A man's success in business depends not only on himself but on the men he helps elect to office. . . .

Housekeeping is woman's business and that her success depends not only on herself but on the way her town is governed. . . .

The control of food, air, light, water, health, education, morals, and all living conditions is today in the hands of the officers of the town. . . .

It is only common justice and common sense to let the woman in the home share in electing the men on whom the comfort of the home depends. . . .

A man does not neglect his business because he votes. . . . A woman will not neglect her home because she votes. . . .

The happiness of a home does not depend on the woman always being in it, but on the kind of woman she is. . . .

In the right kind of home the man's point of view and the woman's point of view are both needed.

Let us try it in government. . . .

As Man to Man

Can men represent women at the polls? No man votes for another man or any woman. He votes for himself. . . . Men think chiefly of how elections will affect business—women think chiefly of how elections will affect the home. . . .

Would men be satisfied if only women chose the officials who were to regulate their business? . . .

Is it a square deal to ask women to be satisfied when only men choose the officials to regulate their homes? . . .

If we trust women with our children can't we trust them with the vote? . . .

Let us admit that laws are made as voters demand and that laws are enforced as voters insist. . . . Give women the vote.

Who Shares the Cost of War?

Who face death in order to give life to men? Women.

Who love and work to rear the sons who then are killed in battle? Women.

Who plant fields and harvest crops when all the able-bodied men are in the trenches? Women.

Who nurse the wounded, feed the sick, support the helpless, brave all danger? Women.

Who see their homes destroyed by shell and fire, their little ones made destitute, their daughters outraged? Women.

Who are sent adrift alone, no food, no hope, no shelter for the unborn child? Women.

Who must suffer agony for every soldier killed? Women. Who are called upon to make sacrifices to pay the terrible tax of war? Women.

Who dares say that war is not their business? In the name of justice and civilization give women a voice in the government and in the councils that make or prevent war.

These Foreigners Must Be Educated: Americanizing the Immigrant (1916)

The document that follows is from a report by Florence S. Wright, a visiting nurse who worked for the Clark Thread Company of Newark. Wright was addressing the National Safety Council, a group that used nurses such as Wright to Americanize immigrant workers.

During the massive wave of immigration from central and eastern Europe that began late in the nineteenth century, social workers, industrialists, and representatives of patriotic organizations began trying to change the behavior of immigrants. They taught English and civics, urged applications for citizenship, and generally stressed the importance of breaking Old World ties. While some immigrants welcomed this, others saw it as an attempt to obliterate their national cultures.

Employers took a particular interest in the campaign. Some did so from a genuine sense that the ability of their immigrant workers to achieve upward social mobility would be enhanced by rapid adoption of American ways, others because they sensed that if immigrant workers embraced American social and political ideals, they might be less likely to build labor unions or organize strikes.

When most of the workers were English-speaking and either American-born or from European countries whose standards of living are not so different from ours, many problems did not arise which now cause us the most anxiety. With laborers coming from the four quarters of the globe, speaking strange languages and bringing with them their own traditions, superstitions, diseases, religions, it becomes necessary for the employer who is awake to his own needs and to those of the country to do something toward educating these masses in habits of cleanliness, health, morality, and thrift, and especially in suitable standards of living and in adapting their lives to changed conditions.

We see an Italian family of six living in three rooms, taking boarders. They do this, not because the man does not earn enough, but to get money to buy a home, and because they were used to being

Florence S. Wright, "The Visiting Nurse in Industrial Welfare Work," *Fifth Safety Council Proceedings* (Detroit: National Safety Council, 1916). Reprinted in Rosalyn Baxandall, Linda Gordon, and Susan Reverby, eds., *America's Working Women* (New York: Vintage Books. 1976).

crowded in Italy. They do not know that conditions which did not injure health in the warm, sunny, outdoor life of the homeland become a menace when every one works indoors and when doors, windows, and cracks are stopped up to keep out the cold. The father is at home with a "cold." The children are anaemic. The mother wonders why no one is well in this country.

A Polish mother refuses to nurse her baby because she wants to work in the mill and gives it condensed milk because "cow's milk gets bad too quick."

A Lithuanian woman buys sausages, new white bread, and coffee as the sole food for her growing family. She had a garden, chickens, and a goat in the old country. Here the "store milk" sours and vegetables seem expensive and not necessary to her. . . .

A Russian father cannot control his boys because they speak a language he does not know and in their new surroundings have become ashamed of the homeland ways. . . .

These instances could be related for hours from memory of actual cases, . . . but is it not proven that these masses of foreigners must be educated in cleanliness, homemaking, and infant care; in fact, that they must be made into good Americans as fast as possible?

No one can do this who does not reach the homes, and who can reach the homes except the visiting nurse?

She goes out in the morning with a list of names and addresses. (Let us hope she is provided with an automobile, for her work is hard and she will not need the exercise of walking.) She finds the Italian family taking boarders. She goes slowly and keeps the family on her list. In time each member will accept her advice without question. The father has his chest examined, is found to be an incipient tuberculosis case, and after a period of rest and education is given outdoor work suited to his strength. The mother is taught to buy and to cook. The children are sent to open-air school. It takes time but in the end the boarders are no longer there, the father is well and doing suitable work, the children are gaining, and the mother is making a home of which the family and the nurse are proud.

Incidentally, the nurse has increased her Italian vocabulary and has six firm friends. Needless to say the unseen employer who sent the nurse also has six loyal friends, although he may never know of their existence.

"A Little Patriotic Affair": New Brunswick during World War I (1917–1918)

President Wilson and his supporters undertook a massive effort to rally the country behind military involvement in World War I. The result was a climate of opinion that led to vigilantism; the forced suppression of socialists, anarchists, and other dissenters; intolerance of "hyphenated Americans"; and in particular, victimization of German Americans. The name of German Valley in Morris County was changed to Long Valley, for example, and German street names in the Ironbound section of Newark were changed as well.

The following episodes from an account of New Brunswick during the war depict the atmosphere of inflamed passions and intolerance of difference.

By unanimous vote of the City Commission, . . . City Attorney Hagerty was instructed to prepare a resolution prohibiting the further sale of German-language newspapers, magazines, or periodicals within the confines of New Brunswick. . . .

A committee from the New Brunswick Board of Trade presented the resolution adopted at the annual meeting of the trade board requesting such action. . . .

It was held that the German-language press greatly retards the assimilation of the German element of our population. . . .

The Board of Education passed a resolution discontinuing the course in German and no new classes were formed.

Samuel Harry Chovenson, of Millville [Cumberland County], a freshman at Rutgers College, was "tarred and feathered" . . . by a group of patriotic college men. In place of the much-used tar, a gallon of good old New England molasses was poured over the young man's anatomy, which was then sprinkled with the stuffings of two pillows from a nearby room.

Chovenson refused to speak on the Liberty Loan,[1] and word of his

1. To help finance the war, Secretary of the Treasury William G. McAdoo launched an aggressive campaign to sell Liberty Bonds to the public. "Four-

John P. Wall, comp., *New Brunswick, New Jersey in the World War, 1917–1918* (n.p., n.d.), Rutgers. Reprinted by permission of the Department of Special Collections and University Archives, Rutgers University Libraries.

seditious actions rapidly went the rounds of the student body, stirring up the patriotic young men. . . .

Chovenson, who was not a citizen, was seized . . . at 4:30 after he had finished drilling with the Rutgers Cadet Corps. He was removed to a room . . . where he was guarded until 9:30. At that hour the young men began flocking to George Street near the Johnson and Johnson plant. In a few minutes' time a group of four hundred men was present. Chovenson was quietly removed to the field along the canal bank. . . .

Here one of the young men announced that there was to be no mob violence. While the crowd waited, the committee in charge stripped Chovenson of his Rutgers Cadet Corps uniform, and, leaving him with nothing but a pair of pants, began to paint him with the molasses. Not a part of his body was left uncovered, the sticky mass of molasses and feathers being applied with great fervor.

At a given signal four husky young men shouldered a plank with Chovenson, who was blind-folded, as their burden, and headed the parade down George Street. At every corner new recruits were added until . . . five hundred men were in line. Signs were carried at the head of the line bearing the inscriptions, "He's a Bolsheviki." "He is against the Liberty Loan and the U.S.A.," and "This is what we do with Pro-Germans." The procession moved . . . in a very orderly manner, the curbs being crowded with people from the theaters who were demanding more severe punishment for the offender.

Numerous soldiers were spectators and were especially anxious to get to the "tar and feathered" young man. The line moved to . . . George and Albany. At this point the blind was removed and Chovenson was allowed to go free. Setting out at a pace only a frightened man can take he headed for his boarding place . . . and that was the last seen of him in New Brunswick.

Acting upon information to the effect that the socialist colony, known as the Fellowship Farm, at Stelton, and the Ferrer Modern School colony nearby were flying red flags instead of the stars and stripes, a company of determined young men from New Brunswick mounted on horseback, visited the colonies, . . . and demanded the removal of the objectionable emblems.

The patriotic demand was complied with in both cases and the red

---

Minute Men" were encouraged to appear before movie audiences or in lecture halls or churches to speak briefly (for roughly four minutes) in behalf of the Liberty Bonds. Any refusal to participate, such as the unfortunate Chovenson's, was considered an act of friendship to Germany.

flags came down without a resort to force, which undoubtedly would have been employed had a refusal been met with.

Those who engaged in the visit to Stelton said: "This was just a little patriotic affair similar to some others which need attention in this section. If the red flags are again hoisted at Stelton there will be less gentleness shown."

The purpose of the whole affair is to keep New Brunswick and the surrounding district free from anarchy, extreme socialism, and revolution.

A Way of Life Denied at Home: Race Relations during World War I (1918)

Fred Morrow, author of the following recollection, attended Bowdoin College. He worked for the National Association for the Advancement of Colored People (NAACP) and CBS before serving in the army during World War II. After the war he earned a law degree at the Rutgers University School of Law. During the Eisenhower administration Morrow was an executive assistant to the President, the first African-American to serve at that level in a presidential administration. But Morrow was frequently criticized by the black community for his defense of the Eisenhower administration's weak record on civil rights.

The memoir from which this comes, Way Down South Up North, *was published in 1973, when its author was vice-president of a major New York bank. The book deserves a wider readership than it has received. It paints a vivid picture of the stern moral fiber of which the Morrow family was made and of the harsh climate of race relations in New Jersey in the years of Fred Morrow's youth.*

In this segment Morrow writes of a contradiction many black Americans felt during World War I. They were fighting a war to uphold abroad ideals that were unmet at home. He also describes a dramatic episode in which his father, a minister, resorted to armed self-defense to protect his family.

The first two segments of this excerpt deal with racism; the last passage introduces the complex question of the relationship between race and class.

The drama of World War I broke into our midst with suddenness and great impact. I was in the fifth grade. . . . The whole country had been quickly mobilized behind the effort, and even in the classroom our patriotism was being tested by participation in buying war bonds and government savings stamps with our pennies. Our little community was galvanized into action. It was typical of the thousands of similar small towns over the nation. . . .

The Negroes in Hackensack of draft age were on edge. No matter how great their patriotism, they could not enlist in the white National Guard and the only alternative, if they wanted to volunteer, was to go to New York and apply for service with the old Fifteenth Regiment of

E. Frederic Morrow, *Way Down South Up North* (Philadelphia: The Pilgrim Press. 1973), 74–79. Copyright © 1985 by The Pilgrim Press. Reprinted by permission of the publisher, The Pilgrim Press, Cleveland, Ohio.

the New York National Guard. The old Fifteenth was a black outfit commanded mostly by white officers, but it was a well-trained and disciplined group and highly rated. About five of the local boys went to New York and joined the Fifteenth, and the news circulated through town like wildfire. They were immediate heroes and the less venturesome youths of draft age were greatly disturbed. My brother Gene, just beginning his freshman year, returned home from college one weekend with dismaying news. Half his classmates had volunteered and he felt it incumbent upon himself to do likewise. However, he would like to have his parents' consent. . . .

The irony of World War I was that Woodrow Wilson eloquently anesthetized the country with the rhetoric that the war was being fought to save democracy. This meant little to Negroes anywhere. President Wilson was notorious for his disinterest in Negroes. . . . Wilson, as governor of New Jersey, had a deaf ear to the pleas of black Jerseyites for greater citizenship participation in state affairs, and as president of Princeton he made no effort to include blacks in the academic life of the university. Furthermore, the United States would be sending segregated armies to Europe. . . . How dastardly to draft, or even permit, blacks to volunteer to fight in separate outfits and to die three thousand miles away from home to give to others a way of life they were not permitted to enjoy in their own country. For black parents who had scrimped and saved and sacrificed to give a son a chance to escape the crippling, stifling ravages of discrimination and segregation, to have to face the question now being asked was a traumatic and sorrowful moment. . . .

Father came to the conclusion that, if Gene wanted to go, he ought to go under the best possible auspices. He felt that effort should be made to apply for admission to the Black Students Officer Training Corps at Hampton Institute, Virginia. Any future need for Negro officers would be met from this corps. After much effort, Gene was admitted to the corps and reported to Hampton for induction and training.

The deadly poison of discrimination cut deeply into our consciousness during the war years. While all the war posters screamed "democracy" and "patriotism" and "contribution," these terms meant different things when directed to the attention of black citizens. For example, the black mothers in Hackensack whose sons had gone off to war wanted to participate in the effort . . . to aid the Red Cross by making bandages and visiting the nearby camps and managing canteens. They applied to the local Red Cross chapter headquarters, but were denied both membership and participation. Volunteers for bond drives and war stamp efforts were accepted on a segregated basis, if at all.

The greatest debarkation center for troops to go overseas was Camp Merritt, near Tenafly, New Jersey, just seven or eight miles from Hackensack. . . .

White southern soldiers on the loose in northern New Jersey towns harassed black citizens unmercifully. Blacks were beaten and molested and insulted everywhere. . . . The summer of 1918, Father was pastoring in Passaic, New Jersey. He commuted by trolley car on weekends, and he often took Mother and the children with him. After the evening service on Sunday, he would return on the ten o'clock trolley to Hackensack. The trolley, passing through the saloon-laden towns of Garfield and Lodi, would pick up dozens of soldiers returning to Merritt, many of them drunk and abusive. Father had some nasty experiences during the summer, and he decided that whenever he took his family he would carry his revolver. One night we were returning from Passaic and at a stop in Lodi the car filled up with white soldiers from the South. They were drunk and disorderly and offensive. They spied us sitting in a group in the middle of the car. My mother had my brother John on her lap and my sister was sitting, terrified, holding my father's hand. The soldiers called us vile names and told my father to get up and dance. As they started toward us to enforce their whims, father stood up, pistol in hand, and said that if they made one more move he'd fire all six shells. We rode the rest of the way with father shielding his family with his body and his pistol cocked for action. . . .

Interest in the purchase of war savings stamps in the classrooms was heightened by a contest which pitted classes against each other. The class that bought the most stamps at the end of each month won a silver star in the huge display board outside the principal's office. . . . The poverty of the black children was evident and painfully blatant. In most black homes, there simply was not extra money to put into war stamps. . . . Only in most exceptional cases did the children have weekly allowances from which twenty-five cents a week could be pinched to make a showing in class.

Some of our white classmates bought one to five dollars' worth at a time and they kept the class in contention in the contest. This kind of situation, denying black children the opportunity to participate in a class function because of economic privations, produced definite and indelible inferiority complexes in them. Their classmates knew that, if these blacks pulled their weight, the class would compete much more strongly and successfully. The whites were too young to reason why the blacks did not perform. But the blacks knew that their embarrassment sprang from the inglorious role their parents played in the job structure of community life.

Nothing for the "Joys of Living": The Cost of Living (1919)

By today's standards, the wage rates and costs of living of the past seem absurdly low. But this is not a helpful way to look at them. Income should first be compared to costs to determine how families fared. Only then, if a comparison to the present is desired, might the relationship of annual earnings to expenses from one period be compared to another.

The following chart was prepared for the personnel manager of Thomas A. Edison Industries. The weekly estimate of $22.48 means that the annual living expenses of a family of five were approximately $1,170. According to the 1920 U.S. census, the average annual wage in 1919 of an employee in the electrical industry in the Newark/East Orange area was $1,085.

This suggests that although wages had risen rapidly in the decade, prices had more than kept pace. The typical working-class family of the day was not able to participate in the developing consumer society with only one wage earner. Family income was generally augmented by the contributions of women, children, other relatives living in the household or boarders.

It should be added that the number of hours worked per week was declining rapidly in these years. Before World War I, perhaps one worker in eight worked only forty-eight hours per week. In 1919 the number had risen to almost half.

Weekly cost of supporting the family of an ordinary laboring man, which averages five persons.

Provisions
Meat (14 pounds/week @ $0.36/pound)	$4.90
Bread (2 loaves/day @ $0.10/loaf)	1.40
Butter (4 pounds)	2.00
Potatoes	.50
Coffee	.43
Tea	.58
Milk and sugar	1.00
Onions*	.15

Letter to Mark Jones, director of personnel, Thomas A. Edison Industries, 1919, Archives, U.S. Department of the Interior, National Park Service, Edison National Historic Site, West Orange, New Jersey.

Provisions (*continued*)

Turnips*	.25
Cabbage*	.30
Subtotal	$11.51

Clothing
Children

6 pairs of shoes @ $3.50/pair	$21.00
6 suits of underclothes @ $1.50 each	9.00
12 pairs of stockings @ 0.35/pair	4.20
3 suits @ $12.50/suit	37.50
1 overcoat	30.00

Man

1 suit	30.00
2 pairs of shoes @ $6.00/pair	12.00
Underwear	5.00

Woman

Dresses, summer	20.00
Winter	25.00
2 pairs of shoes	10.00
Underwear	10.00
Miscellaneous repairs	19.00
Subtotal	$214.70

$$214.70/52 = 4.13$$

Rent	$4.00
Carfare	.84
Heat and Light	1.00
Miscellaneous	
Doctor, medicine, insurance, etc.	1.00
Total	$22.48

You will notice we have been extremely moderate in selecting the various articles necessary to sustain life. All articles here are of medium grade. We have not provided for entertainments, refreshments, or anything that adds to the joys of living.

*Items varied to balance food values evenly.

Strikebreaker or Color-Barrier Breaker?: Race and the Labor Movement (1923)

William Ashby, the author of the following account, was the first black social worker in New Jersey and the founder of the first Urban League chapter in the state. He was one of the leading African Americans of his day. A monument to his memory stands in Newark's Central Ward, and the Department of Community Affairs building in Trenton bears his name.

Ashby recounted the story excerpted here, along with other examples of his efforts to find jobs for black workers, in his memoir, Tales Without Hate, *published in 1980.*

His version of this episode may not fit the facts as perfectly as a historian would like (a general hazard of memory), but it is nonetheless an important document. Its context is the great migration of southern blacks to the North, which began just before World War I and was accelerating in the 1920s. These migrants were lured by the promise of better jobs, decent housing, and greater social equality, but their expectations were going largely unmet. The American Federation of Labor was of little help, issuing occasional calls for organizing black workers, but most AFL unions continued to bar African Americans.

There were isolated employers who were genuinely forward-looking on racial matters, and there were others who were willing to hire black workers (often at lower wages than white workers were receiving) to weaken a union's power by keeping the employees divided against one another.

In this instance, as in so many others, Ashby was ahead of his time. In 1925 the National Urban League set up a department of industrial relations, formalizing its efforts to find industrial employment for black workers.

The *Newark Evening News* reported a strike had broken out at the Sayre and Fisher brick company in Sayreville.

Two days later a man came to my office. I recognized him as one of two partners who operated a private employment firm. I knew something about the methods by which the company conducted its business. While it was true that they would round up workers where fifty, one hundred, or more were needed on a new project, their real job was to bring in hordes of men to break a strike.

William M. Ashby, *Tales Without Hate* (Newark: Newark Preservation and Landmarks Commission, 1981), 98–100. Copyright © 1980 by William Ashby. Used with permission of the Newark Preservation and Landmarks Committee and Mrs. Simon Moss.

I had known them to bring in a trainload of laborers, rounded up in cities where there were large pools of unemployed. Also they sometimes went into the South, rounded up hundreds and chartered boxcars they attached to freight trains in order to reduce the cost of transportation.

I was peeved even at the sight of the fellow. In response to my inquiry about what he wanted, he told me that he would like us to assist him in getting a large crew of men for a brickyard.

"Sayre and Fisher?" I asked.

"Well, yes."

I was mad at the man for . . . his presumptuousness in the belief the Urban League would permit itself to be involved in a labor situation where a strike was occurring, thereby being charged as a strikebreaking organization. My parting words to him lacked much of my normal civility.

The next day I had a call from the director of the Newark Chamber of Commerce. He asked me if I would accept a call from the director of the Chamber of Commerce of Middlesex County, the county in which Sayreville was located. I agreed.

The man asked me to assist him in building up a labor force for Sayre and Fisher.

Now I was really mad. It was as if a conspiracy had developed to put me and the Urban League in a position where we would be the targets for labor unions to shoot at.

"Why do you ask me to break a strike?" I shot at him.

"Mr. Ashby, I give you my word that the strike is over," he said.

"I have seen nothing of it in the papers," I replied angrily.

The next morning he called again. He asked me if I would agree to come to Sayreville to talk with George Fisher, the president of the brick company. . . .

Fisher said, "Mr. Ashby, we are in great need to increase our labor force. We have been for some time. Now we are almost desperate. Above and beyond our regular trade, we have a contract to supply millions of white-face bricks to be used in the stations of a new subway which they are just building in New York. We are way behind in our deliveries. They are pressing us. That telephone may ring any minute asking us to hurry. Our present working force is putting in all the overtime they can stand. Yet we do not catch up.

"You see, practically all of our common laborers are either Hungarians or Poles. At one time it was very easy for us to rebuild our labor needs with the same people. But as you know, since the war the labor source from Eastern Europe has come to a complete halt. I asked friends of mine who operate brick-making plants in Peekskill, N.Y., and Baltimore, what their experiences had been in the use of colored laborers. Both assured me that they had been very satisfactory. I called in my superintendent and my foremen and told them that I was determined to go into the labor market and get colored men to take up our slack.

"When the workers heard this, they told the superintendent that they would strike if they brought Negroes in."

"You have a strike on now?" I said.

"Oh, no, Mr. Ashby. That strike was settled. We gave them the raise in wages they demanded."

"Why are they not at work?" I asked.

"Because they want a guarantee from me that I won't bring in any colored men to work here."

"Are you sure that is the reason?"

"I would not have you come all the way down here to tell you a lie."

"Give me a half hour or so to make up my mind."

I went out of his office and walked a short distance into the town. Groups of men stood about on the streets talking. Not one word of English did I hear. I walked past a grocery store. On the window were letters in Hungarian.

"This is hell," I thought. "It is humiliating enough for me to be forced to accept all sorts of debasement from the descendants of those who have been in the country for a hundred years, and helped to build it. But those fellows just got here yesterday, so to speak. They knew only one sentence in English: 'Me no work with neegars.'"

I was faced with a situation which literally scared me to death. Fisher had given me his word the original strike had been settled. But suppose . . . the strike was still on, and I brought in men to crack it? Condemnation of me and the Urban League would be crushing.

But if I broke a strike that was protracted because the workers refused to work with men of a different color, thereby denying them the right to sell their labor and provide food for their families, would I have shown less regard for the rights of labor than did the strikers themselves?

As I walked through the streets of this little town, I asked myself, "Can the breaking of a strike ever be morally and legally justified? What kind of morality or legality is it that tells me that I must step aside and let a white man work because he is white, while he makes me stay idle and in want because I am a Negro. . . . In the light of labor ethics, if it is right for them to deny me the right to work because of my color, is it wrong for me to deny them the right to work by breaking their strike?" I returned to the brickyard.

"Mr. Fisher, here is my proposition to you. One, I will bring in as many men as you need. But you must pay them $45 a week. That, I know, is five dollars more than you assert your men settled for.

"Two, you shall have to underwrite a fund sufficient for me to advertise in the Negro weekly newspapers, and also place placards all over Newark, telling men that jobs are open to them.

"Three, I will come down here for a week or ten days, disguise myself as a worker and mingle with the men to assist them in their adjustment."

The company sent up trucks to pick up men in front of our building. In less than two weeks, several hundred men had reached Sayre and Fisher Co., for work.

Dr. Abram L. Harris[1] . . . charged me and the Urban League as strikebreakers. I think that I was only a color-barrier breaker.

1. An economist from the University of Chicago, author of *The Black Worker* (1932).

To Protect Their Health and Morals: Regulating Female Employment (1923)

During the Progressive years the idea gained acceptance that women employed outside the home were overworked, underpaid, and generally exploited more appallingly than men. To remedy this, reformers advocated laws that limited the amount of time per week that a woman could work, prohibited women from employment in certain industries, or banned women from working at night.

In the 1920s a serious debate emerged over the wisdom of this protective legislation, as it is known. Critics argued that placing women in a special legal category that accepted their physical inferiority legitimized the notion that men and women would forever inhabit separate spheres. Supporters emphasized the necessity of improving the conditions of working women.

Since the federal Civil Rights Act of 1972, most laws of this sort have been presumed invalid because that law calls for people to be dealt with as individuals, not on the basis of group attributes. Nonetheless, the debate is with us still between supporters of special treatment for women and advocates of total equality. (See document 71.)

Be it enacted by the Senate and General Assembly of the State of New Jersey:

1. In order to protect the health and morals of females employed in manufacturing establishments, bakeries, and laundries by providing an adequate period of rest at night, no female shall be employed or permitted to work in any manufacturing establishment, bakery, or laundry in this state before 6:00 A.M. or after 10:00 P.M. of any day; provided, that nothing herein contained shall apply to canneries engaged in packing a perishable product such as fruits or vegetables.

Acts of the One Hundred Forty-seventh Legislature of the State of New Jersey, Laws of New Jersey (1923), 312–313.

"How New Jersey Laws Discriminate Against Women": The National Woman's Party in New Jersey (1925)

The National Woman's Party (NWP), one of whose pamphlets is excerpted here, was an outgrowth of the most militant wing of the woman suffrage campaign. Founded by New Jersey native Alice Paul, the NWP struggled to win total equality for women, as embodied in the Equal Rights Amendment,[1] drafted by Paul, which is quoted below.

The NWP position was opposed by the League of Women Voters and other groups, which felt that a campaign for total equality would invalidate laws they had championed that gave women special privileges and protections. (See document 70.)

The law of New Jersey has for its framework the common law of England. At common law "the husband had control, almost absolute, over the person of his wife; she was in a condition of complete dependence; could not contract in her own name; was bound to obey him; and her legal existence was merged in that of her husband."[2] . . .

While the legislation of New Jersey has made a steady advance to free the married woman from the shackles of the common law, the position of woman under the law is still not equal to that of man. . . .

The object of the Woman's Party is to advance the interests of women—in the law and in the customs of the people, as well as in every realm of human activity. As its first task, the Woman's Party is working to remove discriminations against women in the law. . . .

The Woman's Party is also working to obtain an amendment to the

1. The Equal Rights Amendment, in a form different from that drafted by Paul and quoted here, was approved by the House of Representatives in 1971 and by the Senate in 1972. In 1982 it died when it failed to receive ratification from the requisite thirty-eight states.
2. Here, and elsewhere, the author is quoting what is probably a well-known legal authority, but I have been unable to identify it.

National Woman's Party, "How New Jersey Laws Discriminate Against Women," 1926, Rutgers. Reprinted by permission of the Department of Special Collections and University Archives, Rutgers University Libraries.

national Constitution stating: "Men and women shall have equal rights throughout the United States and every place subject to its jurisdiction.". . . .

By virtue of the common law a rule prevails in New Jersey "that where the married woman commits an offense . . . in the presence of her husband or . . . under his immediate influence and control, she is presumed to have acted not voluntarily but under his coercion and he is responsible while she is excused, unless the presumption is overcome by competent testimony. In this respect the wife is "accorded the legal status of a servant or slave.". . . .

For illicit intercourse, a married man is punishable only by a fine of not more than $50 or six months' imprisonment or both, while a married woman who engages in unlawful relations is given a fine of not more than $1,000 or three years' imprisonment or both. In other words, for like misconduct a married woman may be compelled to pay a fine twenty times greater than that of a married man, as well as to suffer imprisonment for six times as long. Moreover, the imprisonment of the woman may be with hard labor if the court so directs. . . .

Women workers are subject to special regulations that do not apply to their men competitors. The maximum working hours per week are fixed at fifty-four for women but not for men workers in manufacturing and mercantile establishments, bakeries, laundries, and restaurants. This difference in the treatment of men and women places women at a disadvantage in the labor market since the want of elasticity in the restrictive laws governing their employment undoubtedly closes the door of equal opportunity. Certainly such discriminatory laws perpetuate the harmful assumption that paid labor is primarily a masculine prerogative, and hence tend to encourage the placing of further handicaps upon women. About two years ago a law became effective barring women from working in manufacturing establishments, bakeries, and laundries at night. . . .

The law exempts "from liability to be drawn upon any panel of grand or petit jurors" women who are the "mothers of one or more minor children" (that is, children under twenty-one years of age). . . . The exemption of these mothers . . . lessens their opportunities for service and practically excludes them from an important part of the administration of justice.

The immemorial common law right of a married woman to have as her legal designation any name honestly used by her is denied by New Jersey to the married women attorneys. . . . The legislature recently passed laws stipulating that upon the marriage of a woman attorney . . . she must add after her name a hyphen and the surname of her husband. It is clear, therefore, that a woman who has made a reputation in her profession under her maiden name will find it obligatory upon marriage to "hide her light under a bushel" by taking a "changed and new name," a course certain to result in confusion and a monetary loss. . . .

Will you not help to remove discriminations in the law against the women of New Jersey and other states by joining the Woman's Party and supporting its campaign for "equal rights" legislation?

"Let Me Know Where I Can Get Some Socialist Literature": Criticism of President Hoover (1931)

In the first years after the stock market crash of 1929, popular anger focused on President Herbert Hoover's seeming indifference to the plight of those who suffered as the economy deteriorated. Ultimately, Hoover's program offered too little, too late, given the depth of the crisis, but many historians now feel that he deserves some credit for beginning the active government intervention in the management of the economy for which Franklin Delano Roosevelt is famed.

The September 1931 letter quoted here, from the anonymous C.M. of Madison (Morris County) to Mr. Walter Gifford, chief executive officer of AT&T and chairman of the President's Organization for Unemployment Relief (POUR),[1] mentions some of the policy areas in which President Hoover got into trouble. Hoover believed that the nation's big corporations would manage themselves in a way that would forestall government regulation. But in 1931 prices had risen and most companies had abandoned their pledges to maintain wage levels.

Another important issue was the President's desire to avoid direct federal responsibility for relief. This position in particular undermined Hoover's popularity and led to his massive defeat at the hands of Franklin Delano Roosevelt in the 1932 presidential election.

Dear Sir:

Just listened in on your radio address.

I can't believe that your intelligence allows you to believe that what you said tonight will be swallowed by the rank and file of American working men. Certainly their intelligence tells them that it's the same old "bunkum" handed out every depression.

You said, "This emergency is only temporary and therefore re-

1. The President's Organization for Unemployment Relief, established in 1930. This group had no money in its budget for relief. It sponsored surveys, recommended ways families could economize, and called on garden clubs, women's groups, and business and professional organizations to increase their benevolent activities.

Reprinted in Robert S. McElvaine, ed., *Down and Out in the Great Depression: Letters from the Forgotten Man* (Chapel Hill: University of North Carolina Press. 1983), 45–46. Copyright © 1983 by the University of North Carolina Press.

quires temporary relief." It's going to be the longest temporary relief you ever saw.

And before this thing is over it's going to be national government relief and the working men are to be insured against unemployment and want.

You say wages have and are being reduced only to correspond to reduced cost of living. Why haven't you reduced telephone rates? Ha! Ha! Ha! This is only one instance of hundreds I could tell you of tonight. Light and fuel have not dropped in price—poor man's necessities.

President Hoover called your crowd together a few months ago and you all faithfully promised to keep wages up. Papers were out in heavy type; how you all made such promises. It was only the same old story, not even worth a scrap of paper. You capitalists are up against it this time. And this good old U.S.A. is going to get down to the real facts, that this government is really meant for rule by the people, of the people, for the people.

P.S. . . . As I have a lot of "Hoover Time" on my hands, would like to improve it. Please let me know where I can get some socialist literature.

Carry on the Fight: A Labor Union's Vision (1935)

The 1930s are often considered turbulent years. No area of the country or major industry was untouched by labor conflict in the decade. Many of the young activists in the labor movement of the 1930s saw unions as instruments by which to build a radically new America. They envisaged a militant union movement that would unite all American workers against their employers and break down divisions in the working class created by race and ethnic background and, to a lesser degree, gender.

For the most part the unions identified with this radical or left wing of the house of labor became part of the Congress of Industrial Organizations (CIO), which held its first national convention in Atlantic City in 1937. Local 1733 of the Federation of Silk and Rayon Dyers and Finishers of America, publishers of the pamphlet of which this excerpt was the conclusion, is an exception.

The dyers' union, as it was locally known, was an affiliate of the United Textile Workers of America, a member union of the American Federation of Labor (AFL). The dyers' union was formed in 1933 after a strike in which workers won wages better than those guaranteed by the National Recovery Administration. The next year, after a second strike, the contract was renewed on even better terms. The level of determination of the dyers during this second strike is suggested by the rabbit stew they served on winter mornings to those on the picket lines. The rabbits had been hunted the night before in the surrounding woods.

Unionism means more than the bread and butter gains of industrial struggle. It means educational, athletic, and social activities. The union should be placed side by side with the home as a focal point of the worker's life. Dances and other social functions should be regular union features. A woman's auxiliary should be started. Unionists should gather together for gym classes, hiking trips, and other sports activities.

Of paramount importance is education. Education so that all workers can take a more constructive part in union meetings, and education about happenings in the world today. Classes in English are

Herman Wolf, *After 141 Years: What Dye Workers Have Won in Two Successful Strikes.* (Paterson, N.J.: Federation of Silk and Rayon Dyers and Finishers of America, 1935), 34–36. Reprinted by permission of the American Labor Museum, Botto House National Landmark, Haledon, New Jersey.

necessary; classes on economic and political questions, on the history of the labor movement in America and abroad. Open forums should be run where workers can express their opinions freely, discuss important political questions of the day, and come to realize that only a new economic setup will give them permanent security.

All these things, we say, are functions of a good union. In addition, this contract does not mean that the fight against the boss is over. Not by a long shot. We must be continually alert in our organized shops and we must send organizers to New England and Pennsylvania to bring workers there up to our standard so that in 1936 the union will have every shop in the industry organized. . . .

The dye workers and their union must ever be awake, on the political field as well as the economic. In state capitals and in Congress the dyers' union must carry on the fight for the forty-hour week; for unemployment, old-age, and health insurance; for higher income, gift, and inheritance taxes on the rich. It must fight against the sales tax, against labor injunctions, against the use of state militia and deputized thugs to break strikes. It must fight for all measures of benefit to the workers and against all measures oppressive to the workers.

Above all the union must fight every attempt to curb the liberties of the masses. It must vigorously challenge and defeat any effort to put over an American form of fascism, whether by an American Liberty League[1] of wealthy capitalists, or by a fine-sounding scheme of some demagogue.[2]

In so doing it must fight for the establishment of a genuine labor party on a nationwide scale, for only as this fight is continued and broadened will the dye workers and the rest of the working class of America surge forward. And only as the working masses go forward will the day of real freedom and liberty, the day of the emancipation of mankind be brought nearer.

May it be in our time. . . .

Whether it be a chiseling boss or a big-hearted boss—it is still a boss—and he still won't pay you what you can get through organizing together with your fellow workers.

Organization brings strength and strength brings power.

---

1. The Liberty League was founded in 1934 by conservative opponents of President Roosevelt, whom they compared to Hitler, Stalin, and Mussolini. The League attacked the New Deal program as extravagant, unconstitutional, and socialist.
2. Popular opposition to Roosevelt and the New Deal coalesced around the leadership of four individuals who appealed demagogically to the prejudices and emotions of their audiences: Dr. Francis E. Townsend, U.S. Senator Huey P. Long, Gerald L. K. Smith, and Father Charles E. Coughlin.

The Man on Relief Is Similar to His Neighbor: Welfare during the Great Depression (1936)

When Franklin Delano Roosevelt became President there were upwards of thirty million Americans living in families without regular incomes (almost a quarter of the population). Alleviating their suffering required immediate attention. The Federal Emergency Relief Administration, established by legislation during FDR's first hundred days in office, was the first federal relief program in U.S. history. Gradually, direct relief was replaced by work relief for most recipients, although as the following excerpt suggests, not all those in need could be helped by employment opportunities. The passage comes from a dissertation submitted by Richard A. Lester to the economics department of Princeton University in 1936, based on research he carried out during 1934 and 1935.

Lester suggests the multiplier effect that economic downturns have. A family that has fallen on hard times spends less in the local grocery and, perhaps, delays paying its doctor bill. In turn the doctor and grocer make adjustments that affect others in the community; perhaps they buy less or reduce the hours of employment or the wages of a stock clerk, nurse, or receptionist.

The average man on relief is not so different from his non-relief neighbor, and the fact that his family, rather than his neighbor's, is on relief seems to be due chiefly to circumstances beyond his own control. However, his family usually does contain a larger number of dependent children than his neighbor's. His annual pre-Depression earnings may have been somewhat below the average for his type of work and he is likely to be an unskilled worker.

In 1934 he had been out of steady employment for approximately two and one half years. Disemployment had reduced his standard of living to a point where, after a few voluntary moves or evictions, he was living in cramped quarters, probably without bathroom or modern lighting facilities. Meanwhile, in trying to avoid the stigma of public charity, he had used up all the family's economic reserves that could be liquidated and usually had gone heavily into debt as well. By means of such indebtedness he had forced certain groups in the

Richard A. Lester, "Some Aspects of Unemployment Relief in New Jersey" (Ph.D. diss., Princeton University, 1936), 41–42.

community such as landlords, grocers, and doctors to shoulder a portion of the burden of his involuntary unemployment. If the mortgage on his home was foreclosed or his property was sold for taxes, as was frequently the case, real estate values in the vicinity were affected. When out of a steady job or on relief his income from occasional, temporary work had not been large. Sometimes he tried, . . . by starting a business of his own or by shifting into agriculture, public service, or domestic service, to augment the meager income of the family.

Certain families, overrepresented in the relief population, present special problems . . . because the family lacks a breadwinner or the breadwinner had been handicapped by disease, injury, or prolonged unemployment or is too old for efficient work at the unskilled or semiskilled occupations that he has pursued in the past. Few such family heads would be covered by any system of unemployment insurance and by no means all of them would be covered by old-age assistance, yet they should not be kept on direct relief for the rest of their lives. They constitute a real problem in rehabilitation.

Ben Shahn's Jersey Homesteads
Mural (1937)

In 1937 the Farm Security Administration organized an experimental community in rural Monmouth County, east of Hightstown. A group of Jewish immigrant textile workers and their families were brought to the newly built town to run a triple cooperative: they were to farm, manufacture garments, and market the products of both these ventures cooperatively.

One of the early residents of Jersey Homesteads, as the project was known, was the artist Ben Shahn, who painted the mural detailed here for the venture. Today the mural hangs in the elementary school in Roosevelt, the name the community adopted in 1945 after President Franklin Roosevelt's death.

The detail used for this illustration represents approximately one-third of the enormous work, which is twelve feet tall and forty-five feet long. In the mural Shahn depicted his version of the history of Jersey Homesteads. In the upper left one sees immigrants debarking from a ship and filing past the coffins of Sacco and Vanzetti. Sacco and Vanzetti were Italian immigrant anarchists executed in 1927 for the murder of two employees of a Massachusetts shoe company during a robbery. Their controversial execution influenced Shahn and many others, who felt they had been convicted because of their political beliefs rather than because the evidence against them was convincing. The coffins suggest that America has not been entirely receptive to all immigrants. Below the coffins is the processing center at Ellis Island.

In the center foreground of this section Albert Einstein leads a group of immigrants into America. Einstein was an important supporter of the Jersey Homesteads project, and he symbolizes the other side of the Sacco and Vanzetti story: America as a refuge for the exiles of Europe. Next to this group on one side is a scene on the rooftop of a tenement building and on the other one a garment shop, the places where most immigrants lived and worked.

In the sections of the mural not reproduced here Shahn painted scenes of trade union organizing, WPA-style construction, and the planning of Jersey Homesteads under a picture of FDR who is described as a "gallant leader."

Shahn worked in a style known as social realism in which the artist tried to depict the common experience of the working American.

Original in elementary school, Roosevelt, New Jersey. Reproduced by permission of Bernarda Bryson Shahn.

Forced on Relief Again: A Newark Woman on Welfare (1939)

The following story was told to Irving Zuckerman, a field worker for the New Jersey ethnic survey of the Federal Writers Project, Works Progress Administration (WPA).[1] *Zuckerman described the unnamed blond narrator as an "extremely attractive" woman of "much vitality" who had a relationship with her husband that seemed "stable and of mutual comfort." Their home had a "cheerful and intimate" atmosphere.*

The excerpt indicates some important themes about life during the Great Depression. First, the narrator's father lost his job before the crash, suggesting that the economy was in transition before the onset of the Depression. Second, the speaker much preferred working to receiving direct relief. A third related theme is the important role the WPA played in the lives of those for whom it provided employment in these years.

I was born in the heart of the Third Ward.[2] I don't recall much about my early years, except that most of my activities were confined to playing with my sister and brother. . . .

My father decided . . . to give in to my mother's lifelong wish of living where there were trees and flowers. They looked for a home in the suburbs. . . . First my father swept floors and then he operated a pleating machine in a cleaning and dyeing plant. With lots of skimping and doing without, they were able to save a little money. . . . They found . . . land in Maplewood, which was then mostly woodland, and laid plans for building a little home. We children attended the school system of Maplewood and the contrast was very marked. It was very difficult for us to adjust ourselves to playmates whose fathers were big executives in corporations, after having lived in a poverty-stricken area.

1. The WPA was established under the Emergency Relief Appropriation Act of 1935. During its eight-year existence, the WPA employed more than 8.5 million people and provided financial aid to another 30 million, at a cost of $11 billion. Its 1.4 million projects included 650,000 miles of roads, 125,000 public buildings, 8,000 parks, thousands of theatrical productions, many murals in public buildings, and travel guides and books of folklore and local and regional history.
2. A neighborhood of southeastern Newark, known as one of the city's poorer sections.

David S. Cohen, *America, the Dream of My Life* (New Brunswick: Rutgers University Press, 1988), 202–204.

Life continued more or less quietly until I was in the fourth year of high school. Then a new machine came out in the factory in which my father worked, which made it possible for any child to do his work. A young girl was hired at twelve dollars for a job at which he had formerly been paid seventy-five dollars. From then on our economic conditions became difficult. The difficulty of paying taxes on our home forced the mortgage company to take away the house in which we lived. This was very hard on my mother because for ten years she had carefully . . . cultivated lovely plants and flowers surrounding the house. When we were children we indulged in a sentimental pastime of buying my mother a plant every year at Mother's Day. She had planted these around one side of the house, apart from all the other flowers. When notice came for us to move, she asked the agents if she could please dig up the plants which her children had given her over a period of ten years. They said no; it's part of the property as long as it's in the ground. And so my parents moved to an old deserted house on a dead end street. . . .

A month before my graduation from high school the stock-market crash forced me to go out and look for a job. I had already completed a course in fine arts and hoped to get work in that line. When I finally did get a job, after a six-month search, it was in a sewing factory. . . . I worked here several months making children's cotton dresses. My average salary was six dollars a week. I was laid off there and got a job . . . making the flies on men's cotton pajamas at two cents a dozen. I worked here one week and received $4.92 a week.

Feeling that a change was necessary in my life, I got married. But the only change . . . was that I went to work in another factory. Two months after I was married I discovered that I was pregnant. Because we had no money and lived in one little furnished room, I continued working in the factory. A month and a half before the baby was born the boss told me that I could no longer do the work required of me. I went to the social service for help. . . . Not being able to afford her upbringing and not being able to go to work immediately, I was forced on the relief rolls. My mother offered to have me live with her in the five-room apartment that my sister, my brother, my father, my sister's child, and my mother shared. The three of us—my child, my husband, and myself—moved in with them, making a total of eight. There was, naturally, a lot of crowding, and we weren't very happy.

Fortunately, I soon got a WPA job . . . and we were able to move. This job, plus the few pennies my husband made driving a cab, permitted us some comfort with the child. I worked there for two years and was then laid off under the eighteen-month clause.[3] I have now been forced back on relief, but I hope to soon be back on the project. I've tried everywhere for private employment, but no dice. My countless searches for work have been in vain. My work on the project was interesting and creative. I was very much interested in it and should naturally like to continue it, if possible.

3. In 1939 congressional opponents of the WPA demanded a reduction in the wages paid to employees of WPA projects and a requirement that no one remain on program's rolls for more than eighteen months.

We Saved Their Chestnuts Once: Republican Congressmen on War in Europe (1939)

The article excerpted here was published in the New Jersey Republican, *an Essex County–based weekly newspaper. It appeared a few months before Germany invaded Poland, precipitating British and French declarations of war on the aggressor.*

All seven of the congressmen quoted here were Republicans, as were eleven of the fourteen members of New Jersey's congressional delegation that term.[1]

In the years after World War I Americans were nearly united in their belief that the country should not again involve itself in a European war. Even as war loomed, Americans (although most strongly favored the Allies) wanted the country to stay out of war. As the situation in Europe worsened, isolationism became more and more confined to the conservative wing of the Republican party.

America should . . . not repeat what happened more than twenty years ago and transformed the flower of our young manhood into white crosses on foreign soil. . . .

America . . . should not sacrifice its youth to satisfy the greed of other nations or become involved in their disputes. Protect America? Yes. Spend millions for our own defense? Yes. But to repeat what happened before? No.

A survey among New Jersey's congressional delegation indicates they share the sentiment of their constituents that we should mind our own business.

Says Representative [Robert Winthrop] Kean: "I believe that we should keep out of any war . . . unless the United States itself is in danger."

Says Representative George N. Seger: "As the World War Mayor of

1. Those quoted were Walter S. Jeffries, Margate City, served in Congress 1939–1941; Robert W. Kean, Livingston, served in Congress 1939–1959; Frank C. Osmers, Jr., Haworth, served in Congress 1939–1941, 1952–1965; D. Lane Powers, Trenton, served in Congress 1932–1945; George N. Seger, Passaic City, served in Congress 1923–1940; J. Parnell Thomas, Allendale, served in Congress 1936–1950; Albert L. Vreeland, East Orange, served in Congress 1939–1943.

Bruce Craven, "We Should Keep Out of War," *New Jersey Republican* 1, no. 11 (May 1939):12.

Passaic, one whose two sons served overseas during the whole period of that conflict, I know something of the meaning of war.

"I do not want to see American participation in any more foreign wars. This is a time for Americans everywhere to keep their heads clear, their feet on the ground. . . . By thinking and acting in terms of peace we can avoid war and help the world to avoid war."

Representative Albert L. Vreeland feels that . . . "Europe for a year has intermittently been in the throes of conflict and in all probability will continue to be as long as there are persons using different basic languages and living in so close proximity as they are. . . . The difficulties that arise across the ocean are none of our affair. . . . It is about time we stopped trying to be a police force for the entire globe and tend to our own affairs. . . ."

Representative D. Lane Powers . . . has this reaction: . . . "I can see no reason . . . that we should become embroiled in the conflict which is apparently forthcoming.

"We pulled Europe's chestnuts out of the fire in 1917. We not only lost some of our finest young men in that conflict, but got stuck with the war debts besides. . . . Our interests lie primarily and solely in this Hemisphere."

Representative J. Parnell Thomas . . . says: "I was a participant in the last World War. . . . I see no reason why we should again sacrifice the lives of hundreds of thousands of our young manhood in order to help settle the squabbles abroad.

"Throughout the history of the world the nations of Europe have warred against one another. . . . You and I will never see the day when Europe will be completely at peace. It is, however, their business. If they don't know enough to keep out of war, then I see no reason why we should think that it is our business. . . .

"On the other hand, I firmly believe that we should maintain an unusually strong defense; that we should have the strongest navy in the world and more than adequate land forces. If we do this and if we will mind our own business, we will never have to worry about the possibility of the United States going to war."

Representative Walter S. Jeffries . . . states: "I am utterly opposed to the United States involving itself into a European war. I favor America building a strong defense and preserving the policy of George Washington,[2] to keep out of entanglements and alliances."

---

2. At the conclusion of his presidency George Washington issued a Farewell Address to the nation in which he argued that European interests were only remotely related to the interests of the United States and advised the country to avoid "permanent alliances."

Representative Frank C. Osmers, Jr.,[3] . . . makes this statement: "The last time we engaged in a European war it cost us one hundred thousand men and thirty-two billion dollars directly,[4] and it has been estimated that the total indirect cost of the war to the nation was upward of 333 billions of dollars. For what? To make the world safe for democracy. And today, twenty years after Versailles,[5] there is less democracy on the face of the earth than at any time in the past 75 years.

"We should have learned that while we can dictate a victory in Europe we can not dictate a peace. . . .

"We should lend our influence to peace in Europe, but not our men, our money, or our guns. It is my generation which will have to fight the next war. We will defend the shores of our nation to the last man, but we will not die to defend someone else's political ideology. Let those who make the next war fight the next war."

3. Congressman Osmers resigned his seat in the House of Representatives to enlist in the army on December 8, 1941, the day war was declared. He was awarded a Bronze Star for his meritorious service during the war, and returned to Congress in 1952.
4. The precise figure of American war deaths was 112,432, more than half of those from disease. During the war government expenditures totaled about $26 billion. With interest rates, veterans' benefits, and other costs included, the direct cost to the United States was about $112 billion.
5. The Treaty of Versailles drew up the covenant of the League of Nations and dictated the terms by which World War I was formally ended. The United States Senate rejected the treaty and the U.S. never joined the League of Nations.

DOCUMENT 78

"Our Little Colored Family": A Black Woman Trying to Get a Job (1940)

Helen Jackson Lee came to Trenton in February 1940 with her husband and two children. Widowed by a car accident a few months after she arrived, Lee stayed in Trenton and resolved to find a job with the state government.

Her 1978 book, Nigger in the Window, *recounts her lifelong encounter with racism and sexism in the civil service. She struggled for more than two years merely to find a clerical job with the state. In the excerpt below, her pride in finally landing a job is mixed with bitterness at the paternalism that underlay the episode. In addition the passage reflects Lee's prejudice against recent immigrants who were receiving rights denied to African Americans.*

Ultimately, Helen Jackson Lee worked for the state for nearly thirty years before retiring in 1973. At every step along her way she met and overcame obstacles. Her book is an important record of the efforts of an articulate black woman to find a place in the world in the years before the civil rights movement and affirmative action programs.

In July 1940 I . . . set out to find a job with the State of New Jersey. . . .

People said the State House . . . was just about owned by the Irish; they held the majority of the civil service and political positions. . . . It didn't matter to black people whether the State House belonged to the Irish or not. The important fact was that, with few exceptions, it was all white. Even the groundskeepers, janitors, painters, cafeteria workers were white. What hurt most was that most of the menial workers could hardly speak English. . . . Black women—clerks, stenographers, and secretaries—were out of the picture. . . .

Trenton was a segregated town. While black people could sit anywhere on the buses, they couldn't eat in the better restaurants or hotel dining rooms downtown. And long lines of blacks waited to climb the steps to the peanut galleries . . . of the theaters and first-run movie houses. It was an embarrassment for blacks to watch their leading physicians, school principals, and local leaders standing back while poorly dressed factory workers, some speaking Eastern European dialects, walked in free to sit where they wished. . . .

Trenton was an industrial city with many potteries, steel mills,

Helen Jackson Lee, *Nigger in the Window* (Garden City, N.Y.: Doubleday, 1978), 129–164. Copyright © 1978 by Helen Jackson Lee. Used by permission of Doubleday, a division of Bantam Doubleday Dell Publishing Group, Inc.

factories, and a large auto plant, but the production lines were almost solidly white. Black men swept the floors, moved heavy equipment . . . and performed other burdensome tasks. In the business sections they were almost invisible except as window cleaners, janitors, or elevator operators. There were no black salespeople in the stores, banks, or business offices. They were hired as maids, package wrappers, or seamstresses. . . .

I still clung to the hope that somehow I could become independent, even in a wretched town like Trenton.

In the South, black people scoffed at a widow who didn't put forth an effort to keep her family together. . . . I was determined to . . . show people up North that I was strong and could survive in hostile surroundings. . . .

While the children were in school I searched for work. I went into insurance [and] real estate . . . offices, banks, and department . . . stores. What did I see? A sea of hostile white faces. Wherever I went it was always the same—whites sat behind the desks, the typewriters, the cash registers. . . . As I watched white girls and women operating business machines, the sounds were like siren voices calling me to come in and work. But I couldn't get past the front desk. Where were all my dark-skinned brothers and sisters? They were in there somewhere, but they were pushing the brooms, washing the windows, carrying out the trash, hanging up the garments on store racks, moving in and out of the side doors with packages, and attending public washrooms. There were no black clerks to take my insurance premiums. If I had had any money to save, it would have been a white teller who recorded it. . . .

I had plenty of company looking for work. While the automobile plants were converting to defense plants and hiring masses of white people, they were rejecting black men and women. The excuse was the inability to produce papers to show their citizenship. Since most black people applying for jobs had been born in the South where records of births, especially black babies, were seldom kept it meant endless delays. . . . Meanwhile black applicants watched in anger while droves of Italians, whose mother country was our enemy, walked through the lines showing only a baptismal certificate or naturalization papers. Some blacks blamed the sabotage of airplanes on these Italians when reports of malfunctioning planes came back to the states. . . .

I was still determined to break into the white clerical world. Luckily I passed a state civil-service examination for clerk-typist. That was only the beginning, I knew. My most difficult task would be to get past the front door of state offices so zealously guarded by white defenders of the status quo.

I also had to deal with friends who thought I was a fool to work in an office when I could teach. . . .

In March 1942 . . . I read, "Your name has been certified to this department for the position of clerk-typist." . . . I was nervous when the young blonde receptionist took the certification and disappeared into an inner office. When . . . I saw the look on her face I knew she had sounded the alarm to the interviewer: "It's a colored woman!"

The interviewer made no effort to stand and greet me, simply motioned for me to take a seat directly in front of the desk. . . . Somehow it didn't surprise me when the interviewer said abruptly, "I'm not going to hire you. . . . As long as I'm in charge of personnel, no colored women are going to work in these offices." . . .

I received exactly a dozen notices before I was finally hired . . . at the New Jersey Unemployment Compensation Commission. . . . "When can you start?" Mr. Jordan asked. I felt like shouting, "Right away!" but I held back. . . . Mr. Jordan told me to report in three days. "Welcome to our little colored family," he said as he escorted me to the door. . . .

Later I was to learn that this meant being among the dozen or so Negro employees who were set apart, almost as wards of the Governor, from the other employees at UCC. Governor Hoffman[1] had been labeled by many Negroes as the best friend colored people had in New Jersey. My first Christmas at the UCC I learned . . . that each member of the little colored family was supposed to contribute five dollars toward a gift for the Governor.

1. Harold G. Hoffman was governor from 1935 through 1938. He took up the post of executive director of the Unemployment Compensation Compensation when he left the governorship. A few weeks after Hoffman's 1954 death, convincing evidence was released that showed a pattern of blackmail and embezzlement spanning much of his political career.

Away from the Democratic Ideal: Segregation in the Schools (1941)

The author of the following passage is notable in many respects. Marion Thompson Wright, an East Orange native and daughter of a domestic servant, was the first black historian to receive a Ph.D. from Columbia University. She was the first black woman to write about the history of New Jersey, and one of the first professionals to write about the history of African Americans in New Jersey.

The book, whose foreword is excerpted here, was titled The Education of Negroes in New Jersey *and was Wright's Ph.D. thesis. In it she combined three themes. Primarily, she focused on the manner in which New Jersey's policies had hindered its black citizens in their efforts to provide quality education to their children. She also emphasized the degree to which blacks had overcome the obstacles of discrimination and race prejudice. Lastly, by emphasizing things such as the 1881 law outlawing racial discrimination in public schools, she found reason for some optimism about the possibility for the creation of a socio-legal climate that would encourage black achievement.*

This passage describes the variety of racial patterns to be found in New Jersey's schools in 1939 and 1940 as she was writing her study. The book itself chronicles the historical background of these many forms of segregation, which Wright was hoping to help end.

The national context of Wright's study is significant. In the late 1930s the National Association for the Advancement of Colored People was spearheading an effort to challenge the "separate but equal" doctrine the Supreme Court had established in its Plessy v. Ferguson *ruling of 1896. In its rulings the Court had gradually been demanding hard evidence that separate educational facilities were in fact equal. In 1954, in the famous case of* Brown v. Board of Education of Topeka, Kansas, *the Court abandoned its separate-but-equal doctrine in favor of a view that "separate educational facilities" were "inherently unequal." This ruling put an end to the remaining segregated educational facilities in New Jersey.*

In this state almost every conceivable practice governing the education of Negro children could be found. These practices vary from the complete segregation of these children in the elementary schools in

Marion Manola Thompson [Wright], *The Education of Negroes in New Jersey* (New York: Bureau of Publications, Teachers College, Columbia University, 1940), v, vi. Reprinted by permission.

some of the southern counties of the state to situations in certain of the northern counties where there is a complete integration of the Negro children in the regular schools, which are staffed with teachers appointed according to merit and without regard to their racial identity. Between these two extremes there exist varying combinations of segregation and integration, such as: separate elementary schools and mixed junior and senior high schools; separate elementary and junior high schools and mixed high schools; divided building, one-half for whites and one-half for Negroes; separate classes and teachers for each race within the same building; separate elementary schools for each race on the same school site; separate elementary schools joined by a common auditorium. In some instances the Negro children are taught by Negro teachers in the regular subjects and by white teachers in the special subjects. Strangely enough in the case of one school system with an otherwise segregated setup in the elementary schools, a colored teacher is teaching white . . . classes. . . . Trenton, the capital of the state, is one of the very few places where segregation is carried into the secondary level, for there separate housing[1] is provided as far as the ninth grade.

Added to the provocative situations noted above is the pertinent fact that the state legislature in 1881 enacted a statute which prohibited the exclusion of any child from any public school on account of nationality, religion, or race. Yet there are at present in the state at least seventy separate schools for Negro children. This represents an increase of eighteen such schools within the last two decades. That the tendency is away from rather than toward the democratic ideal in education is clearly evident.

1. She means a separate building.

"Can People Be Heroic Without Knowing It?": Women in Defense Plants (1943)

The author of this passage, Elizabeth Hawes, was not a representative "Rosie the Riveter," as women working in war industries were often called. Hawes was a journalist who went to work at the Wright Aeronautical Plant in Paterson with the intention of writing about her experience. Nevertheless, her book is a valuable document of women's experiences at such plants.

The women with whom Hawes worked faced hostility from the men in the plant for a number of reasons. Some men simply did not believe women belonged in heavy industry. Also, women were threatening because management could use them to lower wages, and there was the real question of who would be employed when the war was over.

From the women's point of view this work provided a sense of pride that few women had experienced from their previous jobs. The work was hard and dirty, the men sometimes oppressive, and the additional burden of domestic responsibilities was great. Nonetheless, many women who did what Hawes did look back on the time they spent in these plants as the best of their lives.

I was . . . directed to go to a trade school at my own expense for two weeks. If Wright's were not then ready to take me on, I'd be kept at school but put on the payroll at 60 cents an hour. . . .

At the Trade School there were more men than gals and Wright's took all the men into the plant after two weeks, leaving us wenches to languish on the payroll. Also, the instructors tried to teach the men more about the machines than they did the gals. As the machines in the school were mere toys, this didn't matter much. . . .

Every one of us girls in my class asked for the third shift—the one that works from midnight to 8:00 A.M. We figured we could arrange the rest of our lives better by working that shift than any other. Two out of twelve of us had children, one being me. . . .

I had a son—Gavrik—age five. He went to a nursery school which opened at 8:45 A.M. and closed at 3:00 P.M.—but had an after school session for the children of working mothers which went until 6:00 P.M. My husband and myself completed the family. . . .

Elizabeth Hawes, *Why Women Cry: or Wenches with Wrenches* (New York: Reynal & Hitchcock, 1943), 58–69, 76–81, 134–137.

In addition to getting Gavrik from school three or four days a week, making his supper, and putting him to bed, I had to do the food buying. . . .

I shopped every Friday morning after I went into the plant, snatched about four hours sleep before getting Gavrik from school, preparing our dinner, and packing myself off to work. I found I could hold out during the eight hours of work from midnight Friday to eight Saturday morning on the four hours sleep and the strength of the knowledge that Saturday night was my night off. . . .

The reason I, like most working mothers, wanted the third shift was because there was no provision on the schedule for anyone but me to take care of Gavrik in the daytime if he got sick and couldn't go to school. I knew that in such an emergency I could give up my sleep and catch up sometime, somehow. . . .

It was a huge place, this Wright Plant Seven. . . . Sections and departments flowed endlessly into and out of one another, divided only by streets along which tooted little trucks. Around the machine-blinded corners, people on bicycles shot out at you. Each department centered around a cluster of little wooden buildings housing the foreman and sub-foreman, as well as the cribs where some of the tools we needed for work were stored. . . .

Helene, also a working mother, and I were put into the same section of a department which did every kind of thing to make a gear. Our job was grinding the outside of the gears on what are known as OD grinders. Adjacent to us was a section which did the inside grinding on ID grinders. OD and ID stand for outside and inside diameter, respectively.

We polished off the long, round part of the gears and also the flat surfaces of the flanges. A gear is apt to look quite like a candlestick in its early stages. You later discover that most of the stick part is there merely so you can hold the piece in your machine and gets cut off in the end. . . .

Most of the women who are going to the machines now never did a piece of creative work in their lives. The nearest many of them ever came to it was creating children and there nature controls everything after the first round.

These women used to be sandwich makers, telephone operators, servants, salesgirls, secretaries, or housewives. Their jobs, though they might have been vital, were uncreative in the extreme. When you work the machine that makes the bit that turns the motor that raises the plane that's going to soar in the clouds—or a piece of the Frigidaire, for that matter, that's going to keep the food from rotting—when you do that, you feel creative. . . .

It is a constant fight, if you work on the third shift, to make any kind of adjustment to the rest of the world. You come home about 8:30 A.M., eat some breakfast or dinner or whatever you call it. Then you know you'd better get to bed quick because if you have to get your child from school or want to have dinner with your husband, or anyone who has normal working hours, you must be up around 5:00 P.M. So you force yourself to try and sleep immediately after work.

If you have children coming home for lunch, or the cleaning to do, or if you shop every day for food, your sleep gets sandwiched in between household jobs. If you do all the daily laundry, as almost every woman in the plant did, instead of catching up with your sleep on Sunday, you wash and iron all day. . . .

Our section began with Rodger, who'd once been a grinder for five years and then spent six selling some household device all over the country; Jessie, who'd been a teacher and had two sons in the army; Helene, mother and former housewife whose husband had gone to war; myself. Then came Janet who'd worked in an embroidery shop, been married five months, and was waiting for her tool-designing husband to stop being deferred; Sylvia, a Negro wife and mother whose husband had a job in Washington; Bill and Charlie, both ex-liquor salesmen, and a jolly little Scotch woman named Nelly who had worked in England in a plant during the last war. . . .

One . . . time I . . . heard one of the theme songs many of the men sang over and over to themselves as they looked around them. "Women, women, women; What's going to happen after the war? Will the men ever get their jobs back?" . . .

The women talked a little about the letters they did or didn't get from their husbands or sons or lovers. But almost never was the war mentioned directly.

At first it used to get me down a little. And then I thought perhaps the war is such a terrible thing, nobody wants to speak about it. Maybe they care so much, they can't talk of it. . . .

In the locker room, the talk ran along more or less like this:

"When do you do your shopping?"

"Oh, first thing when I get off the bus. Then I usually do a little cleaning when I get home."

"When do you sleep?"

"I get a nap before the kids come home for lunch, and before they get back from school. Usually sleep a little after dinner."

"I only had three hours sleep yesterday. Thought I'd never get the laundry done."

"I couldn't get to work last night because my husband is sick and now my kid's got it too."

"Why are you here so early every night?"

"Oh, you know, after the dishes are done and all, well, it's really time for the family to go to bed. So I come on over here in an early bus and rest here."

"And beans were thirty-five cents. I just won't buy them."

Night after night, the same talk: the price of food; the sleep or the no sleep; the sick children or husbands; the hours it took to get to work; the food we bought to eat at work, warmed over from the early morning, sometimes outright bad.

Can people be heroic without knowing it?

"Gosh Darn This War": Correspondence Between a Young Woman and Her Husband at War (1943–1944)

The letters excerpted here went between Marian Merritt, a night duty nurse, and her husband, Private First Class Harold B. Merritt of the 163rd Signal-Photo Company. Harold Merritt went overseas in August 1943. We don't know much about the Merritts beyond what we learn from this correspondence. Harold returned safely from the war, so we may assume he and Marian picked up where they had left off, as they so deeply desired.

These letters provide an intimate glimpse into the thoughts and feelings of Harold and Marian Merritt and by extension the thousands of young couples whom the war separated and whose strenuous efforts to make up for lost time caused the "baby boom" of the late 1940s and the 1950s.

September 20, 1943
My darling,

Today was another uneventful one, as is usual these days. I slept well, . . . dreamt of you. . . .

Last night I was talking over the Army nurse situation with some of the girls in the hospital and I've just about made up my mind to go into the service. You're away now and no doubt will not be home until this thing is over, so I'd like to know what you think about it. There's no possibility, because I'm married, of overseas duty so I'd just be assigned to some base hospital here in the country—unless, of course, I volunteered for it. It will give me something to do and I'll see the country too; then I'll feel that I'm doing something to help too. If I thought that you'd be coming home between now and the end of the war, I wouldn't even suggest this, honestly darling. So let me know what you think.

November 8, 1943
Darling,

Here it is our sixth anniversary and I'm sitting here reliving in my mind all that happened on that day of days, . . . feeling so alone. . . . I

Manuscript Group #1337, New Jersey Historical Society. Reprinted by permission of the New Jersey Historical Society.

just hope that we won't have to spend too many more without each other. It seems so long since I've been in your arms. . . . We were so happy six months ago. . . .

I'm hoping for a letter one of these days—there haven't been any for eleven days now. But I've faithfully written every day hoping that you would benefit by it. It's at times like this that everything looks so dismal. If I only knew where you were. Of course I have an idea, but then we never can be sure of anything these days, can we darling: nothing but our love.

November 29, 1943
My Darling:

I wanted to ask you about . . . a thing which came to mind last night while reading an article in *Reader's Digest*. . . . It has to do with our plans after the war is over and I get home—particularly in connection with where we would live, which would also have control over a lot of other things. . . . The article . . . stated things would be high priced—homes, material, furniture, furnishings, cars, etc. So I wondered whether you had thought about our living at my house or yours for a while until we were organized, [could] rent an apartment somewhere, or what other alternatives you had in mind, hon. Of course we can't make any decisions until we are together to talk it all over. But write and give me your opinion about the matter.

Didn't tell you yet how much I love you, darling, but you know I do and always will—desperately.

December 6, 1943

A year ago . . . you were leaving to go back from your Thanksgiving furlough. It doesn't seem possible that so much could have happened in so short a time. But that's life, I guess. I don't quite know you see, I haven't really lived mine yet. I'm waiting for you to come home, dear, so we can do it together.

December 7, 1943
My dearest darling:

Seven months ago tonight was my last single night . . . and a girl never forgets things like that. But really dear it's not that I'm thinking about, it's all that came after it during the three wonderful months that followed with the best husband in the world. . . . I've thanked God so many times for all that, believe me darling; it's just too bad it didn't last a while longer.

Now that we've been at war for two years I was beginning to hope that it would be all over before long and then tonight's paper had a headline which read, "War with Germany will probably be over by next December 7," which sounds a bit discouraging I'd say. Of course it's newspaper stuff and we never really know what's going on over there I guess. But it's not the kind of thing any of us like to read. . . .

Don't let me discourage you. . . . I'm getting the little things ready that we'll need for our home and I'll be here no matter how long it takes, waiting with open arms to have you back where you've always belonged—with me. . . . I'll never be able to do enough for you, to make up for all we've missed.

December 10, 1943

I didn't sleep so well today. . . . I kept thinking about you, wondering as I often do just how long it will be before we'll be together again. . . . I know that God will take care of everything and one of these days our patience will be rewarded. . . .

About my going into the service, . . . I do realize I have a job home here—an important one—and I'm going to try to do a good one just for you. Loving you as I do there's no need to explain any further, so don't worry, my dearest, I'll be here planning for our future, taking care of the little things that come up and waiting faithfully for the one I love to come home.

December 11, 1943

One thing I want you to do, hon, is on December 31 at 5:00 P.M. it will be midnight here so just for a couple minutes stop and think about me, hon, and all the things that have happened and I'll do likewise here. So even though we can't be together in body, we will be in mind. Of course we always are anyway, but we'll make this just a little bit extra special, dear. I know that both our prayers will be that another year will see us together once more living and loving the way that we always planned.

December 30, 1943

My own darling:

Today was pretty cold, just like a usual winter's day. Bessie and I went to Midvale and had a nice visit with [your] folks. . . . I . . . slept real well for a change. But no wonder my darling. I had your flannel pajamas on and slept in your bed. . . .

Since Monday I've had thirteen wonderful letters from you, my dearest one, and . . . I'm feeling so happy since they came. I'm full of pep. My energy seems to be boundless. I'm so very happy in the thoughts that this new year will bring you back to me. That is if God hears our fervent prayers, and I'm sure he does. . . . You mean everything in this world to me.

January 5, 1944

On the way in the hospital I met . . . my favorite maternity doctor. . . . I got to know him well when I worked up there last year. . . . So tonight the first thing he did was ask me whether or not I'm pregnant. . . . I said no, of course, and proceeded to ask him how I could be, without you here; so he said I should hurry up and when I do to come to him. . . . I told him there was nobody that wanted a baby any more than I do, but it was just an impossibility right now. Of course when we do have our twins I wouldn't think of letting anyone but him deliver me. . . .

January 20, 1944

My Darling:

How is Doc Wabbit's little bunny today? Just as lonesome as ever, and don't we know it. Gosh darn this war anyhow. It certainly is proving very inconvenient. . . .

I know it may sound monotonous to express our true feelings for each other, but I don't want you to stop, hon, for now. It is all we can do until we are together and it helps so much.

January 29, 1944

My dearest darling:

When I stop and think of how completely happy we could be, darling, it just about breaks my heart. To realize that this awful thing will go on indefinitely, that I can't even begin to plan for our future together. . . . I long to see you darling, to be with you. . . . The worst part is that we don't know how much longer it will be and I'm so lonesome and heartsick now. I don't know what to do at times. You mean so much to me and here's a couple of what should be our best years taken right out of our lives, these years when we should be enjoying ourselves and our love together. Nothing I do, not anything, seems right or complete because you're not here to share it with me as you should be.

Peace and Problems

NOTABLE EVENTS

1950   Korean War begins

1953   Korean War ends; Rosenbergs executed; New Jersey Turnpike opens

1954   Supreme Court *Brown* decision; Garden State Parkway opens

1955   Montgomery bus boycott

1956   Elvis Presley releases "Hound Dog"; Salk polio vaccine approved

1957   Soviet Union launches Sputnik I; baby boom peaks (4.3 million births)

1958   Eating clubs at Princeton University issue ethno-religious quotas

1959   Castro takes power in Cuba; D. H. Lawrence's *Lady Chatterley's Lover* banned from mails

1960   Sit-in in Greensboro, North Carolina; birth control pills approved for sale; televised presidential debates; John F. Kennedy elected President

1961   Peace Corps founded; Bay of Pigs invasion; Freedom Riders test segregation in the South; Eisenhower warns of "military-industrial complex"

1962   Rachel Carson publishes *Silent Spring*; John Glenn orbits globe; Marilyn Monroe dies; Cuban Missile Crisis

1963   Betty Friedan publishes *The Feminine Mystique*; march on Washington; Kennedy assassinated

1964   Beatles perform in the United States; President Johnson signs comprehensive civil rights law

1965   President Johnson expands American involvement in the Vietnam War; antiwar demonstrations; Malcolm X assassinated; Watts riot in Los Angeles

1966   National Organization for Women (NOW) established; Mildred B. Hughes is first woman elected to state senate

1967   Race riots in Newark, Detroit, and other cities; Thurgood Marshall becomes first black Supreme Court justice

1968   My Lai massacre in Vietnam; Martin Luther King, Jr., assassinated, riots in 125 cities; Robert F. Kennedy assassinated

1969   Stonewall riot; Apollo II moon landing; Woodstock festival; first women undergraduates enroll at Princeton University

1970   Invasion of Cambodia; American university students killed in demonstrations

1971   Twenty-sixth Amendment (eighteen-year-olds vote) takes effect; Attica prison riot

1972   Nixon visits China; George Wallace shot

1973   American Indians protest at Wounded Knee, South Dakota; *Roe* v. *Wade*; Vietnam cease-fire agreement; state supreme court declares unconstitutional the property-tax–based system of funding public schools

1974   Hank Aaron breaks Babe Ruth's home run record; Richard M. Nixon resigns from the presidency

1975   Last American forces leave Vietnam; first state income tax initiated

1976   Casino gambling legalized in Atlantic City

1979   Three Mile Island nuclear power plant accident; Shah of Iran deposed, hostages taken; Soviets invade Afghanistan

1980   Ronald Reagan elected President; five southern counties vote to secede from New Jersey in nonbinding referendum

1981   Hostages released in Iran

1983   New Jersey Supreme Court issues Mount Laurel II decision

1984   Geraldine Ferraro becomes first woman major-party candidate for Vice President

Selected New Jersey Population Statistics, 1950–1990

Year	1950	1960	1970	1980	1990
Population (× 1,000)	4,835	6,067	7,171	7,365	7,730
% Female	50.7	51.0	51.6	52.0	51.7
Race					
% White	93.3	91.3	88.6	83.2	82.4
% Black	6.6	8.5	10.7	12.6	13.8
Other	0.1	0.2	0.7	4.2	3.8
% Urban	86.5	88.5	88.9	89.0	n.a.
People per square mile	651.9	818.0	966.8	993.0	1,042.2
N.J. % of U.S. population	3.2	3.4	3.5	3.3	3.1

ADDITIONAL SOURCE: New Jersey State Data Center, *Total Population, 1980–1990* (Trenton, 1991).

Church, Fire Brigade, and Children: Cranbury Township (1956)

Briton James Morris, author of the following description of Cranbury (Middlesex County), is one of the best-known travel writers in the English language. A few years before this piece was published, for example, he covered the first expedition to climb Mount Everest, the highest mountain on earth. In 1972, James Morris became Jan Morris after surgery completed the transformation from male to female that Morris had begun a few years earlier with hormone treatments.

Jan Morris has written about many places in the world—from suburban New Jersey to Calcutta—and published in magazines as diverse as Better Homes and Gardens *and* Rolling Stone. *The book from which this excerpt comes was awarded a prestigious British literary prize. In Morris's description of Cranbury one can detect the voice of the foreigner in some of his observations, but one also reads the comments of a perceptive observer of small-town life.*

I lived for a time with my wife and children in a little . . . village called Cranbury. . . . It is just a small market center, where farmers do their shopping and a few commuters to the city have established their homes. . . .

The place is at its best on a frosty evening in winter, when . . . the white weatherboard houses of Main Street shine in the moonlight. On such nights the people of Cranbury often go skating on the village pond, to the accompaniment of music from loudspeakers mounted on the roof of the fire station. . . . There are farmers in check shirts and ear muffs, moving with unexpected grace. Girls waltz pointedly in pairs, wearing blue ski trousers and white jumpers.[1] A man who looks like an insurance agent steers a ponderous course over the ice, his black hat still sedately on his head. Small children totter in desperate instability toward the bank and boys with toboggans shoot about like rockets. Various men with a tendency toward authority stand in municipal attitudes on the perimeter.

Across the road in the fire station the fire engines stand vigilantly gleaming. . . . The fire station is a center of activity in Cranbury,

1. A British term for a pullover sweater.

James Morris, *As I Saw the U.S.A.* (New York: Pantheon, 1956), 10–17. Reprinted by permission of the Peters Fraser & Dunlop Group Ltd.

following an old American tradition. For many years all fire brigades were amateur and voluntary, and it became a basic duty of the rural American male to join the local brigade; fire fighting became a social function and the fire brigade acquired the status of a team or club. In Cranbury this system still prevails. The fire chief is the local garage man, and very proud he is of the smartness and alertness of the brigade. . . .

It is a fairly well-heeled village and there is a good deal of comfort in these white houses. Everyone has a refrigerator, of course, and most people have television; many also possess washing machines, dishwashers, gadgets for making waste matter swill away down the sink, cookers that time themselves and ring a bell when the meat is done, radios that wake you up with a cup of coffee, electric sewing machines, white telephones, and microphones to transmit the sounds of sleepless babies. Almost every family has its car . . . and the slimmest daughter handles it like a lorry[2] driver. Almost every house has its central heating and from time to time a truck arrives to pump oil through heavy pipes into the basement furnaces. . . .

The predominant influence in Cranbury is . . . the Presbyterian church whose white steeple rises gracefully above the housetops. Religion in such a place as this is at once devotional, philanthropic, and social. On Sunday mornings Main Street is crowded with the cars of the churchgoers, and the sidewalks (lined with trees) are full of people dressed very decidedly in their Sunday best. . . . The boys wear bow ties and coats with fur collars, the girls frilly party dresses.

You can hardly escape the advances of a lively American church of this kind. Almost before you have settled in your house you find yourself irrevocably committed to one activity or another. It may be the Stitch-and-Chatter group on Thursday, or the Helping Hand Club on Monday evenings. Perhaps there is a bazaar, or a discussion group, or a Bible study class, or even dinner at the minister's. . . . So friendly are these approaches, and so sincere, that you can scarcely object to them. . . .

They not only contribute to a healthy (if slightly priggish) climate of thought, but also perform works of active good. Each year bands of migrant workers, mostly Negroes, arrive in the district to help with the potato harvest. They are very poor, and often ruthlessly bullied by the Negro contractors who have engaged them and brought them from the South in lorries. They live in shacks and huts provided by the farmers, communing only with themselves, strangers to the country, like Israelites in Egypt. Every year the good people of Cranbury, through their various societies, take care of these unfortunates, ar-

2. A British term for truck.

ranging for the schooling of their children, providing meals and occasional outings. . . .

Life in Cranbury revolves around the church, the fire brigade . . . and the children. . . . "We love our children," say the road signs outside many American towns; rather as a Tibetan hamlet might announce its belief in rebirth, for indeed it goes without saying. . . .

The little American . . . often turns out to be wonderfully good material. I remember the little boys of Cranbury, muffled to the ears, of course, in protective clothing, out in the snow with a shovel in their hands and a dollar in prospect, working hard and cheerfully . . . to clear the garden path. I remember with gratitude the girls who would come to our house, in between dates, to look after the baby with great care and competence. The truth is that American children develop national characteristics disconcertingly early. This is the land of opportunism, and the children realize it soon. The boys see no point in unnecessary hardship or risk, but are greedy for . . . useful knowledge and will work well for fair reward. The girls seem to know before they leave the nursery that a good marriage must be their goal, and regulate their lives accordingly. . . . The first clause of a "program for education" produced by the National Education Association of America reads: "All youth needs to develop salable skills and those understandings and attitudes that make the worker an intelligent and productive participant in economic life." For the boy, this mouthful means a grasp of the methods of self-advancement; for the girl, a neat hand with a lipstick . . .

Anyway, the Cranbury children . . . are both friendly and well-mannered. On the frozen lake in the moonlight they look enchanting, but then so does almost everyone (though nobody could claim ethereal charm for the man in the black hat). . . . In the eighteenth century Crèvecoeur[3] posed the celebrated question: "What is he, the American, this new man?" [One] might well go to Cranbury for an answer. . . . A characteristic citizen, the elderly man leaning against the wall of the fire station, . . . knows little of Europe and its values, but is quite willing to learn; dislikes and distrusts authority, but is ready to cooperate if nicely asked; can be a fearful bore, but tries to reach his conclusions fairly; enjoys watching the skating, but will be up early next morning; cares not two hoots for smart Princeton or dazzling New York; owns a fine car and a sound bank balance, but still approaches life with some humility.

3. Michel-Guillaume Jean de Crèvecoeur (1735–1813). A Frenchman who lived in Orange County, New York, from 1769 to 1780. During this period he wrote *Letters from an American Farmer*, in which he posed the question quoted by Morris.

Income Distribution (c. 1960)

The late 1950s and early 1960s were one of the longest and steadiest periods of prosperity in United States history. During these years the view became prevalent that the labor problem had been solved. American workers seemed to be part of a homogenous American middle class. The violent conflicts between labor and capital that had marked the previous seventy or eighty years were a relic of the past. Surveys found that nearly 60 percent of American families had annual incomes between three thousand and ten thousand dollars. This compared very favorably to the less than a third of Americans whose standard of living was middle class in the last year of prosperity before the Great Depression.

Pictures are not the only type of nonverbal evidence that historians have at their disposal; statistics are another. Although they are imperfect representations of reality, they may be no more flawed than other types of data that historians use. Statistical evidence from the past needs to be approached with the same care as the other kinds of material in this volume.

The following table depicts the range of annual incomes in twelve New Jersey municipalities as reported in the 1960 U.S. census. All columns but the last one are percentages. The figures represent the percentage of families in the municipality named in the first column whose annual income fell into the range represented at the top of each column.

There are wide ranges of wealth evident in these towns and cities. For example, there was a variation in median family income of more than ten thousand dollars between the community with the highest (Millburn) and that with the lowest (Atlantic City).

Older cities had the lowest median incomes. Atlantic City, Camden, Newark, and Trenton all had at least three in eight families with incomes below five thousand dollars.

Residential suburbs of Bergen, Essex, and Union counties had the highest incomes. In Englewood, Fair Lawn, Millburn, and Livingston a third or more of the resident families earned over ten thousand dollars annually.

New Jersey Almanac: Tercentary Edition (Upper Montclair, N.J.: New Jersey Almanac, 1964), 703–707.

Family Income in Selected Cities, by Percentage of Families in Income Ranges and by Median Family Income

Income range	$0–$4,999	$5,000–$9,999	$10,000–$14,999	$15,000–$24,999	Over $25,000	Median family income
City						
Atlantic City	63.1	30.1	4.7	1.3	0.9	$4,108
Bayonne	30.3	52.0	13.5	3.9	0.4	$6,423
Camden	42.7	46.0	8.8	1.9	0.2	$5,471
Englewood	23.4	40.7	18.3	9.9	7.8	$7,827
Fair Lawn	11.2	55.2	23.4	8.2	2.1	$8,346
Levittown	9.2	70.2	17.6	3.0	0.1	$7,654
Livingston	8.7	46.1	30.4	12.0	2.9	$9,566
Millburn	9.6	24.0	19.7	24.4	21.3	$14,145
Morristown	24.7	48.2	17.8	7.1	2.9	$7,339
Newark	43.8	44.4	9.2	2.5	0.5	$5,454
Pennsauken	20.6	55.0	19.1	4.2	0.9	$7,276
Trenton	38.5	44.8	11.5	3.9	0.5	$6,707

"Don't Be a Dishwasher!": Promoting Electrical Appliances (1963)

The prolonged prosperity of the postwar American economy led to a rapid rise in the disposable income of American families. As earnings rose so did the appetite for appliances and amusements such as televisions or dishwashers. The advertisement reprinted here was published in a magazine called Suburban Life. The magazine's title reflected the rapid growth of suburbs in New Jersey, and its articles were aimed at the suburban families who were producing the "baby boom" of these years.

It suggests three themes. First of all, the suburban family was premised on a full-time housewife and mother who sublimated her own needs in order to provide a nurturant and supportive environment for her husband and children. The year this ad ran author Betty Friedan criticized as The Feminine Mystique this idea that women could only fulfill themselves as mothers of families. Her runaway bestseller helped catalyse the women's movement.

The second argument, that labor-saving devices meant more free time, just doesn't wash. In 1965 a national survey found that the average American woman spent twenty-eight hours a week doing housework and twenty-six caring for her children. This fifty-four hour work week was roughly the same as that found by researchers in the decades before both world wars. The level of drudgery that housework requires had been reduced, but it still took time. With the dishwasher, in particular, the point is clear. Doing the dishes was often a task husband and children had helped with, but now with the new machine, it was so simple that mom could be left to do it and she could be expected to get the dishes cleaner than in the past.

The third noteworthy point concerns the source of the advertisement. It came from the company that sold electricity, and the advertisement was part of a larger campaign on its part to increase the consumption of electricity. The figure seen standing on the dishwasher is Reddy Kilowatt, the company's mascot in this effort.

BUY A
DISHWASHER

HAVE MORE TIME TO SPEND WITH YOUR FAMILY

An automatic dishwasher gives you more free time and your whole family benefits! Just flick a switch and the job is done. And space is no problem. A portable dishwasher can be used in any kitchen.

Don't be a dishwasher! Buy one at your favorite store!

New Ways on Top of Old Patterns: Willingboro in the Early 1960s

The United States is the most suburban nation in the world. Approximately 45 percent of Americans live in communities that consist mostly of owner-occupied, single-family homes lying an appreciable distance from their places of work. The trend toward this housing pattern has been under way for more than a century, but it accelerated in the decades after World War II.

Three communities—one on Long Island, New York, one outside Phila-delphia, and one in Burlington County, New Jersey—built by Levitt and Sons epitomize the postwar suburbs. The following excerpt comes from the summary chapter of a classic of American sociology: Herbert Gans's The Lev-ittowners, published in 1967 based on research (including two years' resi-dence in the community) Gans carried on from 1958 to 1962.

Most of the literature of the day was critical of suburban living, disparag-ing the monotony and conformity of the suburbs. Gans paints a different picture and simultaneously raises challenging questions about enduring class differences in America.

Levittown has . . . three basic shortcomings. . . .

One is the difficulty of coping with conflict. Like the rest of the country, Levittown is beset with conflict: class conflict between the lower-middle-class group and the smaller working- and upper-middle-class groups; generational conflict between adults, children, adolescents, and the elderly. . . .

The second shortcoming, closely related to the first, is the inability to deal with pluralism. People have not recognized the diversity of American society and they are not able to accept other life styles. Indeed, they cannot handle conflict because they cannot accept plu-ralism. Adults are unwilling to tolerate adolescent culture and vice versa. Lower-middle-class people oppose the ways of the working class and upper middle class, and each of these groups is hostile to the other two. Perhaps the inability to cope with pluralism is greater in Levittown than elsewhere because it is a community of young fam-ilies who are raising children. Children are . . . easily influenced by new ideas. As a result, their parents feel an intense need to defend

Herbert J. Gans, *The Levittowners* (New York: Vintage Books, 1967), 413–420.

familial values; to make sure that their children grow up according to parental norms and not by those of their playmates from another class. . . .

Working-class people do not want to be joined by lower-class neighbors or to be forced to adopt middle-class styles. Lower-middle-class people do not want more working-class neighbors or to be forced to adopt cosmopolitan styles, and upper-middle-class people want neither group to dominate them. . . . These . . . are fears about self-image. When people reject pluralism, they do so because accepting the viability of other ways of living suggests that their own is not as absolute as they need to believe. The outcome is the constant search for compatible people and the rejection of those who are different.

When the three class groups . . . must live together and share a common government, every group tries to make sure the institutions and facilities which serve the entire community maintain its own status and culture and no one is happy when the other group wins. If working-class groups can persuade the Township Committee to allocate funds for a firehouse, middle-class groups unite in a temporary coalition to guarantee that a library is also established. When the upper-middle-class group attempts to influence school policy to shape education to its standard, lower-middle-class residents raise the specter of Levittown aping Brookline and Scarsdale,[1] while working-class people become fearful that the schools will neglect discipline or that taxes will rise further. Consequently each group seeks power to prevent others from shaping the institutions that must be shared. . . . They do not demand lower taxes simply for economic reasons (except for those few really hard pressed) but in order to be sure that community institutions are responsive to their familial values and status needs. . . .

The third shortcoming . . . is the failure to establish a meaningful relationship between home and community. . . .

Levittowners deceive themselves into thinking that the . . . home is the single most influential unit in their lives. Of course, in one way they are right; it is the place where they can be most influential, for if they cannot persuade the decision-makers, they can influence family members. Home is also the site of maximal freedom, for within its walls people can do what they want more easily than anywhere else. . . . Levittowners have not yet become aware of how much they are a part of the national society and economy.

In viewing their homes as the center of life, Levittowners are still

1. Prosperous suburbs of, respectively, Boston and New York, known for the quality of their school systems.

using a societal model that fit the rural America of self-sufficient farmers. . . . Yet even though Levittowners . . . continue to be home-centered, they are much more "in the world" than their parents and grandparents were. . . . This generation trusts its neighbors, participates with them in social and civic activities, and no longer sees government as inevitably corrupt. Even working-class Levittowners have begun to give up the suspicion that isolated their ancestors from all but family and childhood friends. Similarly, the descendants of rural Protestant America have given up the xenophobia that turned previous generations against the Catholic and Jewish immigrants. . . .

These and other changes have come about not because people are now better or more tolerant human beings, but because they are affluent. For the Levittowners, life is not a fight for survival. . . . Income and status are equitably enough distributed so that neighbors are no longer treated as enemies, even if they are still criticized for social and cultural deviance. By any yardstick one chooses, Levittowners treat their fellow residents more ethically and more democratically than did their parents and grandparents. . . .

But beyond these changes, it is striking how little American culture among the Levittowners differs from what de Tocqueville[2] reported . . . a century ago. Of course, he was here before the economy needed an industrial proletariat, but the equality of men and women, the power of the child over his parents, the importance of the voluntary association, the social functions of the church and the rejection of high culture seem to be holdovers from his time, and so is the adherence to the traditional virtues: individual honesty, thrift, religiously inspired morality. . . . Still other eternal verities remain; class conflict is alive as ever, even if the struggle is milder and the have-nots in Levittown have much more than the truly poor. Working-class culture continues to flourish. . . . Affluence and better education have made a difference, but they have not made the factory worker middle class, any more than college attendance has made lower-middle-class people cosmopolitan.

What seems to have happened is that improvements and innovations are added to old culture patterns, giving affluent Americans a foot in several worlds. They have more knowledge and a broader outlook than their ancestors and they enjoy the advantages of technology, but these are superimposed on old ways. While conservative critics rail about technology's dehumanization of modern man, the Levittowners who spend their days programming computers come

2. Alexis de Tocqueville was a French aristocrat who published *Democracy in America* (1835) after an 1831 visit to the United States. It remains the most widely quoted study of American life ever written.

home at night to practice the very homely and old-fashioned virtues these critics defend. For example, they have television sets, but they watch much the same popular comedies and melodramas their ancestors saw on the nineteenth-century stage. The melodramas are less crude and vaudeville is more respectable—the girls dance with covered bosoms—but Ed Sullivan's program is pure vaudeville and *The Jackie Gleason Show* even retains traces of the working-class music hall. The overlay of old and new is not all good, of course; the new technology has created methods of war and destruction which the old insularity allows Americans to unleash without much shame or guilt, and some Levittowners may find work less satisfying than their ancestors. But only some, for the majority's parents slaved in exhausting jobs which made them too tired to enjoy the advantages of suburbia even if they could have afforded them.

The Summer of 1967: The Newark Riots

In the summer of 1967, residents of Newark, Plainfield, Englewood, and other cities took part in violent demonstrations that led to the loss of many lives and the destruction of tens of millions of dollars' worth of property. Variously termed riots, civil disorders, racial turmoil, or urban unrest, these upheavals are easily the most dramatic events to have taken place in New Jersey during the half-century since World War II.

In their aftermath, incumbent politicians were swept out of office (Newark Mayor Hugh Addonizio and members of his administration were indicted on fraud and corruption charges), and many new social programs—federal, state, and local—were initiated.

The riots were extremely controversial. Even today, more than a quarter of a century later, those who were touched by these events find them difficult to discuss dispassionately. Many questions are still debated. Among them: Were these riots the cause or the consequence of the general decline of the cities? Did they produce more positive or negative results? And, of course, What are the long-term solutions to the problems that underlay these disruptions?

No small set of brief documents can do justice to an episode as complex as this, but the following four excerpts represent a range of voices. The first piece comes from black nationalist Amiri Baraka's autobiography. In it Baraka recalls driving through the riotous streets of Newark on the first night of the turmoil. Shortly after leaving the bar where this excerpt ends, Baraka and his two associates were arrested on charges of weapons possession. Their arrests added to the charged atmosphere of the aftermath of the riots. The three were initially convicted of the charges, but their convictions were overturned on appeal when a man whom they took to the hospital was found to testify in their behalf.

The second excerpt is from the "Report for Action" issued by the group Governor Richard J. Hughes commissioned to study the riots. This report is widely considered to be the best of all the official reports on the urban riots of the 1960s.

Amiri I. Baraka, *The Autobiography of Leroi Jones* (New York: Freundlich Books, 1984), 258–261. Reprinted by permission of Lawrence Hill Books.

Report for Action (Trenton: New Jersey Governor's Select Commission on Civil Disorder, 1968), x–xii.

Tom Hayden, *Rebellion in Newark: Official Violence and Ghetto Response* (New York: Vintage Books, 1967), 5–12. Copyright © 1967 by Tom Hayden. Reprinted by permission of Random House, Inc.

Road to Anarchy: Findings of the Riot Study Commission of the New Jersey State Patrolmen's Benevolent Association, Inc. (1968), ix, x.

The third document is from an essay written by Tom Hayden, a leader of the New Left.[1] Hayden, a founding member of Students for a Democratic Society (SDS), was in Newark in 1967 working with an SDS organization called The Newark Community Union Project. Some observers felt the riots were instigated by Hayden and his supporters.

The last piece is from the summary of a report by the state Patrolmen's Benevolent Association.

One afternoon I heard something about a demonstration . . . about a cabdriver who'd gotten beaten by the police the night before. When we got there, there were maybe fifty to one hundred people. . . . It was obvious to me that it was not like a picket line at a strike or the lighter kinds of demonstrations. . . . There was a presence on the line and in the scattered crowd that gathered on the other side of the narrow street. . . . It was like the air itself was a container for something that was pushing against it trying to break out. . . .

After an hour or so . . . we . . . started to go home, rolling slowly . . . over to Springfield Avenue.[2] It seemed there were knots of people, ever moving, people were in small groups, looking, peering, as if they too sensed what was ready to loose itself. . . .

Later in the afternoon . . . some of the young boys who came in and out of the Spirit House[3] rushed in. "They're breaking windows on Springfield Avenue" was the word. Outside . . . you could see people in motion, like a slow-motion flick speeded up. Moving in all directions.

We stood for a second, all of us from in the house. Then Shorty, Barney,[4] and I jumped in the bus. . . . We were around the corner and onto Springfield Avenue. When we got there the shit was already on! Further up the street you could see figures moving fast. The sun was falling to hide them quick. Suddenly, sirens. We could see some smoke, hey, then glass started to break close to where we were.

The spirit and feeling of the moment a rebellion breaks out is almost indescribable. Everything seems to be in zoooom [*sic*] motion, crashing toward some explosive manifestation. . . . In rebellions life goes to 156 rpm and the song is a police siren accompanying people's breathless shouts and laughter.

All that was pent up and tied is wild and loose, seen in sudden

1. A term applied to those members of the generation of college students in the 1960s who were radicalized by the civil rights movement and the war in Vietnam.
2. A major commercial street, a center of the rioting and the scene of much of destruction.
3. The center of Baraka's cultural activities.
4. Close associates of Baraka at Spirit House.

flames and red smoke, and always people running, running away and toward. We wheeled the wagon around and began to head up toward what looked like the eye of what was growing mad and gigantic and hot. We went straight up Springfield, not fast, not slow, but at a pace that would allow a serious observer to dig what was happening. . . .

Boxes of stuff were speeding by, cases of stuff: liquor, wine, beer— the best brands, shoes, appliances, clothes, jewelry, food. Foodtown had turned into open city, some dudes jumped the half a story out the window to the ground. There were shifts of folks at work. The window breakers would come first. Whash! Glass all over everywhere. Then the getters would get through and get to gettin'. Some serious people would park near the corner and load up their trunks, make as many trips as the traffic would bear. Some people would run through the streets with shit, what they could carry or roll or drag or pull. Families worked together, carrying sofas and TVs collectively down the street. All the shit they saw on television that they had been hypnotized into wanting they finally had a chance to cop. The word was, "Cop and blow! And don't be slow."

Then the fire setters . . . would get on it. Crazy sheets of flame would rise behind they thing. Burn it up! Burn it up! Like Marvin[5] had said: Burn, baby, burn! They were the most rhythmic, the fire people. They dug the fire cause it danced so tough, and these priests wished they could get as high and hot as their master, the flame.

Now we circled and dashed, zigzagged, tried to follow the hot music's beat. We were digging, checking, observing, participating; it was a canvas, a palette no painter could imagine. A scale no musician could plumb. (Why do you think Trane and Albert[6] sounded like that? They wanted the essence of what flailed alive on all sides of us now.)

The police were simply devils to us, beasts. We did not understand then the scientific exegesis on the state[7]—though we needed to. Devils! Beasts! Crisscrossing in their deadly stupor of evil. The people were like dancers whirling around and through the flames. A motorcycle leaped through Sears' window with a blood, head down, stuck to it, booting and smoking up Elizabeth Avenue. Rifles strapped to his back. The last firearms sold legally in Newark disappeared in all

5. I don't know whom Baraka is referring to. The slogan "Burn, baby, burn" came to be associated with the Watts riot of 1965 because it was used by a Los Angeles disk-jockey popular with black listeners.
6. Tenor saxophonists John Coltrane and Albert Ayler were experimenting with an atonal style known as free jazz in this period.
7. A more sophisticated understanding of the operation of police power that Baraka was later to develop.

directions out of Gene's[8] and the same Sears. Devil-cars spinning meanwhile as they shot at everything that moved, everything with any grace.

We moved through looking until the rage and madness' dazzle had reached its peak. I thought it must be like what a war is, to be in the middle of it. Then we saw people getting hit. The devils were spraying the dancers; they were enraged by their own poison. We saw a man fall near Springfield and Belmont and the police quickly swallowed him up. We had to move quickly, and keep some distance and the correct angle between ourselves and them. At Belmont and Spruce we saw another brother hit, he fell into a sitting position, shot through the leg. Blood streamed down his pants and the case of shit he was carrying was smashed to the ground. . . . We pulled up and dragged him into the van, then we sped off toward City Hospital. . . .

We went down to the Key Club for a drink. As wild as it seemed, there were people in there, a few, sipping and talking low about what was loose in the streets. We met . . . another hip Newark boy, we went past his crib and passed the peace pipe[9] around, talked some more about what the future held for ourselves and our people.

That this report had to be written is a manifestation of a deep failing in our society, for many of the problems that it analyzes should have been solved by now. . . .

The record of history does not augur well for action. Although violence has marked the path of many ethnic and social groups, the major issues that were in contention in those conflicts have long since been resolved. But one great issue remains unresolved: the place of the Negro in American society. It is this issue that almost tore the nation apart one hundred years ago. It is this question that led to the Chicago riot of 1919, the Harlem riots of 1935 and 1943, and the mounting disorders in our cities in the years since World War II. . . .

The distance between white and black is growing. . . . Distrust and anger are on the rise on both sides.

There is a clear and present danger to the very existence of our cities. Consequently, more is demanded than argument over the respective shortcomings, responsibilities, and prejudices of white and black. The way to use time now is for action.

The burden of responsibility weighs most heavily on those . . . with control over the resources that will be needed to produce tangible

8. A local sporting goods store.
9. Smoked marijuana or hashish.

results. But much of what needs to be done and much of what this Commission is recommending does not cost money and cannot be bought.

The central issue with which this nation has temporized for the past one hundred years—to make equality real for the black man—was bound, sooner or later, to land on the doorstep of each of us. And had not the Negro been patient and forbearing, it would have landed there before.

We need fewer promises and more action from political leaders and government officials.

We need fewer press releases from police commissioners on community relations and more respect by patrolmen for the dignity of each citizen.

We need fewer speeches from employers and union leaders on equal opportunity in the future and more flexible hiring standards now.

We need more principals, teachers, and guidance counselors who want their students to succeed instead of expecting them to fail.

We need more social workers who respect and foster a client's pride instead of treating him as an irritant or a child.

Suburban residents must understand that the future of their communities is inextricably linked to the fate of the city, instead of harboring the illusion that they can maintain invisible walls or continue to run away. . . .

If the events of last July had one effect, it was to show that we can no longer escape the issue. The question is whether we shall resort to illusion, or finally come to grips with reality.

The illusion is that force alone will solve the problem. But our society cannot deliver on its promises when terror stalks the streets, and disorder and lawlessness tear our communities apart. No group of people can better themselves by rioting and breaking laws that are enacted for the benefit and protection of everyone. Riots must be condemned. The cardinal principle of any civilized society is law and order. It is vital to all. . . .

At the same time, we recognize that in the long run law and order can prevail only in conditions of social justice. . . . Reality demands prompt action to solve the long-neglected problems of our cities.

Inherent in these problems is the virus of segregation. It cannot be treated with palliatives. It must be attacked at the source. It is rampant in urban bodies no longer healthy enough to fight disease of any kind and which will increasingly suffer frustration and disorder unless old and outdated approaches are abandoned and new solutions sought in the metropolitan and regional context.

Such solutions require a coordinated attack on many fronts, and they will take time. But a beginning can be made quickly. The way to begin is at home, in the way we do business on our streets, in our shops, our schools, our courts, government offices, and wherever members of the black and white communities meet.

Much of the community predicted that Newark's riot would be triggered by a police incident. . . . The police are seen as direct carriers of intimidation, harassment and violence. Dominated by the Italians who run Newark politics, tainted by alleged underworld connections, including a token of about two hundred fifty blacks among its fourteen hundred members (all of them in subordinated positions), the police department seems to many Negroes to be an armed agency defending the privileges of the city's shrinking white community. . . .

On the front lines against the police . . . were the men between fifteen and twenty-five years old from the projects and the nearby avenues. They were the primary assailants and the most elusive enemy for the police. They were the force which broke open the situation in which masses of people began to participate. Few of them had ever been involved in civil-rights organizations. . . .

The youth were . . . breaking windows where the chance appeared, chanting "Black Power," moving in groups through dark streets. . . . A small number entered stores and moved out with what they could carry; they would be replaced by others from the large mass of people walking, running, or standing in the streets. Further back were more thousands who watched from windows and stoops and periodically participated. Those with mixed feelings were not about to intervene against their neighbors. A small number, largely the older people, shook their heads. . . .

For the most part the rioting was controlled and focused. The "rampaging" was aimed almost exclusively at white-owned stores and not at such buildings as schools, churches, or banks. The latter institutions are oppressive but their buildings contain little that can be carried off. To this extent the riot was concrete rather than symbolic. . . .

Police behavior became more and more violent as the looting expanded. . . . Their tactic seemed to be to drive at high speeds with sirens whining down major streets in the ghetto. Thus they were driving too fast for rock-throwers while still attempting a show of force. . . .

It seems to many that the military, especially the Newark police, not only triggered the riot by beating a cab-driver but then created a climate of opinion that supported the use of all necessary force to suppress the riot. The force used by police was not in response to snipers, looting, and burning, but in retaliation against the successful uprising of Wednesday and Thursday nights. . . .

To the conservative mind the riot is essentially revolution against civilization. To the liberal mind it is an expression of helpless frustration. While the conservative is hostile and the liberal generous toward those who riot, both assume that the riot is a form of lawless, mob behavior. The liberal will turn conservative if polite methods fail to stem disorder. Against these two fundamentally similar concepts, a third one must be asserted, the concept that a riot represents people making history.

The riot is certainly an awkward, even primitive, form of history making. But if people are barred from using the sophisticated instruments of the established order for their ends, they will find another way. . . . The riot is not a beautiful and romantic experience, but neither is the day-to-day slum life from which the riot springs. Riots will not go away if ignored and will not be cordoned off. They will only disappear when their energy is absorbed into a more decisive and effective form of history-making.

These tactics of disorder will be defined by the authorities as criminal anarchy. But it may be that disruption will create possibilities of meaningful change. This depends on whether the leaders of ghetto struggles can be more successful in building strong organization than they have been so far. Violence can contribute to shattering the status quo, but only politics and organization can transform it. The ghetto still needs the power to decide its destiny on such matters as urban renewal and housing, social services, policing, and taxation. Tenants still need concrete rights against landlords. . . . Welfare clients still need a livable income. Consumers still need to control the quality of merchandise and service in the stores where they shop. Citizens still need effective control over those who police their community. . . . In order to build a more decent community while resisting racist power, more than violence is required. People need to create self-government. We are at a point where democracy—the idea and practice of people controlling their lives—is a revolutionary issue in the United States.

We Americans have been asked in recent months to believe: that white racism causes black riots; that riots are spontaneous explosions without planning or direction; that a consistent pattern of police brutality is evident in the Negro ghettoes of our nation's cities, and is a cause of rioting; and that rioting is directly traceable to poor housing, to substandard eduction, to joblessness. . . .

The Riot Study Commission of the New Jersey State Patrolmen's Benevolent Association categorically and totally rejects these conclusions as unsubstantiated and unwarranted.

We find instead that our nation is moving toward two societies; one bound by the rule of law and the other exempt from law.

We find instead that the lawlessness on our nation's streets feeds on and is nurtured by the weakness of official response. As the excuses and apologies for lawlessness grow, so does the lawlessness.

We charge that a conspiracy exists of radical elements, dedicated to the overthrow of our society—and that this conspiracy is aided, perhaps unwittingly, by people at the highest levels of government and society. . . .

The future of our free society will be in grave doubt, unless and until all Americans rededicate themselves to the preservation of law and order; for without law there can be no peace, and without order there can be no progress. . . .

While this committee was at work the riot reports of the President's Advisory Commission and of Governor Hughes' commission were released, and both—in the words of former Vice President Richard Nixon—"put the blame for the riots on everybody but the rioters."

We were all lectured . . . on the evils of police brutality, the dangers of police "overreaction" in the face of rioting, the failures of police to understand the sociological implications of a riot, the inefficiency and incompetency of police when rioting occurred. . . . This report is our answer.

Actions or Appearances?: Radical Feminists Protest Miss America (1968)

About two hundred women participated in the September 1968 protest at the Miss America pageant in Atlantic City, but the significance of the event outweighs the low number of participants. It was brought into millions of homes by television, and it was widely covered in the press, thus announcing to the nation the arrival of what is arguably the most far-reaching of all the movements for change of the 1960s: feminism. An unfriendly writer referred to this protest as the Boston Tea Party of the women's liberation movement.

At the demonstration itself the women marched, chanted, and sang. They carried signs with such slogans as: "I am a woman—not a toy, a pet, or a mascot," and they crowned a live sheep Miss America. Although the protesters were characterized as "bra burners," nothing was actually burned on this occasion.

The following document is an excerpt from a flyer announcing the protest. Some elements of the document remain part of the feminist critique of American society; others are more reflective of the anarchist-inclined counterculture of the 1960s.

On September 7th in Atlantic City, the annual Miss America Pageant will again crown "your ideal." But this year . . . we will protest the image of Miss America, an image that oppresses women in every area in which it purports to represent us. There will be: picket lines; guerrilla theater; leafletting; lobbying visits to the contestants urging our sisters to reject the pageant farce and join us; a huge freedom trash can (into which we will throw bras, girdles, curlers, false eyelashes, wigs, and representative issues of *Cosmopolitan, Ladies' Home Journal, Family Circle*, etc. Bring any such woman-garbage you have around the house.) . . . It should be a groovy day on the Boardwalk in the sun with our sisters. In case of arrests, however, we plan to reject all male authority and demand to be busted by policewomen only. (In Atlantic City, women cops are not permitted to make arrests—dig that!)

Male chauvinist-reactionaries on this issue had best stay away, nor are male liberals welcome in the demonstrations. But sympathetic men can donate money as well as cars and drivers.

Reprinted in Robin Morgan, ed., *Sisterhood Is Powerful: An Anthology of Writings from the Women's Liberation Movement* (New York: Random House, 1970), 521–524.

Male reporters will be refused interviews. We reject patronizing reportage. Only newswomen will be recognized.

We Protest:

1. *The Degrading Mindless-Boob Girlie Symbol.* The Pageant contestants epitomize the roles we are all forced to play as women. The parade down the runway blares the metaphor of the . . . county fair, where the nervous animals are judged for teeth, fleece, etc. and where the best "specimen" gets the blue ribbon. So are women in our society forced daily to compete for male approval, enslaved by ludicrous "beauty" standards we ourselves are conditioned to take seriously.

2. *Racism with Roses.* Since its inception in 1921 the Pageant has not had one black finalist. . . . There has never been a Puerto Rican, Alaskan, Hawaiian, or Mexican-American winner. Nor has there ever been a *true* Miss America—an American Indian.

3. *Miss America as Military Death Mascot.* The highlight of her reign each year is a cheerleader-tour of American troops abroad—last year she went to Vietnam to pep-talk our husbands, fathers, sons, and boyfriends into dying and killing with a better spirit. . . . We refuse to be used as mascots for murder.

4. *The Consumer Con-Game.* Miss America is a walking commercial for the Pageant's sponsors. Wind her up and she plugs your product on promotion tours and TV. . . .

5. *Competition Rigged and Unrigged.* We deplore the encouragement of an American myth that oppresses men as well as women: the win-or-you're-worthless competitive disease. . . .

6. *The Woman as Pop Culture Obsolescent Theme.* . . . What is so ignored as last year's Miss America? This only reflects the gospel of our society, according to Saint Male: women must be young, juicy, malleable—hence age discrimination and the cult of youth. And we women are brainwashed into believing this ourselves!

7. *The Unbeatable Madonna-Whore Combination.* Miss America and *Playboy's* centerfold are sisters over the skin. To win approval, we must be both sexy and wholesome, delicate but able to cope, demure yet titillatingly bitchy. Deviation of any sort brings, we are told, disaster: "You won't get a man!!"

8. *The Irrelevant Crown on the Throne of Mediocrity.* Miss America represents what women are supposed to be: unoffensive, bland, apolitical. If you are tall, short, over, or under . . . weight . . . forget it. Personality, articulateness, intelligence, commitment—unwise. Conformity is the key to the crown—and, by extension, to success in our society.

9. *Miss America as Dream Equivalent To—?* In this reputedly democratic society where every little boy supposedly can grow up to be

President, what can every little girl hope to grow to be? Miss America. That's where it's at. Real power to control our own lives is restricted to men, while women get patronizing pseudo-power, an ermine cloak, and a bunch of flowers; men are judged by their actions, women by their appearance.

10. *Miss America as Big Sister Watching You.* The Pageant . . . attempts to . . . enslave us . . . in high-heeled, low-status roles; to inculcate false values in young girls; to use women as beasts of buying; to seduce us to prostitute ourselves before our own oppression.

DOCUMENT 88

Opening Pandora's Box?: A Debate on Environmental Policy (1972)

Another of the far-reaching reforms born in the 1960s was the environmental movement. On Earth Day in 1970 Governor William T. Cahill signed legislation that created a state Department of Environmental Protection, symbolizing broad public support for protecting the natural resources that enhance the quality of life. Other aspects of environmentalism included intensified efforts to curb pollution, the founding of many new environmental organizations willing to use legal action to further their goals, and the drafting of many new laws or regulations to protect the environment.

The debate excerpted below illustrates many of the themes of political environmentalism. It comes from a hearing held in May 1972, the second of two discussions of a bill sponsored by Assemblymen James J. Florio and Thomas H. Kean (both of whom subsequently served as governors of the state), among others. The legislation under consideration allowed any citizen to go to court to prevent damage to the environment. This bill did not pass, but similar legislation was enacted in 1974, during the legislative session that followed.

Arthur H. West [President, New Jersey Farm Bureau]: . . . We have feared for some time that the current environmental movement would lead to extreme proposals. We Americans are prone to go too far when we set out to correct an ill. In our zeal to stop air and water pollution and to improve the environment we need to stop and think before going too far. . . .

C. Russell Kramer [State Chamber of Commerce]: . . . Enactment of this bill would be a substantial deterrent, in our opinion, to any future coordinated industry/government efforts to abate pollution. The greatest practical gains in industrial pollution control have been made through cooperation between industrial companies and regulatory officials in working out effective programs based upon reasonable timetables. To have the legislature encourage civil litigation on these problems rather than cooperative efforts would appear to be counterproductive.

The federal government and the state of New Jersey now have . . . pollution-control agencies . . . staffed by many technologically competent scientists, engineers, and specialists who devote full time to

Public Hearing before Assembly Committee on Air and Water Pollution and Public Health on Assembly Bill No. 569 (Protection of Natural Resources), 1972.

the study of pollution and its abatement. . . . To allow the well-thought-out regulations, pollution standards, and plans of these agencies to be disrupted by lawsuits brought by well-meaning but technologically uninformed citizens would harm the overall pollution abatement program. . . .

Assemblyman Wilkerson [William G. Wilkerson, M.D., a Democrat from Jersey City]: . . . Is that the biggest problem that you see . . . this direct access to the courts for relief?

Mr. Kramer: That's correct. And without showing any harm. . . .

Assemblyman Wilkerson: . . . Do you think that, as far as ecology is concerned, we . . . who are responsible for getting . . . laws on the books to prevent pollution should wait until our citizens have been harmed before they have a right to ask for relief?

Mr. Kramer: . . . I think you should go along with the machinery you created and not permit anyone who shows no individual harm to bypass all of this machinery and go directly to the courts. . . .

Assemblyman Kean [Thomas H. Kean, Republican of Livingston]: . . . This legislation recognizes that every citizen is entitled to a decent and clean environment, one in which our atmosphere is free of poison, our streams and rivers clear of industrial and residential waste, and our surroundings free of noise and clamor. . . . These are things government has an obligation to provide to the people it serves. . . .

The opponents of this law . . . now praising the Department of Environmental Protection . . . are the very people who opposed every attempt . . . to strengthen the Department . . . and generally have opposed every piece of legislation that we have passed to help our environment. . . .

Assemblyman Wilkerson: . . . Isn't this going to demand more money? If this money was taken and given to the Department to use in hiring more agents and put them out in the field to do just the thing that all of us want done, wouldn't this . . . be more efficient? . . .

Assemblyman Kean: It isn't just efficiency that I am after. . . . I am after giving the citizen some access beyond the bureaucracy. . . .

It has not been good enough . . . to say we have a number of people on the payroll, therefore if you have problems call the government . . . because government at all levels has been very often unresponsive to citizen demands. . . .

Commissioner Sullivan [Richard J. Sullivan, the state's first commissioner of environmental protection]: . . . This delicate environment that we all inhabit can have abstract, obtuse, oblique effects upon all of us over the longer term, and if, in order to institute an action, somebody has to show that the risk of emphysema to him or the risk of typhoid fever from polluted water is imminent, then there is no point in adopting this bill.

Frank J. Oliver [League for Conservation Legislation]: . . . A law such as this . . . would have been useful in 1961 when the governor and his appointed Commissioner of Conservation and Economic Development sold 715 acres of the state forest—the Worthington Tract—to a power company. . . . State lands are held in trust for the owners, the citizens of the state, and the sale of this land for non-recreational purposes could have been challenged by the citizens if A-569 had been in effect. . . .

The present concerns about conservation and ecological systems relate to a state of harmony between man and his total environment. Man is gradually . . . developing an awareness of a new morality—a land ethic in its broadest sense. This new conscience must find effective expression in the development of fresh legal concepts. . . .

The people of the state of New Jersey are asking for legislative recognition that, in matters involving their quality of life in environmental terms, they have the right to seek adjudication of their grievances. . . .

Francis E. P. McCarter [Chairman, State Bar Association, Committee on Conservation and Ecology]:[1] . . . What New Jersey needs in this area is not one other law which is completely unrelated to existing law but rather a codification of existing laws. . . . We now have a patchwork of unrelated, inconsistent, and sometimes conflicting laws in the area of air, water pollution, and so on. . . . Adding this law on top of it is going to make the capacity of any industry or municipality in this state to know what its obligations are and what its budget should be to meet those obligations, next to impossible. . . .

An individual who feels that, let's say, the stream in his neighborhood is being polluted by a factory has only to go to his local board of health, swear out a complaint and the board of health must prosecute that in the municipal court. Now this means that the thing can be brought on within a matter of a couple of weeks at the most and nothing could be quicker than that.

In the present state of our society in which the ecology has taken the place of motherhood, the flag, and the Bible, there is nobody who really wants the bad publicity of being found guilty of polluting the environment, certainly no business which sells to the public wants that kind of publicity. . . . Publicity is what people fear more even than the fine, as onerous as the fine can be. . . .

John Reed [Chairman of the Environmental Committee, New Jersey Builders Association]: . . . This bill, number 569, has a resemblance in hazard to the opening of Pandora's box. . . .

The essence of this . . . is that of a stop-work type of bill. . . .

1. Mr. McCarter was speaking for himself, not the bar association.

Permitting the individual . . . to have access to a court on the likelihood of damage . . . is both unnecessary and dangerous to the overall interest of the state.

We totally oppose this bill. . . . We believe it could seriously impair our ability to build housing for the people of New Jersey. . . . It does not seem possible to us, in dealing with the cleaning up of many, many years of environmental problems, at tremendous expense with complicated technology, that we can afford to go to anything which could continually change our standards. Obviously we could not anticipate who might sue on what subject or when. . . .

At the present moment . . . we are required to put underground the telephone company lines, the electric company lines, the sanitary water lines, the sanitary sewer lines. . . . So we must put trenches in the ground. It is not within the known technology to build without muddying a nearby stream. This bill would even allow them, on the threat of our muddying the stream, to stop all major subdivisions in the state of New Jersey. I believe it is not important whether we have one or more lawsuits. I think the first lawsuit filed of this type would be sufficient to slow down industry and start creating a rise in unemployment. . . .

Peter Buchsbaum [Staff Counsel, American Civil Liberties Union of New Jersey]: . . . The ACLU of New Jersey . . . regards this freedom as being no less essential to the quality of life than the more traditionally recognized liberties which the ACLU has long defended. . . .

I would like to make a specific comment . . . regarding the ability of people to sue via the board of health. . . . There is a severe jurisdictional problem. . . . You have different boards dealing with different areas. If you have a problem in Kearny, for instance, on the Passaic River, you may have to go to the Passaic Valley Commission, you might not be able to go to the Township of Kearny. So the relief would not be immediately available. . . .

The low fines which would probably be obtained from boards of health would not be significant in deterring pollution and I don't believe the publicity . . . would be significant either.

Lastly, in many cases the municipalities themselves are involved in pollution. . . . You wouldn't expect to get much from the local board of health in that kind of a situation. . . .

Richard Zimmer [Vice-Chairman, New Jersey Steering Committee, Common Cause]: . . . In a recent poll of Common Cause coordinators in New Jersey we found that preserving the environment ranked second in importance only to ending the Vietnam War. But Common Cause supports A-569 not simply because the goal of this legislation is to protect the environment; Common Cause is especially enthusiastic about this bill because for the first time the average citizen will be enlisted in the battle. . . .

In times like these, when the very foundations of democracy are under great stress, when public confidence in traditional political methods is declining, when the citizen is becoming more and more estranged from his leaders, it is imperative we look beyond traditional political methods and try to develop new ways to bridge the gap between the individual and the government which is supposed to serve him. . . .

If properly implemented A-569 will allow citizens to work in harmony with elected officials and state agencies to improve our environment.

DOCUMENT 89

Constitutional Rights Cannot Wait for Political Consensus: The Supreme Court Addresses the Housing Problem (1983)

In 1971 the South Burlington County chapter of the National Association for the Advancement of Colored People sued Mount Laurel Township over the exclusion from the township of mobile homes, the lowest-cost housing available. In 1975 the state supreme court ruled that because Mount Laurel restricted home ownership to people with high incomes, its zoning ordinance was unconstitutional; this ruling undermined the long-standing power of a municipality to control the use of privately owned land within its boundaries.

The court went on to say that all townships with land available for housing development were obligated to make possible the building of a "fair share" of the affordable housing needed in the region in which the municipality was located. But this complicated and controversial ruling, now known as Mount Laurel I, created no mechanism by which it could be enforced.

The court decision excerpted here,[1] known as Mount Laurel II, was issued in 1983 because municipalities and local courts were ignoring the earlier ruling. Mount Laurel II is one of the most far-reaching decisions in recent New Jersey history; it has had national implications, influencing courts, and even some legislation, in other states. The decision, written by Chief Justice Robert Wilentz, required municipalities to remove all obstacles to the construction of affordable housing within their boundaries, and it set up a mechanism by which low- and moderate-income housing construction could be enforced.

Shortly after this decision was issued, the legislature created a Council on Affordable Housing, which assigns to municipalities quotas of affordable housing.

The constitutional power to zone . . . must be exercised for the general welfare. When the exercise of that power by a municipality affects something as fundamental as housing, the general welfare includes more than the welfare of that municipality and its citizens: it also includes the general welfare—in this case the housing needs—of

1. The textual notes marked with asterisks are from the court decision.

Reports of Cases Argued and Determined in the Supreme Court of New Jersey 92 (1983), 204–205, 208–220.

those residing outside of the municipality but within the region that contributes to the housing demand within the municipality. Municipal land use regulations that conflict with the general welfare . . . are unconstitutional. In particular, those regulations that do not provide the requisite opportunity for a fair share of the region's need for low- and moderate-income housing conflict with the general welfare and violate the state constitutional requirements of substantive due process and equal protection. . . .

The basis for the constitutional obligation is simple: the state controls the use of land, all of the land. In exercising that control it cannot favor rich over poor. It cannot legislatively set aside dilapidated housing in urban ghettos for the poor and decent housing elsewhere for everyone else. The government that controls this land represents everyone. While the state may not have the ability to eliminate poverty, it cannot use that condition as the basis for imposing further disadvantages. And the same applies to the municipality to which this control over land has been constitutionally delegated.

The clarity of the constitutional obligation is seen most simply by imagining what this state could be like were this claim never to be recognized and enforced: poor people forever zoned out of substantial areas of the state, not because housing could not be built for them but because they are not wanted; poor people forced to live in urban slums forever not because . . . other attractive locations could not accommodate them, but simply because they are not wanted. It is a vision not only at variance with the requirement that the zoning power be used for the general welfare but with all concepts of fundamental fairness and decency that underpin many constitutional obligations.* . . .

*Unfortunately, this unpleasant "vision" is to a large extent already with us, as can be seen by comparing the poverty and decay of Newark and Camden with the prosperity of many of their suburban neighbors.

Since World War II there has been a great movement of commerce, industry, and people out of the inner cities and into the suburbs. At the same time, however, exclusionary zoning made these suburbs largely inaccessible to lower-income households. Beside depriving the urban poor of an opportunity to share in the suburban development, this exclusion also increased the relative concentration of poor in the cities and thereby hastened the flight of business and the middle class to the suburbs. A vicious cycle set in as increased business and middle-class flight led to more urban decay, and more urban decay led to more flight. . . .

The provision of lower-income housing in the suburbs may help to relieve cities of what has become an overwhelming fiscal and social burden. It may also make jobs more accessible for the unemployed poor. Deconcentration of the urban poor will presumably make cities more attractive for businesses and upper-income residents to return to. . . .

A brief reminder of the judicial role in this sensitive area is appropriate, since powerful reasons suggest, and we agree, that the matter is better left to the legislature. We act first and foremost because the constitution of our state requires protection of the interests involved and because the legislature has not protected them. We recognize the social and economic controversy (and its political consequences) that has resulted in relatively little legislative action in this field. We understand the enormous difficulty of achieving a political consensus that might lead to significant legislation enforcing the constitutional mandate better than we can, legislation that might completely remove this court from those controversies. But enforcement of constitutional rights cannot await a supporting political consensus. So while we have always preferred legislative to judicial action in this field, we shall continue—until the legislature acts—to do our best to uphold the constitutional obligation that underlies the Mount Laurel doctrine. That is our duty. We may not build houses, but we do enforce the constitution.** . . .

We reassure all concerned that Mount Laurel is not designed to sweep away all land use restrictions or leave our open spaces and natural resources prey to speculators. Municipalities consisting largely of conservation, agricultural, or environmentally sensitive areas will not be required to grow because of Mount Laurel. No for-

---

Cities, while most directly affected, are not the sole victims of exclusionary zoning. The damage done by urban blight and decay is in no way confined to those who must remain in our cities. It affects all of us. Violent crime and drug abuse spawned in urban slums do not remain within city limits, they spread out to the suburbs and infect those living there. Efforts to combat these diseases require expenditures of public dollars that drain all taxpayers, urban and suburban alike. The continuing disintegration of our cities encourages business and industry to leave New Jersey altogether, resulting in a drain of jobs and dollars from our economy. In sum, the decline of our cities and the increasing economic segregation of our population are not just isolated problems for those left behind in the cities, but a disease threatening us all. Zoning ordinances that either encourage this process or ratify its results are not promoting our general welfare, they are destroying it.

**In New Jersey, it has traditionally been the judiciary, and not the legislature, that has remedied substantive abuses of the zoning power by municipalities. A review of zoning litigation and legislation since the enactment of the zoning enabling statute in the 1920s shows that the legislature has confined itself largely to regulating the procedural aspects of zoning. The judiciary has at the same time invalidated or modified zoning ordinances that violated constitutional rights or failed to serve the general welfare. . . . Although the complexity and political sensitivity of the issue now before us make it especially appropriate for legislative resolution, we have no choice, absent that resolution, but to exercise our traditional constitutional duty to end an abuse of the zoning power.

ests or small towns need be paved over and covered with high-rise apartments as a result of today's decision.

As for those municipalities that may have to make adjustments in their lifestyles to provide for their fair share of low- and moderate-income housing, they should remember that they are not being required to provide more than their fair share. No one community need be concerned that it will be radically transformed by a deluge of low- and moderate-income developments. Nor should any community conclude that its residents will move to other suburbs as a result of this decision, for those "other suburbs" may very well be required to do their part to provide the same housing.

Troubled Times: Bruce Springsteen Describes a Declining Factory Town (1984)

Freehold native Bruce Springsteen is one of rock music's biggest stars. He began his career performing in clubs along the New Jersey shore, most notably at the Stone Pony, a bar in Asbury Park.

Springsteen writes parables of people who dream of running from the declining industrial towns where they live because their prospects are so bleak. Sung in a big, gravelly voice accompanied by a thumping back beat, his songs are vignettes taken from Springsteen's personal knowledge of closed factories and weakened labor unions. His lyrics often provide striking images with which his audiences identify.

The song that follows is characteristic Springsteen, with two exceptions: its protagonist is not a teenager, and the theme of race relations is not a common one for him. Recorded in 1984, the song suggests a father who fears that his son will grow up in a world of diminished opportunities.

My Hometown

I was eight years old running with
a dime in my hand
into the bus stop, to pick
up a paper
for my old man
I'd sit on his lap
in that big old Buick
and steer as we drove through town.

He'd tousle my hair
and say, son take
a good look around;
this is your hometown.

Bruce Springsteen, "My Hometown" *Nebraska* (Columbia Records, 1984). Copyright © 1984 by Bruce Springsteen. Reprinted by permission.

This is your hometown.
This is your hometown.
It's your hometown.

In '65
tension was running high
at my high school.
There was a lot of fights
between blacks and whites.
There was nothing you could do.
Two cars at a light
on a Saturday night,
in the back seat there was a gun.
Words were passed;
in a shotgun blast,
troubled times had come
around

To my hometown.
To my hometown.
To my hometown.
Now Main Street is whitewashed windows
and vacant stores;
seems like there ain't nobody
wants to come down here no
more.

They're closing down the
textile mill
across the railroad tracks.
Foreman says these jobs are going boys,
and they ain't coming back
to your hometown.

Your hometown.
To your hometown.
To your hometown.

Last night me and Kate,
we laid in bed
talking about getting out.
Packing our bags,
maybe heading south.

I'm 35
we got a boy
of our own now.
Last night I sat him up
behind the wheel
and said son take a good look around.
This is your hometown.

Abbott v. Burke, 4 (1997)

*Difficult legal arguments underlie the court case from which the following ex-
cerpt comes, but the basic issue is not complicated. The state constitution requires the legislature to provide a "thorough and efficient" education to every
school-age child. Advocates for students from inner-city school districts have
been arguing since 1970 that New Jersey's heavy reliance on property taxes
for funding public schools creates inequities that discriminate against low-
income and minority children in poor districts. The New Jersey Supreme
Court first concurred in 1973, finding that the state's school funding mechanism creates unconstitutional disparities in educational opportunity. More
than thirty years have passed since that ruling, and New Jersey continues to
struggle to improve the level of funding and the quality of education in its
urban schools. The legal arena in which this has played out is known as Ab-*
bott v. Burke, *for one of the plaintiffs and the state commissioner of education when the cases began.*

The first Abbott *ruling came in 1981 when the court ruled that the state
must offer urban children an education equal in quality to that of their suburban peers. In 1990 the court raised the stakes, requiring the state to equalize
educational funding between suburban and urban districts and to provide
supplemental programs to reduce disadvantages. In 1994 the court, having
grown impatient, gave the state until 1997 to comply with its 1990 ruling.*

*The Comprehensive Education Improvement and Financing Act (CEIFA),
which she signed in 1996, was Governor Christie Whitman's stab at the problem. It introduced core curriculum content standards to measure performance
and required spending in urban districts to be no more than $1,200 per pupil
below the suburban average.* Abbott 4, *excerpted here, declared CEIFA unconstitutional and ordered state officials to immediately increase funding for
urban schools to parity with suburban schools.*

Since this ruling, the court has issued six more Abbott *decisions, and the
list of states dealing with similar problems has reached twenty-one. Because
New Jersey has been a leader in the effort to help poor families advance
through education, the* New York Times *wrote, in 2002, that* Abbott *"may
be the most significant education case" since the U.S. Supreme Court's school
desegregation rulings in the mid-1950s.*

With the promulgation and adoption of substantive standards that define a thorough and efficient education, New Jersey joins a trend in

Abbott v. Burke, 119 N.J. 287 (1997).

favor of a standards-based approach to the improvement of public education. The movement for standards-based reform began in the late 1980s, and emerged as the principal strategy of educators in the early 1990s. . . . The content and performance standards prescribed by the new statute represent the first real effort on the part of the legislative and executive branches to define and to implement the educational opportunity required by the Constitution. It is an effort that strongly warrants judicial deference. . . .

Our function, however, is to determine whether the new approach encompassing content and performance standards, together with funding measures, comports with the constitutional guarantee of a thorough and efficient education for all New Jersey school children. The standards themselves do not ensure any substantive level of achievement. Real improvement still depends on the sufficiency of educational resources, successful teaching, effective supervision, efficient administration, and a variety of other academic, environmental, and societal factors needed to assure a sound education. Content standards, therefore, cannot answer the fundamental inquiry of whether the new statute assures the level of resources needed to provide a thorough and efficient education to children in the special needs districts. . . . [Since] CEIFA does not in any concrete way attempt to link the content standards to the actual funding needed to deliver that content, we conclude that this strategy, as implemented by CEIFA, is clearly inadequate and thus unconstitutional as applied to the special needs districts. . . .

Clearly the delivery of an adequate education requires efficiency in spending. The need to eliminate waste, to increase efficiency, and to maximize the education dollar—a need that is believed to be more acute in the Special Needs Districts (SNDs)—does not lessen the need for resources. Both additional money and reformation of the way in which that money is spent are required to improve the conditions in failing school districts. . . . The facilities in the Special Needs Districts are collectively much older and far more in need of repair than those in the other districts. The same amount of money cannot possibly be sufficient in all districts without taking into consideration the age and present condition of the facilities. . . .

CEIFA is incapable of providing a substantive educational opportunity to public school children in the poorer urban districts that will enable them to achieve a thorough and efficient education. It is, consequently, unconstitutional in relation to the special needs districts. This continued deprivation of the constitutional right to a thorough and efficient education necessitates a remedy. We consistently have recognized that no single remedy can assure the provision of a constitutionally thorough and efficient education to the children in the special needs districts. ("We realize our remedy may fail to achieve the constitutional object, that no amount of money may be able to erase the impact of the socioeconomic factors that define and cause these pupils' disadvantages. We realize that perhaps nothing short of substantial social and economic change affecting housing, employment, child care, taxation, [and] welfare will make the difference for these students . . . ." [citing *Abbott*, 2]

The judicial remedy is necessarily incomplete; at best it serves only as a practical and incremental measure that can ameliorate but not solve such an enormous problem. It cannot substitute for the comprehensive remedy that can be effectuated only through legislative and executive efforts. The finiteness of judicial power, however, does not diminish the judicial obligation to vindicate constitutional rights. Plaintiffs seek affirmation of their constitutional right to an opportunity that will enable them to achieve a thorough and efficient education, that is, a level of education that will allow them to assume a place in society as competitive and effective workers and contributors—an educational opportunity that is now to be defined and measured by the content standards of the new act. Accordingly, the interim remedy that we mandate to effectuate that right is the improvement of regular education through increased funding. The increased funding shall assure parity in per-pupil expenditures between each SND and the budgeted (as opposed to predicted) average expenditures of . . . [other] districts by the commencement of the 1997–1998 school year . . . Further, we continue to insist that the State address special education needs by determining and implementing those supplemental programs essential to relieve students in the special needs districts of their unique disadvantages.

Our Constitution requires that public school children be given the opportunity to receive a thorough and efficient education. That constitutional vision irrefutably presumes that every child is potentially capable of attaining his or her own place as a contributing member in society with the ability to compete effectively with other citizens and to succeed in the economy. The wisdom giving rise to that vision is that both the child and society benefit immeasurably when that potential is realized. Our Constitution demands that every child be given an equal opportunity to meet his or her promise. CEIFA is deficient in that it does not provide adequate resources to help the most educationally deprived children to achieve that promise or to effect change in our most needy schools. . . . Students in all of those districts will continue to attend school in substandard school buildings and under appalling conditions that frustrate, undermine, and ultimately defeat education. Nothing will be done under the act to attract the most qualified teachers to those environments or to improve teaching. None of the needs-based supplemental programs that we repeatedly have ordered will be implemented, save perhaps preschool and kindergarten, by the year 2001.

It is against that backdrop, and the inescapable reality of a continuing profound constitutional deprivation that has penalized generations of children, that one must evaluate an alternative, "wait and see" approach. That approach usually is both prudent and preferred in constitutional jurisprudence, and the Court has taken that approach in the past. . . . In light of the constitutional rights at stake, the persistence and depth of the constitutional deprivation, and in the absence of any real prospect for genuine educational improvement in the most needy districts, that approach is no longer an option. Presented with no alternative remedy by either the plaintiffs or the State, and without a realistic alternative arising out of the new act itself, the Court must resort to judicial relief. In fashioning that relief, the Court never has believed that equality of expenditures alone will translate into an educational opportunity in Irvington that is comparable to the one provided in Millburn. The judicial funding remedy, indeed, is likely to be approaching inutility. Only comprehensive and systemic relief will bring about enduring reform. . . . Although it remains our hope that needed comprehensive relief eventually will come from those branches of government more suited to the task, there can be no responsible dissent from the position that the Court has the constitutional obligation to do what it can to effectuate and vindicate the constitutional rights of the school children in the poverty-stricken urban districts. Plaintiffs' motion is granted.

Sprawl (2002)

A prolonged period of below average rainfall began in New Jersey during the summer of 1998. From March 2002 to January 2003, the entire state was under emergency drought restrictions, which limited car washing, lawn watering, and other water uses. The following cartoon, by syndicated artist Jimmy Margulies, was drawn in this period. But Margulies does not call our attention to the amount of rainfall; he raises a more complex problem.

Most people think of sprawl in terms of the disappearance of farms and open space that comes as suburbs spread and development covers ever more land. We blame traffic congestion and air pollution on sprawl. When we see strip malls on a rural road or big box retail stores where woods used to be, we think it's a shame. But sprawl may be more than shameful. Uncontrolled sprawl threatens New Jersey's ability to remain a place that offers a comfortable standard of living.

It was recently estimated that the number of acres under development in New Jersey increased three times faster than the population grew. Since rain runoff from impervious surfaces such as roads and parking lots carries pollutants into streams and rivers, it is not surprising that water quality declines in areas of new development. But sprawl not only diminishes the quality of our water, it also reduces the quantity of the water supply. When roads, parking lots, driveways, and roofs replace meadows, forests, and wetlands, rainwater that formerly hit the ground, percolated through the soil, and replenished underground aquifers is instead swept away by gutters and sewer systems.

We don't generally think about how water reaches our homes and offices until there is a problem. But because sprawl reduces the supply as it increases demand, some experts fear that water could become scarce in certain areas of New Jersey even in years of average rainfall. Although we usually associate battles over water supply with the American West, sprawl, and the attendant water shortages and other problems it brings, threaten to be New Jersey's issue in years to come.

"The Boom Was a Story about Someone Else": The New Jersey Economy in the 1990s (2002)

The excerpt below comes from a report written by Leslie McCall, a Rutgers University demographer, that was commissioned by New Jersey Policy Perspective, an organization in Trenton that conducts research on public issues it hopes to influence. In this report, however, Professor McCall offers a description of changes in wage and income distribution; she neither analyzes the causes of the patterns she finds nor offers prescriptions for changing them.

The report touches on two related themes. One is that income became more unevenly distributed in the last decade; the other that the ranks of the working poor grew. The issue of income inequality is divisive. It underlies basic differences between political liberals and conservatives. Does the American dream require equality of condition, or merely equality of opportunity? For many conservatives, the harsh realities of economic inequality are softened by a belief that social equality creates the possibility of upward mobility. Liberals question this easy equation because in the last few decades the degree of economic inequality has increased, not lessened, and the prospects for rising above the socioeconomic level of one's parents seem more remote.

Conservatives and liberals also differ on the causes of poverty. Where liberals see a system that traps the poor in failing schools, dead-end jobs, substandard housing, and insufficient health insurance, conservatives see a world in which hard work cures all ills and they call attention to the personal and moral failings of the poor. Complicated problems have more than one cause, of course, but work on solutions can't begin until the problems are recognized.

This report offer[s] a comprehensive portrait of changes in earnings and income, adjusted for inflation, during the decade of the 1990s. Our main finding is that New Jersey was unable to convert one of the longest expansions in state history into real wage and income gains for the majority of workers and households. Indeed, for most New Jersey residents the boom was a story about someone else. Contrary to popular perceptions, the New Jersey economy in the 1990s was not a prosperous one for most people, especially when compared to the 1980s and to other states in the country. Moreover, the distance between

Leslie McCall, *The State of Working New Jersey: Putting the Boom in Perspective* (Trenton: New Jersey Policy Perspective, 2002). Reprinted by permission.

those at the top and the bottom of the economic ladder widened substantially, and living standards stayed more or less the same for those in the middle. . . .

Three general trends stand out.

- New Jersey ended the last decade with a negative record of wage growth for the bottom half of workers, for all education groups except college-educated women, and for all racial groups of men. As a result, top/bottom, racial, and education-based wage disparities stood substantially higher at the end of the decade than at the beginning.
- Despite putting in more hours at work, total household income declined for the bottom 60 percent of households. It increased only for the top 20 percent. As a result, inequality between high-income and low-income households rose for all household types and for all racial groups, especially for whites.
- The share of workers making wages that would put a family . . . under the poverty line also increased over the decade, as did the share making wages less than 150 percent of the poverty line . . .

The 1980s brought higher median wages to most groups of workers in New Jersey, even though in the rest of the country median wages were lower at the end of the 1980s than they were at the end of the 1970s. . . . But in the 1990s things turned for the worse for the median worker as well as for several subgroups of workers. The median wage continued to rise between 1989 and 2000 only for women as a whole (by 0.2 percent per year) and for white women and black women (by 0.8 percent and 0.3 percent per year, respectively). For Latina women, and all racial groups of men, the median hourly wage was lower in 2000 than in 1989, despite the longest expansion in recorded history. . . . Although median wages declined for each of the three racial groups of men, median wages declined more for blacks and Latinos than for whites. As a result, the racial wage gap between whites and blacks and between whites and Latinos grew over the 1990s. In 1989, black men earned 73 cents for every dollar earned by white men and Latinos earned 67 cents. By 2000, these amounts had declined to 69 cents for black men and 61 cents for Latino men relative to white men. Although racial wage gaps are not as large among women as among men, and median wages rose for white women and black women, the gaps widened for women over the 1990s as well. Black women earned 84 cents for every dollar earned by white women in 1989, and 79 cents per dollar in 2000. Latinas earned 78 cents on the dollar in 1989 and 69 cents in 2000.

There is good news of a sort: the gender gap in wages narrowed for every racial group. But the bad news is that this was based not only on wages for women increasing but also on wages for men decreasing. Overall, women ended the decade of the 1990s earning 76.5 percent of what men earned, up from 68.8 percent in 1989. The equivalent figures for blacks were 86.9 percent in 2000 and 77.4 percent in 1989; for whites, they were 76.3 percent in 2000 and 67 percent in 1989; and for Latinos, they were 86.3 percent and 77.9 percent. . . .

The *average* wage . . . actually posted an increase over the 1990s. Not only has the average wage become higher over time, but the average wage is quite a bit higher than the median wage ($18.25 versus $14.44 in 2000). The reason is that the median wage shows what is happening in the middle, while the average wage is skewed by gains at the top. It is possible, therefore, for the average wage to go up even as the earnings of most workers go down. This signals a rise in wage inequality between workers at the top of the wage distribution and everyone else. . . . Moreover, this widening gap in the 1990s between those at the top and bottom of the wage distribution followed on the heels of similar rises in the 1980s.

Although New Jersey's economy has been growing more unequal for nearly two decades, the form it has taken has varied over the period. In the 1980s, rising inequality came from the top and middle of the distribution pulling away from the bottom 20 percent. There were no real wage declines for workers . . . only stagnation at the very bottom. But during the 1990s wage trends took a striking turn for the worse. For the bottom half of the wage distribution, wages declined, while wages continued to grow for the top 30 percent. In fact, wages *increased* the most for workers at the very top . . . and wages *decreased* the most for workers at the very bottom. . . .

Much the same story can be told about trends in wages broken down by years of schooling. In general, wages for New Jerseyans who never went to college have been declining since at least 1980. Those who have not completed high school fared the worst: their median wage dropped 17.6 percent during the 1990s. Among men in this group, the median wage dropped by more than 30 percent. Declines were not as significant among women, nor were they as significant for those with a high school degree or some college. . . . Workers with four years or more of college were the only group to make any gains in the 1990s. But here, too, the record is mixed. All of the gains in the 1990s were due to strong advances made by college-educated women. Their median wage rose by 15 percent between 1989 and 2000, while the median wage for college-educated men fell slightly by 1 percent. . . .

In sum, New Jersey ended the last decade of the twentieth century with a negative record of wage growth for the bottom half of workers, for all except the college-educated, and for all racial groups of men. Only workers at the top or with a college-education made significant gains. . . .

The stagnation and decline of wages for a large share of the work force puts more pressure on families to work harder just to maintain current living standards. This "time squeeze" has become a well-known trend. More family members enter the paid labor force. They work longer hours. They take on second jobs. With many families already having exhausted these options, they have no more spare time left to balance the commitments to work and family. As families lose the ability to compensate for lower wages, their total household incomes begin to decline as well.

In addition to sending more family members into the labor market, especially mothers with young children, a common strategy for families to increase their income is for family members to log longer hours on the job. Overtime pay, when available, makes this option even more attractive. The average number of hours worked in the paid labor force in New Jersey has increased over the past decade. There was a small increase in the number of hours at work for men, who worked roughly 41 hours a week on average, and a somewhat larger increase for women . . . [who] were putting in an extra week of full-time work by the end of the decade. . . . For married couple families with children, where the household head was between the ages of 25 and 54, the total number of hours worked for all family members rose . . . the equivalent of nearly two extra full-time weeks of work. . . .

Since most individuals and families worked harder than ever in the 1990s, one might expect their household incomes to have gone up. But they did not. Instead, total household income declined for the bottom 60 percent of all households . . . . Median household income declined from $55,897 in 1989 to $52,541 in 1999, a 6 percent loss over the decade. Meanwhile, the top 20 percent of households were better off at the end of the 1990s than they were at the end of the 1980s. . . .

Because income growth was concentrated among high-income households, inequality between high-income and low-income households increased substantially over the course of the 1990s. . . . The level of racial inequality remains astonishingly high. . . . While black and Latino households did not lose ground relative to whites, neither did they make any progress in eliminating the already very significant racial gap in income. . . . The bottom line is this: households at the top were better off in 1999 than households at the top in 1989, while households at the bottom were worse off in 1999 than households at the bottom in 1989.

The decline of real wages and real incomes at the bottom of the wage and income distributions plays an increasingly important role in fostering poverty and the kind of economic hardship experienced by the working poor. . . . The working poor . . . increased from 13.2 percent of the work force in 1989 to 15.2 percent in 1999, an increase of 15 percent over the decade. . . . Whites, blacks, and Latinos all ended the decade with a larger percentage of workers earning poverty level wages. . . . Latinos are much more likely to earn poverty-level wages (25.3 percent in 1999) than either African-Americans (15.8 percent) or whites (12.6 percent). . . .

Although the official poverty line was originally designed to estimate the minimum threshold of income needed to survive in a crisis situation, a more realistic estimate of the basic cost of subsistence . . . is at least 150 percent of the poverty line. If this were used as the benchmark [of] a "living wage," . . . the share of the work force that does not earn a living wage for its family size increased from 27.5 percent in 1989 to . . . 29.9 percent in 1999. . . .

It is important to note the quite high levels of employment in jobs that do not furnish a living wage. Roughly half of Latinos, a third of blacks, and a quarter of whites do not make a living wage. Almost one-quarter of all men and more than one-third of all women have low-wage jobs. Women are over 40 percent more likely than men to make less than a living wage. . . .

When the earnings of all other family members and other sources of income such as child support are included, and various types of social welfare assistance are also taken into account, the incidence of poverty among the families of low-wage workers was 8.8 percent in 1999. This is a nearly 70 percent increase from 1989, when the figure was 5.2 percent. If the more realistic standard of self-sufficiency is assumed—150 percent of the official poverty line—then we see that 20.1 percent of low-wage workers live in poor families. In other words, even when all sources of public and private income are included, one of every five low-wage workers and their families still live below an adequate level of self-sufficiency. . . . To say that an increasing share of the *work force* falls into the working poor category—earning poverty-level wages or low wages—or that an increasing share of *low-wage workers* are living in poor families, is not the same as saying that the population as a whole is becoming more impoverished. Rather, it says only that the conditions of *individual* workers at the bottom of the wage distribution, and in particular demographic groups, is deteriorating. . . .

On a wide range of indicators of material hardship, New Jersey not only performs better than average, it often ranks among the very best states. . . . In 1999, New Jersey ranked third with a poverty rate of 7.8 percent, compared to the average poverty rate in the United States of

11.8 percent. A more comprehensive measure of material hardship is the share of persons in families with income below basic family budget[s] . . . including housing, child care, health care, food, transportation, and taxes. . . . On this measure . . . New Jersey had the thirteenth lowest share of individuals living in families with incomes that did not meet these basic needs. . . . Still, though, 21.0 percent of individuals in the state did find themselves in this situation (as compared to 27.6 percent in the nation as a whole).

The study from which these data come . . . found that, in the U.S. as whole, 15.8 percent of the population experienced at least one "critical" hardship—defined as missing meals, not receiving necessary medical care, or doubling up with friends or family—and 45.4 percent of individuals faced at least one "serious" hardship—defined as worrying about having enough food, using the emergency room as the main source of medical care, being unable to make housing and utility payments, and so on. In New Jersey, these figures are lower, especially regarding those who experience serious hardships (34.7 percent), though of course, once again, the number of individuals in such situations is surprisingly high. . . .

The New Jersey economy took a turn for the worse during the 1990s. . . . While those at the very top of the labor market continued to make solid gains in the 1990s, earnings and incomes were stagnant or falling for the rest of the work force. . . . Despite working harder and acquiring more skills, middle-class families have suffered a decline in their living standards. And a larger number than previously has fallen into the ranks of the working poor. Unfortunately . . . economic growth does not necessarily raise living standards the way it did during previous periods of expansion. And as a result, we cannot simply rely on a rising tide to lift all boats.

"I Am a Gay American": Governor James McGreevey Resigns (2004)

The television cameras focused on Trenton in August 2004, as Governor James McGreevey threw the following political grenade at a press conference. The married McGreevey announced to a stunned audience that he was gay, that he had been having an affair with a man, and that he would resign the governorship in three months' time.

His brief statement movingly conveys a sense of the tensions McGreevey felt living as a closeted homosexual. His coming out was an extraordinary moment in the national discussion of homosexuality, and this document suggests simultaneously that American society has progressed toward recognizing that homosexuality is normal, and that many obstacles remain in the path to complete acceptance of gay men and women in civic life.

But historians read political pronouncements for what they don't say as well as for what they do, and Governor McGreevey's announcement left unanswered questions. Was he really resigning because he was gay and had been unfaithful to his marriage vows? By framing the issue in terms of personal liberties, the governor diverted attention from a more serious issue: McGreevey had designated his lover—an Israeli citizen—to be New Jersey's homeland security advisor, despite the man's lack of qualifications for the job; and he was threatening to go public, perhaps in an attempt at extortion.

This went beyond the widespread practice of politicians rewarding friends with jobs. Governor McGreevey's administration was the target of many cronyism and conflict-of-interest allegations. In this case, he put defense against terrorism in New Jersey, home to a quarter of those who died at the World Trade Center on 9/11, in the hands of a man who could not qualify for a federal security clearance.

It will take time before we know how history explains the McGreevey resignation.

Throughout my life, I have grappled with my own identity, who I am. As a young child, I often felt ambivalent about myself, in fact, confused.

By virtue of my traditions, and my community, I worked hard to ensure that I was accepted as part of the traditional family of America. I married my first wife, Kari, out of respect and love. And together, we

Text available at: http://www.cnn.com/2004/ALLPOLITICS/08/12/mcgreevey.transcript/

have a wonderful, extraordinary daughter. Kari then chose to return to British Columbia.

I then had the blessing of marrying Dina, whose love and joy for life has been an incredible source of strength for me. And together, we have the most beautiful daughter.

Yet, from my early days in school, until the present day, I acknowledged some feelings, a certain sense that separated me from others. But because of my resolve, and also thinking that I was doing the right thing, I forced what I thought was an acceptable reality onto myself, a reality which is layered and layered with all the, quote, "good things," and all the, quote, "right things" of typical adolescent and adult behavior.

Yet, at my most reflective, maybe even spiritual level, there were points in my life when I began to question what an acceptable reality really meant for me. Were there realities from which I was running? Which master was I trying to serve?

I do not believe that God tortures any person simply for its own sake. I believe that God enables all things to work for the greater good. And this, the forty-seventh year of my life, is arguably too late to have this discussion. But it is here, and it is now.

At a point in every person's life, one has to look deeply into the mirror of one's soul and decide one's unique truth in the world, not as we may want to see it or hope to see it, but as it is.

And so my truth is that I am a gay American. And I am blessed to live in the greatest nation with the tradition of civil liberties, the greatest tradition of civil liberties in the world, in a country which provides so much to its people.

Yet because of the pain and suffering and anguish that I have caused to my beloved family, my parents, my wife, my friends, I would almost rather have this moment pass. For this is an intensely personal decision, and not one typically for the public domain. Yet, it cannot and should not pass.

I am also here today because, shamefully, I engaged in [an] adult consensual affair with another man, which violates my bonds of matrimony. It was wrong. It was foolish. It was inexcusable. And for this, I ask the forgiveness and the grace of my wife. She has been extraordinary throughout this ordeal, and I am blessed by virtue of her love and strength.

I realize the fact of this affair and my own sexuality if kept secret leaves me, and most importantly the governor's office, vulnerable to rumors, false allegations, and threats of disclosure. So I am removing these threats by telling you directly about my sexuality.

Let me be clear, I accept total and full responsibility for my actions.

However, I'm required to do now, to do what is right to correct the consequences of my actions and to be truthful to my loved ones, to my friends and my family and also to myself. It makes little difference that as governor I am gay. In fact, having the ability to truthfully set forth my identity might have enabled me to be more forthright in fulfilling and discharging my constitutional obligations.

Given the circumstances surrounding the affair and its likely impact upon my family and my ability to govern, I have decided the right course of action is to resign. To facilitate a responsible transition, my resignation will be effective on November 15 of this year.

I'm very proud of the things we have accomplished during my administration. And I want to thank humbly the citizens of the state of New Jersey for the privilege to govern.

Index

About the Editor

Howard L. Green is the founder of Public History Partners (publichistorypartners.com), a consulting firm that offers research and writing services to museums, historical organizations, and government agencies. He studied American history at the State University of New York at Albany and at Rutgers University. Mr. Green has published in the fields of oral history, public history, and New Jersey history. He was the editor of the New Jersey Historical Commission's Ethnic Life Pamphlet Series and the chair of the State Historic Sites Review Board. He compiled these documents as a project of the New Jersey Historical Commission, where he served as research director for many years.